TEACHER *AS* CURATOR

TEACHER AS CURATOR

Formative Assessment *and* Arts-Based Strategies

LISA DONOVAN   **SARAH ANDERBERG**

Foreword by Beth Lambert

TEACHERS COLLEGE PRESS

TEACHERS COLLEGE | COLUMBIA UNIVERSITY

NEW YORK AND LONDON

Published by Teachers College Press,® 1234 Amsterdam Avenue, New York, NY 10027

Front cover photo by Victor Tongdee / iStock by Getty Images.

Library of Congress Cataloging-in-Publication Data

Names: Donovan, Lisa, author. | Anderberg, Sarah, author.
Title: Teacher as curator : formative assessment and arts-based strategies
    / Lisa Donovan, Sarah Anderberg.
Description: New York, NY : Teachers College Press, 2020. | Includes
    bibliographical references and index.
Identifiers: LCCN 2020023716 (print) | LCCN 2020023717 (ebook) | ISBN
    9780807764480 (paperback) | ISBN 9780807764497 (hardcover) | ISBN
    9780807779149 (ebook)
Subjects: LCSH: Arts in education—United States. | Interdisciplinary
    approach in education—United States.
Classification: LCC NX280 .D66 2020   (print) | LCC NX280 (ebook) |
DDC
    700.71/073—dc23
LC record available at https://lccn.loc.gov/2020023716
LC ebook record available at https://lccn.loc.gov/2020023717

ISBN 978-0-8077-6448-0 (paper)
ISBN 978-0-8077-6449-7 (hardcover)
ISBN 978-0-8077-7914-9 (ebook)

Printed on acid-free paper

Manufactured in the United States of America

Contents

Foreword

As the director of Innovative Teaching and Learning for a state education agency, I know that the creative process is at the heart of innovation, and that innovation is critical to the future success of the public education system. To successfully adapt to the rapid changes of today's world, we need to transform K–12 education into an agile education system that is more effective and resilient through educator-driven innovation. This will require that educators be equipped with skills and strategies that empower them to think and respond innovatively about their practice.

In *Teacher as Curator: Formative Assessment and Arts-Based Strategies*, Lisa Donovan and Sarah Anderberg deepen the artistry of teaching and offer methods for collecting and curating evidence of learning. By focusing and documenting decisions made in the classroom, the authors show the importance of mapping progress and sharing what really happens throughout a lesson sequence. Often these moments of teacher and student development and growth go unnoticed. The authors present a case for making visible what often goes missed in the art of teaching—the way skilled educators navigate the often-unanticipated waters of student expression, reaction, and emergent thinking. The art of teaching has to do with the educator's ability to elicit, understand, and inspire student voice and agency to help students make meaning. This book seeks to heighten that aspect of teaching and offers a method for documenting moments of educator brilliance that often happen intuitively, and that significantly impact the lives of students.

There is more to good teaching than delivering information. When teachers shift from holding all the information to translating that information into facilitated, meaningful learning experiences for their students, it only makes sense that their roles evolve. By curating the evidence of the learning they collect and inspiring powerful learning for their students, teachers create learning experiences that will impact the lives of their students long after they leave the classroom. Innovative teaching shifts the focus from delivery of content to engaging students as important partners in the process of learning through critical thinking, collaboration, and reflection.

By centering the role of formative assessment as a critical aspect of teaching and learning, the authors demonstrate how assessment can be woven into lesson planning in seamless and meaningful ways. The arts are shown to be strategies for assessment that also lead to deep learning. The Maine Department of Education was one of the early pilot sites of this work, where interdisciplinary teams of teachers developed model arts integration units and assessment. This effort helped build the capacity of teachers to identify and curate evidence of learning in their classrooms. Teachers became skilled as reflective practitioners and made significant growth in evaluating their own work and the work of their students. Professional learning over 3 years empowered educators to claim their expertise and embrace the opportunities for learning that assessment provided. This created a sense of pride of classroom work worth documenting and sharing with the field.

The authors of *Teacher as Curator: Formative Assessment and Arts-Based Strategies* have collected learning stories for the educator to demonstrate the complexity of learning. They describe learning stories as maps instead of outlines (i.e., traditional lesson plans) that document the stops along the way and allow teachers and students to make detours. The authors and featured educators show how these detours are essential parts of learning as they guide the reader through a process that permits them to think critically about their own lessons while offering practical, implementable strategies to incorporate students' ideas as critical aspects of teaching and learning. Each assertion in this book is supported by classroom practices that educators can try out right away. The authors truly believe in the expertise of educators, and this book is about heightening and broadening that expertise. The voice of the teacher is apparent throughout as the authors share how teachers have carried out the strategies in relatable ways.

Creativity and innovation are fundamental to all disciplines and are an essential part of the learning process. As those of us at the policy level work to realize a vision for innovation and creativity to transform our current education system, I am so grateful to these authors for elevating teacher and student voices and valuing the deep expertise of the educators whose partnerships are critical to our success.

Beth Lambert
Director of Innovative Teaching and Learning
Maine Department of Education

Preface

This book has been years in the making. In our professional lives, we have witnessed firsthand the power of the arts to transform lives of students, teachers, administrators, parents, and the list goes on. We have also seen the arts marginalized throughout the United States. While there is a resurgent focus on arts and creativity, we are cognizant that there are many educators who have not fully tapped the power of the arts and creativity in their classrooms.

Having spent decades exploring arts integration with educators across the arts education workforce (arts educators, teachers who integrate the arts, teaching artists, arts organization leaders, and arts faculty in higher education), we have interacted with thousands of educators. Lisa has worked around the United States and internationally to promote expertise in arts integration training and assessment. Sarah's expertise has evolved from secondary and postsecondary teaching to administration and leadership at the regional, state, and national levels. Together, we have explored varied perspectives on the impact of arts education and researched many approaches to arts-integrated and culturally responsive arts learning in different contexts (rural, urban, and everything in between).

The idea of this book emerged from a sense that the arts could themselves serve as a dynamic vehicle for formative assessment. *Formative assessment* refers to the many methods teachers employ to conduct evaluations of student understanding, learning needs, and progress during a lesson or unit. Formative assessment measures help teachers identify specific learning challenges in-process and develop strategies and modifications to help students achieve (Great Schools Partnership, 2014).

We have been especially curious about the process of *curation* and how it can be an important component of ongoing, formative assessment. We have blended our knowledge of the arts, formative assessment, and lesson design to guide educators through a process that taps into student and teacher creativity. This approach has been explored and tried by K–university educators across the United States as they have thoughtfully considered collecting and curating evidence through processes that involve arts integration. Our hope is that as you read through these chapters you will find insights in our stories and the stories of the educators we feature. At the center of this work has been a focus on and support for the diverse students that we serve.

We believe that reflecting on learning in new ways, documenting stories of learning moments to be shared and studied, and learning from careful attending to planning, review of evidence, and engagement in creative practices in the classroom will yield new insights to educators that will, over time, influence the field in the best possible ways. Consider reading this book with a pen in hand and a reflective journal or pad by your side so that you might reflect on your own practices. We suggest that you think about the educational theories to which you subscribe and investigate further how you might heighten creativity in your own life setting, whether it is a classroom or other environment. How might this effort serve as a launching pad for other creative endeavors for you and your students? Our intent in this book is to braid together research, design, authentic assessment, and storytelling in unique configurations that might trigger new ways to nurture creativity, innovation, and deeper knowledge and understanding. We hope that we may in some way help you unleash new joys in your teaching and find ways to deepen, broaden, and intensify your practice and that, as you do, you see the possibilities that exist through creative endeavor.

Acknowledgments

We wish to thank our collaborators in the field who have supported the evolution of this work. Our arts and education partners have contributed to the development and piloting of the strategies and content of this text. Through these collaborations, we have been able to glean information and perspectives from teachers, administrators, and leaders of arts organizations. We are indebted to the following arts innovators for their support of this work.

The Berkshire Regional Arts Integration Network team (BRAINworks) is a federally funded grant program that provides professional development in arts integration for Berkshire County educators across pre-K–12 classrooms and content in western Massachusetts. We are thankful for the collaboration with Dr. Kim Roberts-Morandi, Director of Curriculum and Instruction, North Adams Public School District and Codirector of BRAINworks; Dr. Barbara Malkas, Superintendent, North Adams Public School District; Dana Schildkraut, Content Coordinator and arts integration specialist, Massachusetts College of Liberal Arts; and Leslie Appleget, Grant Project Coordinator, North Adams Public Schools.

The Maine Arts Integration Resource Project team is part of the Maine Department of Education's 3-year project that worked to support visual and performing arts teachers as they applied our protocols for gathering and presenting evidence of learning through documentation. We are thankful for the leadership of Beth Lambert, Director of Innovative Teaching and Learning for the Maine Department of Education.

The Partners in the Arts team at the University of Richmond (VA) and the Richmond (VA) Public Schools who sponsored professional learning opportunities for teachers and teaching artists to develop processes aligned to curatorial lesson design and formative assessment. We are thankful for the collaboration with Rob McAdams, Director and Faculty, Partners in the Arts, University of Richmond, Richmond, VA; Autumn Nabors, Director of Curriculum and Instruction, Richmond Public Schools, Richmond, VA; and Stacy Hull and Katie Fauth, Program Assistants for Partners in the Arts.

We are grateful for the work of the California County Superintendents Educational Services Association (CCSESA) Statewide Arts Initiative. CCSESA's overall mission is to strengthen the service and leadership capabilities of California's 58 County Superintendents in support of students, schools, districts, and communities. The Arts Initiative works through CCSESA's infrastructure at the national, state, regional, county, and local levels to build and strengthen learning for California's 6.2 million students. We are thankful for the leadership of the CCSESA staff as well as the 58 county superintendents and their staff. In addition, we would like to thank the members of the state Curriculum and Instruction Steering Committee (CISC) Arts Subcommittee representing all regions in California, and the educators and arts leaders who have contributed to strategies and resources on the CCSESA Arts website (https://ccsesaarts.org). We also want to thank Create CA (www.createca.net), a coalition of dedicated and innovative leaders who are committed to building capacity for arts learning and creativity in California's schools. Create CA's mission is to ensure that all students are able to reach their full potential by advancing an education model that promotes creativity and the arts for the 21st-century workforce. We want to thank Pat Wayne, Create CA Program Director, and the Create CA Leadership Council for supporting our partnership and for inspiring our work.

In addition, we want to acknowledge funders who have created spaces for the development of this work, including the U.S. Department of Education, the National Endowment for the Arts, the William and Flora Hewlett Foundation, and the Stuart Foundation.

We are grateful to the following educators and students who have contributed to this work and who have thoughtfully integrated the arts and creativity into their curriculum:

- Educators featured in the CCSESA Arts Lesson Compendium
- Nick Bergheimer, Middle School Social Studies teacher, and students Gia Hazelgrove, Makailah Moore, and Meredith Munnaly for their amazing political cartoons (Figure 6.1), Binford Middle School, a Turnaround Arts School, Richmond, Virginia
- Mary Brooks, STEAM Educator, Arlington, Massachusetts
- Theresa Cerceo, Arts Educator, Dr. Levesque Elementary School and Wisdom Middle/High School, Maine School Administrative District #33, St. Agatha, Maine
- Denise Chesbro, 3rd Grade Teacher, and her students at Abbott Memorial School, Florida, Massachusetts
- Aijung Kim, Teaching Artist, and her students, Partners in the Arts, University of Richmond, Richmond, Virginia
- Dana Schildkraut, Arts Integration Specialist, and the students she served at Berkshire Regional Arts Integration Network, Massachusetts College of Liberal Arts, North Adams, Massachusetts
- Tess Hitchcock, Arts Educator, Visual Arts at the International School of Florence, Italy, and her students. Formerly, Tess served

as a middle school art educator at the Hall-Dale Middle School, Farmingdale, Maine

- Pat Winkle, 2nd-grade teacher, and her students at Egremont Elementary School in Pittsfield, Massachusetts

We are especially grateful for the staff at Teachers College Press: Susan Liddicoat, Kathy Caveney, and Lori Tate, who all skillfully contributed to the editing of our manuscript; and our acquisition editor, Sarah Biondello, who provided ongoing guidance and support.

This work would not have been possible without the love and support of our spouses, Rick Donovan and James Anderberg. We also want to thank Lisa's sons, Alex and Jack Donovan, as well as Sarah's mother, Dr. Cathryn Spelts, for their ongoing inspiration and encouragement.

Arts-Integrated Learning and Creativity

> The creative process is not a mysterious, amorphous, "anything goes" experience. Rather, it has been studied and is found to involve many related interacting phases . . . including imagining or perceiving; sharing; reflecting; creating; and exploring or experimenting. Teachers must facilitate students' engagement throughout the creative process. (Silverstein & Layne, 2010, p. 58)

Imagine a classroom where students are thriving and just can't wait to come to school each day. What comes to mind? Perhaps you imagine a sophisticated modern school where students are interacting with professionals performing great tasks together. Maybe you envision a classroom environment that is designed for hands-on investigation where tables are pushed together, and students are collaborating on group projects. Or possibly, you visualize students sitting in a circle of chairs on one side of the room involved in a discussion and see another group of students creating artwork on the other side of the room.

A flourishing classroom may not look like a traditional classroom with seats in a row and a teacher at the front lecturing. Frankly, it might not look like most elementary, secondary, and postsecondary classrooms today. Unfortunately, many of our schools reflect curriculum, facilities, and processes that operated 50, 60, 70 years ago (Kurani, 2016). The reality is that many of our students are falling through the cracks in antiquated settings with infrequent opportunities for creative and innovative practice.

CREATIVITY IN OUR SCHOOLS

The world is changing so quickly that it's hard to imagine what jobs will look like 10 years from now. Mala Sharma (2019) in the *Adobe Blog* claims, "What we do know, however, is that creative skills will be key to the success of students and job seekers—their superpower, if you will—whatever the future of work may bring." Adobe's research study *Get Hired: The Importance of Creativity and Soft Skills* (2019) cites as its top finding: "There needs to be a greater emphasis on developing creative and soft skills so students can succeed in the future workplace. In addition to more focus on the development of these skills, students need to better understand how vital these are to their career growth" (p. 31).

Educators and parents often see the value in creativity to solve complex problems and prepare students for work in a creative, global economy and advocate strongly for programs that involve creativity and the arts; however, access to the arts continues to be uneven. While some students have creative engagement and arts access, others do not, which perpetuates the inequities in our educational system.

Adobe's global study *Creative Problem Solving: Essential Skills Today's Students Need for Jobs in Tomorrow's Age of Automation* (2018) revealed that current policies are not always working in favor of educators and students, highlighting that "72% of educators and 62% of policymakers and influencers say that current educational practices hurt more than help educators' ability to nurture creative problem solving" (p. 6).

Much is needed to reform our curriculum and provide learning opportunities for our students that include creative problem solving and critical thinking. While it will take visionary decision makers, focused policies and priorities, and increased funding to fully integrate creativity into the classroom for all students, we recognize the power of the practitioner to document promising practices that make the case for building creative capacity in our young people.

Creativity Invokes Critical Thinking

As distance learning has increased due to the COVID-19 pandemic, educators have focused more keenly on how teaching can be effectively implemented in virtual formats. Considering our current technological explosion with an ever-increasing plethora of online platforms, games, and systems for communication and problem solving, it is not surprising that many students find themselves disconnected from traditional practices of school. In some cases, the stark contrast between what is accessible online and what is offered at school contributes to a divide that further disenfranchises our students. As educators look for innovative practices to motivate, engage, and expand capacities of students, it is our belief that employing creative processes through an ongoing reciprocal feedback loop model can have a profound impact on teaching and learning. Tuning into what students feel is relevant and interesting brings their voices forward and opens the door for creative expression. The feedback loop suggests that students' ideas and responses are a critical aspect of how we customize learning to meet students' needs, strengths, and interests.

The concept of the *feedback loop* allows students to give and receive feedback on a task in real time. As students receive timely feedback, they are able to adapt, change course if needed, and make adjustments to revise, refine, and expand their learning. The process is reciprocal for the teacher. Students provide teachers with important feedback that allows them to assess their own instruction and make adaptations and adjustments, in order to meet the needs of the students (Education Technology Insights, 2019). See Chapter 1 for more information on the feedback loop.

There is more to good teaching than delivering information. The feedback loop suggests that students' ideas and responses are a critical aspect of how we understand teaching and learning. Innovative teaching shifts the focus from delivery of content to engaging students as important partners in the process of learning through critical thinking, collaboration, and reflection (Fuglei, n.d.). By *critical thinking* we refer to the ability to reason effectively, use systems thinking, make judgments and decisions, and solve problems (National Education Association, 2012).

We maintain that arts and creativity deepen the processes involved in critical thinking that allow students to analyze information and make reasoned judgments and discoveries. When students engage in problem solving, reflection, and artistic exploration that inspires deeper consideration of content, they find innovative solutions, connections, and fresh insights (National Education Association, 2012). When arts are factored into the equation, students thrive.

Creativity in the Classroom

We are finding that a learning environment that nurtures creative thought and expression is the catalyst for student transformation and achievement. For decades research regarding integrated learning has surfaced many benefits, such as increased engagement, a sense of ownership, increased divergent thinking, language acquisition, and more. While creativity can be incorporated into any subject area, grade level, or educational setting, opportunities for creative expression are significantly attained through the visual, media, and performing arts. Students learn how to generate ideas, translate curricular ideas into new forms, engage deeply with content, and perform, illustrate, synthesize, and express their understanding through a myriad of processes that allow them to take ownership of content, while building skills that will serve them well in life and work.

Teachers who make space for creativity in the classroom allow students to ask questions, thoughtfully analyze, reflect, and problem-solve. Wonder is a by-product of creativity (Beers, 2011) as students imagine "what if . . ." By providing license for curiosity and metacognition, students make meaning through active discovery.

As educators navigate the shifts and trends of educational policy that influence what happens in pre-K–university classrooms, researchers are acknowledging that the missing ingredients for success are lack of engagement, agency, community, and creativity. The Partnership for 21st Century Skills Framework (Battelle for Kids, 2019) expounds on the content knowledge, themes, and skills that should be incorporated into classroom instruction across the curriculum. They include the following literacies: (1) creativity and innovation; (2) critical thinking and problem solving; (3) communication; and (4) collaboration. These are often known as the 4 Cs. We will elaborate more fully on these literacies in Chapter 1. These literacies can be best achieved through interdisciplinary learning that includes the arts. When teachers incorporate interdisciplinary themes and skills in instructional practice, students can recognize the interrelationship of ideas and make connections across academic subjects. "When students create bridges of understanding across academic content, they move their understanding to higher levels and build lifelong habits and skills that cut across all content areas" (Beers, 2011, p. 5).

Teachers may be hesitant to teach creativity and the arts, particularly if they have not had the opportunity to learn in and through the arts themselves. Our experience has proved time and again that when teachers experience firsthand the depth of learning that happens when they engage in creative learning opportunities, they can see the possibilities for their students. While many barriers exist that could deter educators from implementing quality learning through arts integration, perhaps the greatest challenge for the teacher is to overcome personal fears. Beghetto writes, "The key is to have the courage to take the beautiful risks necessary for supporting our students' (and our own) creativity" (Beghetto, 2018/2019, p. 23). Often this involves trying new ideas and methodologies that begin to open up fresh learning opportunities and other creative endeavors. As teachers step into the unknown and take small steps toward integrating creativity into the classroom, new exciting learning emerges that further propels significant changes in teaching practice and methodology.

ARTS INTEGRATION

Arts integration is a pedagogy in which teachers engage students in learning by connecting content in one subject to learning in dance, media, music, theater, and/or visual arts. The Kennedy Center (n.d.) in Washington, D.C., a nationally recognized leader for arts education, defines arts integration as "an approach to teaching in which students construct and demonstrate understanding through an art form." Teachers engaged in an arts-integrated pedagogy may design lessons through which students act out the scientific concept of the movement of the sun, reenact a historically significant moment in time, or illustrate main concepts by creating a storyboard or book.

Drawing from a review of research across sources, Workman (2017) notes that arts education and integration can have powerful effects on students' success "defined not just by student test scores, but also critical skills, such as creativity, teamwork, and perseverance" (p. 1). She suggests these skills are strong "predictors of long-term success in college, careers, and citizenship as test scores" (p. 1).

We believe that integrating the arts across the curriculum can not only build creative capacity in our students but can also foster achievement across academic disciplines. Integration opens new possibilities for students to make connections, apply knowledge, and find relevance in their learning.

School district and postsecondary educators are exploring new avenues for incorporating the visual, media, and performing arts into the core curriculum through interdisciplinary learning and arts integration. We have worked with teachers who are practicing arts integration to engage students more deeply with outstanding results.

For example, a study conducted by Bellisario and Donovan (2012) explored how teachers who had been trained in arts integration understood the relevance of this methodology in their classrooms. Teachers reported that arts integration led to "deep learning." This means students explore topics from multiple perspectives and learn more about the present and past human experience. They make sense of the content and translate it in meaningful ways. The connections are limitless. They develop a sense of ownership and personal relevance of content and engagement.

Foundational Elements of Arts Integration

As you move through this book, we ask you to notice the foundational elements of arts integration at work. We identify the following characteristics of strong arts integration:

- Parallel structures of learning that deepen students' understanding of an academic subject alongside an arts subject. The vocabulary, elements, and skills of one subject are taught concurrently with the vocabulary, elements, and skills of an arts subject such as dance, media arts, music, theater, and/or visual arts.
- Connected and unified learning that allows students to deepen their experience of content through artistic expression.
- Visible learning in which students demonstrate their understanding of content through artistic processes (creating, performing, presenting, producing, responding, and connecting).
- Assessment of what students know and are able to do based on

their providing evidence of understanding in and through one or more art forms.

Research About the Benefits of Arts Integration

While a plethora of benefits can be tied to integrated arts learning, it is important to also recognize the contributions of science and brain research that reinforce the cognitive impact the arts have on the brain. We are beginning to learn from scientists and practitioners what many educators have suspected for decades—that cognitively, students are operating at higher levels when they engage in creative, spontaneous activity, and when they are problem solving. The Arts Education Partnership created a repository of credible research studies in their website, ArtsEdSearch (https://www.artsedsearch.org), which have demonstrated how the arts impacts student achievement, productivity, attendance, and language acquisition as well as a wide range of other capacities. Convincing evidence continues to grow as demonstration projects and research-driven models demonstrate the multiple benefits of an arts-empowered curricula (Miller & Bogatova, 2018; Snyder et al., 2014; Zambon, 2013).

According to David Sousa (n.d.), "The arts are not just expressive and affective, they are deeply cognitive. They develop essential thinking tools—pattern recognition and development; mental representations of what is observed or imagined; symbolic, allegorical and metaphorical representations; careful observation of the world; and abstraction from complexity" (para. 8). As we explore how arts learning opens possibilities for creativity, innovation, and problem solving, we acknowledge that an important attribute of arts-integrated learning is demonstrating understanding of key content. McDougall et al. quote Margaret Wertheim, noted author and artist, as saying, "art is a resource for learning science and mathematics. . . . Art enchants us . . . and draws us in.' . . . Her work today involves experiments with the creation of embodied representations of mathematical ideas that are normally only encountered in symbolic form" (McDougall et al., 2012, p. 13).

Learning in Arts Integration

We want to underscore that arts integration cannot supplant sequential, standards-based arts learning in each of the disciplines of dance, media arts, music, theater, and visual arts. The content and rigor of solid discipline-based learning is needed so that students come to know the vocabulary, elements, and skills of the disciplines. While not every teacher has had training or educational courses in the arts, there are still ways to use strategies in the classroom that provide opportunities for students to connect learning in the arts with other subjects, as we will demonstrate in this book.

Whether you have had deep experiences in the arts, or you are new to the idea of interdisciplinary arts learning, we can help you find ways to incorporate strategies that will enliven your coursework and allow students opportunities to express their understanding. Here is an example that points to the power of integrating the arts in the classroom:

> In David Cooper's sixth grade social studies class, we see students learning about Greek mythology through the arts. David has his students apply their knowledge of social studies when looking at ancient artwork in the classroom and then later at a field trip to the Getty Villa. As a final performance of understanding, David's students work together to plan and perform a Greek or Roman talk show. This performance of understanding shows students applying their knowledge of Greek mythology in a new and creative context. (Jones, 2014)

In this book we include illustrative examples of how teachers from many content areas and grade levels use the arts as a means to capture examples of learning in and through the arts. The results? Flourishing classrooms!

ARTS AS A MEANS OF FORMATIVE ASSESSMENT

What has yet to be fully tapped is the power of the arts to serve as a means for formative and summative assessment. *Formative assessment* is characterized as diagnostic assessment used in the process of learning to gather information about how the student is progressing and how the teacher can improve teaching to meet the needs of students. Considered to be a low-stakes form of assessment, formative assessment involves methods that allow students to demonstrate their understanding and application of knowledge and skills during the learning process. *Summative assessment* is used at the end of a lesson or unit to determine student achievement. Generally, summative assessment is considered an evaluative form of assessment and can take the form of an end of lesson or unit test, project, or culminating activity that reflects students' knowledge and achievement.

For teachers who are consistently required to document learning through endless paperwork and test scores, the arts provide an avenue for bringing assessment to the center of the learning process while supporting many targeted learning outcomes. H. Richard Milner IV (2018) writes that "assessment should help us learn about students, not sort them. . . . While measurement allows us to understand the dimensions of student outcomes, our focus must be on the inputs, that is, the learning and development opportunities of students in their individual contexts" (p. 88).

In this book we explore the methodology of formative assessment in and through the arts and demonstrate how arts integration can provide opportunities for deeper learning through thoughtful lesson design. We also explore the relevance of curation in the classroom and provide ways to curate evidence of learning in order to make meaning of student learning and analyze progress.

Curation in the Classroom

A core thread of this book is the idea of "teacher as curator." Focusing through the curatorial lens will change the way you make choices about the design of your lesson plan, teaching strategies, and formative assessment tools, and the way you collect, organize, and review evidence. A curator selects, foregrounds, and presents ideas and information. This lens will add a new level of intentionality and expertise to your process. And this can have a profound effect on your work. Earlier in our careers, we probably would not have attached the word *curator* to teaching practices. One generally thinks of a curator as a person in a museum who is responsible for the care, selection, and presentation of artifacts or pieces of artwork. Broadening that definition to capture key capacities that instructors often do daily, we say that they can and should collect evidence that informs their understanding of what students know and can do and then curate that evidence. We will unpack a process for you that will allow you to start thinking about formative assessment through the lens of artistic processes and curation. As part of the curation of evidence, we will model how teachers can draw data from multiple sources, encouraging robust documentation.

Documentation as a Way of Knowing

A central theme of the book is documentation—documentation of planning, of learning moments, of reflections during the process of teaching as well as insights gleaned after the teaching and learning process. We explore documentation of insights gained as well as documentation to be shared with students and external stakeholders. Documentation is not as much about creating a chronology as it is about developing a narrative that elaborates on the events, protocols, and processes that point to growth and further learning. In referring to Reggio Emilia approaches, Tiziana Filippini notes that "documentation is not just a technical tool, but an attitude toward teaching and learning. . . . In this sense, documentation is an essential tool for listening, observing, and evaluating the nature of our experience" (Filippini, as cited in Turner & Wilson, 2009, p. 6).

The Reggio Emilia approach foregrounds children's curiosity and allows play and exploration to lead teaching and learning. Following World War II, parents in a small city in northern Italy created a school focused on developing children's critical thinking. "The Reggio Approach believes it is important to document and display children's work while at the same time giving careful attention to the way you present that information" (Reggio Emilia, n.d.). Founder Loris Malaguzzi wrote the poem "100 Languages of Children" "in which he acknowledged the 'infinite ways that children can express, explore, and connect their thoughts, feelings and imaginings'": (Early Learning and Kinder, 2018).

You will see that documentation can reveal the layers of rigor that exist in the creative process, making the case for how arts integration leads to deep learning in our classroom. Documentation brings forward your insights about the classroom. Documentation can lead to change.

Project Zero, the research arm of Harvard's School of Education, has framed five features of documentation through their Making Learning Visible initiative. Those ideas have informed our investigation of "teacher as curator":

- Documentation involves a specific question that guides the process, often with an epistemological focus.
- Documentation involves collectively analyzing, interpreting, and evaluating individual or group observations; it is strengthened by multiple perspectives.
- Documentation makes use of multiple languages (different ways of representing and expressing thinking in various media and symbol systems).
- Documentation makes learning visible; it is not private. Documentation becomes public when it is shared back with learners—whether children, parents, or teachers.
- Documentation is not only retrospective; it is also prospective; it shapes the design of future contexts for learning. (Making Learning Visible, 2005)

These features inform our approach to documenting arts-based approaches in the development of lesson plan to learning story.

INFLUENCE OF PEDAGOGICAL RESEARCH

All educators carry a backpack of research and educational theory that fuels their teaching practice. What is in your backpack? As we ponder our collective experience and what has helped to inspire our professional practice, we recall several key studies that provide a conceptual base for this book. We recognize that you have your own set of practices that help determine your unique journey in education. The creative nexus for innovation stems from melding foundational theories of practice with new concepts and research-based strategies that often yield new methodologies and groundbreaking directions in learning. At first glance, the new information can be disruptive—as it forces teachers to drop assumptions and to think about their methodologies from different perspectives. The outcome is that a teacher can curate educational research and theory and customize instruction geared for specific student populations. Our experience has been that innovative teaching and learning grounded in arts integration is the "elixir" that keeps students wanting to come to class. Arts integration opens doors to learning across the curriculum that provide students opportunities for innovation, creative expression, and experiential learning that brings relevance to their lives.

We came to many new insights in the writing of this book. Perhaps most significant is that we discovered that at the nexus of research, theory, and practice, we stand on the shoulders of great practitioners (teachers) and researchers who have forged new ways of thinking to impact the field of education. Research informs our practice. Seminal giants of research, some of whom we mention here, have influenced our progression. It is in the blending of many models that we have found rigor, enhanced strategies, and new understandings. In this book we offer arts-based approaches to collect evidence of student learning in meaningful ways. We also include theoretical frames that have informed our thinking, including the Backward Design for Learning by Wiggins and McTighe, the Universal Design for Learning by the Center for Applied Special Technology, and the work on Project Based Learning, Integrated Learning, and Visible Learning done by Harvard University's Project Zero.

Backward Design for Learning

Backward design is an instructional approach that begins with identifying expected goals in the classroom and designing learning activities using "backward mapping." The rationale for backward design is that starting with the end goal in mind helps teachers determine what students should know and be able to do and the assessment measures that will indicate that students have achieved their goals. Teachers first identify specific standards and learning targets, and then design activities, assessments, and projects in their lesson-design process to achieve those goals. Grant Wiggins and Jay McTighe popularized this methodology in their book, *Understanding by Design* (1998, 2008), which has been adopted by school districts across the United States. Many additional resources based on this research have since been developed.

Universal Design for Learning

An important body of work that has influenced our thinking has been Universal Design for Learning (UDL), developed by the Center for Applied Special Technology a nonprofit research and development organization. CAST describes UDL in the following way: "Rooted in the learning sciences—including neuropsychology, human development, and education research—*Universal Design for Learning* (UDL) is a set of principles that informs and guides our work in educational research and development" (CAST, n.d.).

The frame of UDL provides a compelling rationale for arts integration. Its tenets invite educators to move away from assuming learning issues emanate from students. Rather, UDL suggests that the obstacles to learning lie in the way teachers construct and teach the curriculum. UDL promotes creating new access points to the curriculum.

The concepts of Universal Design for Learning connect what is known about neuroscience research and the brain with the intentional curriculum and instruction elements that build greater accessibility for all kinds of learners, including special needs students and students from other cultures. UDL invites educators to consider how they can diversify teaching strategies by providing multiple ways of representation, multiple means of engagement, and multiple means of action and expression. We will dive deeper into these concepts in Chapter 4.

Project Zero: Studio Habits of Mind

Lois Hetland and her team at Harvard University's Project Zero (introduced earlier) designed a pedagogical framework titled Studio Thinking, which identified eight dispositions that an artist uses. This framework includes dispositions and structures that provide educators with "accessible, ordinary language" that can help educators share and translate habits of mind developed by participation in the arts and show applications of arts learning across disciplines and provide artists with an analytical lens for their work (Hetland et al., 2007).

These dispositions point to key characteristics of critical thinking and arts creation that can be applied across the curriculum. The dispositions are: Develop craft, engage and persist, envision, express, observe, reflect, stretch and explore, and understand art worlds (Hetland et al., 2013). As Mariah Rankine-Landers (2015) explains, "Studio Habits of Mind (SHoM) empower students to articulate their learning in any subject matter, and provide an entry point for learning based on individual choice and need. They are not hierarchical, and they can be used in guided instruction or constructivist teaching modalities."

BLENDING THEORY AND PRACTICE: A JOURNEY THROUGH THIS BOOK

As an educator, *you are the expert!* We recognize that you alone know your students and what they need. Our goal is to make apparent the vital importance of teacher and student voice. As Allison Rodman (2018), founder of The Learning Loop, emphasizes, "Teachers don't want to be passive receivers of 'best practices,' but co-designers on a journey of self-discovery"

(p. 18). As you journey through this book with us, we hope you find many possibilities for your instruction and that you explore new ways to magnify your voice and the voices of your students.

In Chapter 1 we discuss the topic of assessment as an underutilized component of classroom practice that can advance student achievement and create opportunities for change. We dive into the power of authentic, classroom-based, formative assessment through the arts, which provides students opportunities to demonstrate their knowledge and skills as well as their learning progress. In Chapter 2 we explore the meaning of culturally and linguistically responsive arts learning, provide a conceptual base for understanding the assets of diverse student populations, and point to methods that honor the backgrounds and traditions in ways that cultivate equity and access in the classroom.

In Chapter 3 we discuss the art of curation in the classroom and how this can be a significant part of lesson design involving formative assessment. In Chapter 4 we demonstrate how we can "reclaim" the lesson plan and feature eight curatorial lenses for reviewing and deepening the lesson plan. In Chapter 5 we introduce a protocol for documenting teaching and learning through curation maps that help teachers trace a teaching and learning journey through a lesson or unit and provide examples from teachers who have used this process. In Chapter 6 we focus on developing learning stories and their impact for documenting and sharing growth in the classroom. In Chapter 7 we introduce arts-based assessment strategies that can help unlock creativity in the classroom and provide unique ways for students to express their understanding of content across the curriculum.

We hope that this book will leverage your own knowledge and practice and that you consider the research and pedagogies that have influenced your teaching, so that perhaps you, too, will find new perspectives as you amalgamate and curate information, make meaning, and advance creativity in your classrooms. Now, let's adjust our kaleidoscope to explore creative possibilities for the students we serve.

CHAPTER 1

A New Lens for Assessment

Formative assessment . . . is an ongoing process that mirrors integral aspects of the artistic process itself: Students are given criteria that describe high-quality performances, provided with feedback, and encouraged to revise their work. (Arts Assessment for Learning, n.d.)

This chapter addresses the often-emotional response teachers have to the idea of assessment and explores how formative assessment is central to teaching and learning. We invite educators to consider possibilities of formative assessment as an important part of the instructional process. We will highlight the importance of arts-based, creative assessment as a means for students to demonstrate understanding and find their voice and ownership of the content they are learning.

REFRAMING ASSESSMENT

Assessment Gets a Bad Rap

When you hear the word "assessment," what comes to your mind? Let's face it. Assessment is a loaded word and invokes many emotions. Consider the script below with excerpted voices in an "interview theater piece," where voices were placed in juxtaposition with each other to keep inflection and the use of slang to bring forward the personalities of the speakers. The piece was performed at the New York University Assessment Conference and director Philip Taylor worked with actors to create the opening chant as actors walked in. As you read a portion of the script below, note the intensity of feeling about assessment. ("MCAS" refers to the Massachusetts Comprehensive Assessment System.)

> *Repeat chant three times in unison speeding up each time. March as you speak.*
> **All Actors:**
> Lockstep! Cookie Cutter! MCAS!

Question! Pressure Points! Imagination!
Actor 1:
Testing was something that was done to [us]
you know
that was almost how a teacher handled it
because that was how it was presented to them
Actor 2:
I'm gonna come in and test your kids and then…
Actor 1:
I'm gonna tell you whether you're good enough. (Donovan, 2006)

Emotional Response to Assessment

We find that there is a deep emotional response by many educators regarding the negative impacts of assessment. Getting a handle on assessment is critical to a teacher's success in the classroom. Think about a moment of assessment in your teaching. What comes up for you? Teachers often tell stories about students' anxiety with assessment, describing how they race through computer testing to get it done or how students are pulled out for testing again and again. Some teachers share an overall sense that assessment takes students out of the learning process. Others have expressed that they think assessment is a punitive measure that reflects on their quality as teachers and is used for the wrong measures. Leaders tell stories about rankings and scores that often neglect to provide a holistic view of the child. What does the word *assessment* mean for you?

Think about a story of meaningful teaching and learning in your classroom. What emerges? When we have asked teachers to share stories with this prompt, poignant moments of learning for teachers and their students were shared using language that included words like *powerful, connection,* and *insights*. After some reflection, teachers realized that the stories they shared described deep learning in their classrooms and were truly linked to assessment. This begs the question: How did we get so far away from the power of assessment as an authentic and significant part of the learning process?

Challenges with Current Assessment Practices

Kulasegaram and Rangachari (2018) discuss the challenges that many of us have experienced in current implementation of assessment: from lockstep approaches that don't support the varied ways students learn, to overemphasis on narrowly focused tools and practices that are at odds with values of lifelong learning. They maintain that current assessment practices promote "unrealistic expectations of certainty" and do not fully prepare students for future learning. They suggest that in the current landscape, assessments often "discourage the embrace of ambiguity and creativity." Often success on assessments can be equated with quality learning rather than markers of competence. The authors caution us to think about the dangers of putting too much emphasis on narrow measures, indicating that "this misalignment will negate high-quality teaching and reinforce suboptimal outcomes for students" (p. 6).

Brenda Fyfe concurs that policy on outcomes often serves to limit how we see students. She says, "I am concerned that some of our documents on best practice in the U.S. still have the tendency to narrow and limit our image of the child [student], boxing them into predetermined expectations about learning" (Fyfe, as cited in Gandini & Kaminsky, 2004, p. 6). In our complex educational systems, we need to balance standardized testing and measuring of student outcomes with other measures that encourage self-directed learning opportunities for students.

We have heard similar thoughts echoed in our work with educators and have witnessed the struggle. Professionals often let the barriers discourage them from harvesting the benefits of assessment. The word *assessment* has been used in so many ways that it often leads to misunderstandings and misconceptions. One common misunderstanding is that assessment equals evaluation and grading. Many educators see assessment as a one-way process where the teacher attributes a grade for the students' work. Others think that assessment is only formalized bubble-sheet testing. Formalized assessment is undoubtedly tied to accountability in education and measures of student achievement. We acknowledge the purposes of formalized testing and assessment, and while views vary on the subject, we know that in the current landscape of education, frustration with assessment suppresses the power that can result from authentic, classroom-based, formative assessment processes and practices. According to Gallo et al. (2006), "Beyond simply planning lessons, teaching those lessons, and refining students' skills, it is time to *make a commitment* to integrate practical assessments into teaching" (p. 50, emphasis in original).

AUTHENTIC ASSESSMENT

Getting Clear on the What and Why of Assessment

According to Bryan Drost (2016), "'Assessment' comes from the Latin word *assidere,* which means to sit beside the learner." Drost goes on to ask, "But how does one really sit beside the learner? I believe it is about putting the 'me' back into assessment, a 'me' that is a part of the teacher–student relationship inherent in the definition. From my perspective, this 'me' refers to the fact that assessment has always been meant to be useful for the 'me' who is the teacher—the one who has to improve the learning of kids tomorrow—and the 'me' who is the student trying to gain knowledge and improve skills."

Authentic assessment refers to the monitoring of learning in which students apply their knowledge and skills in relevant, meaningful ways. Students are provided opportunities to work in authentic contexts reflecting real-world applications that create meaningful learning experiences while preparing students for the future.

Central to the idea of authentic, formative assessment is that students are actively participating in meaning-making rather than just remain passive participants who are receiving information in the classroom. Use of well-orchestrated formative assessment measures can have a transformational effect on teachers and their teaching. In a very real way it flips a switch, shining a bright light on individual teaching decisions so that teachers can see clearly (and perhaps for the first time) the difference between the intent and the effect of their actions (Moss & Brookhart, 2009).

Jon Mueller (n.d.) suggests that it's not an "either/or." Rather, authentic assessment can complement traditional assessment. He brings it home in this example:

> If I had to choose a chauffeur from between someone who passed the *driving* portion of the driver's license test but failed the *written* portion or someone who failed the driving portion and passed the written portion, I would choose the driver who most directly demonstrated the ability to drive, that is, the one who passed the driving portion of the test. However, I would *prefer* a driver who passed both portions. I would feel more comfortable knowing that my chauffeur had a good knowledge base about driving (which might best be assessed in a traditional manner) and was able to apply that knowledge in a real context (which could be demonstrated through an authentic assessment).

Using different approaches to assessment can provide us with a variety of ways to understand student learning. While we advocate here for increased use of formative, authentic assessment and identify ways in which the arts provide new strategies for these assessment approaches, we also acknowledge the power of a balanced approach that includes traditional approaches.

Feedback Loop

Incorporating a feedback process into classroom instruction allows for ongoing observation of student growth and learning. Through this kind of ongoing, evolving assessment, the teacher is really looking for a wide range of evidence of understanding by employing different checkpoints for evaluation and engaging in dialogue with students to help make meaning of their learning and growth. The teacher and student work together in an evolving cycle of investigation and reflection. The diagram in Figure 1.1 captures some of the key processes involved in the curatorial process first mentioned in the Introduction. The center of the diagram represents the ongoing process of the *feedback loop*, which means that the teacher continually checks for understanding and solicits feedback from students while also reciprocally providing feedback to the students as well. At the top of the diagram (Step 1), the cycle begins as the teacher sets clear learning targets and makes those visible and understandable to students. Following clockwise on the diagram, you will see the second component (Step 2) of identifying arts strategies and determining what evidence will be collected in a lesson or unit that will demonstrate that students have met the learning target. Once these are determined, the teacher next (Step 3) designs a lesson or unit that includes the strategies and evidence gathering processes that will help students meet the learning targets. The next step in the cycle (Step 4) is that the teacher ignites the instruction of the unit. The teacher allows students to explore content, apply learning, and revise as students engage and find ways to express their learning through inquiry, trial, and revision. The teacher continues to curate evidence (Step 5) that is emerging through the teaching and learning process. The teacher and the students curate evidence by finding key artifacts that demonstrate how students have achieved and met designated learning targets. The evidence is analyzed by the teacher with the students and conveyed in a learning story. The learning story (Step 6) can be developed independently or through a collaborative process with teacher and students or by groups of students, depending on the chosen format. The cycle repeats as a new learning target is identified. We will explore the topic of "teacher as curator" more fully in Chapter 3.

Creating a feedback loop can not only engage educators in reflecting on their teaching practice, but also actively engage students in thinking about their work and thinking about their thinking. In other words, assessment should draw out metacognitive thinking for students as well as teachers. Sometimes teachers are so anxious for students to find the correct answers that they omit discussions of the processes, strategies, and steps that produce the answer. Asking students to describe their thinking while they solve a problem seems to beget even more thinking. Students must learn more than how to find answers; they must become aware of the cognitive processes that produced the answer (Costa & Kallick, 2009, p. 46).

Metacognition and reflection are very much a part of the feedback loop. Metacognition really has much to do about thinking about our thinking. Through metacognition both teacher and students become mindful about their learning and decision-making. Metacognition has been linked to positive student outcomes as it is vital that all involved in the teaching and learning process reflect and make meaning as well as make translations to other content. This is where the feedback loop becomes so vital, so that students (and teachers) take ownership of their learning and intentionally provide

Figure 1.1. Teacher as Curator

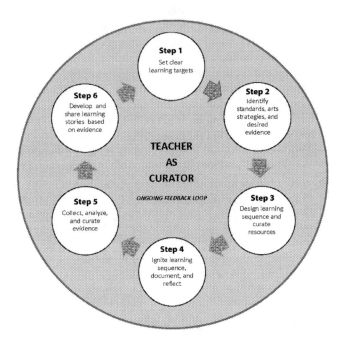

ongoing feedback. This perpetual interaction drives learning outcomes as both teachers and students monitor learning progress.

Meredith (2015) describes the feedback loop as "a process of checking for and affirming understanding that is specific, non-evaluative, manageable, and focused on a learning target." Students can't succeed if they don't know what outcomes are expected. Teachers can't improve their teaching if they don't have the opportunity to reflect on what the evidence of learning reveals about the teaching process. Beyond formalized tests and quizzes (which have their place in our classrooms), it is important to think about the checkpoints that also provide ongoing feedback. Bottom line: There are many ways to consider the question, "How are we doing?" Margaret Heritage (2011) writes,

> The essential purpose of formative assessment as a practice is to move students' learning forward while their learning is still in the process of developing. This stands in contrast to other forms of assessment, which evaluate learning after a period of teaching. Formative assessment practice operates as a feedback loop in which both teachers and students play active, distinctive, yet complementary roles in enabling learning by consistently working to build and consolidate student understanding and skills during the course of a lesson. (p. 18)

Figure 1.2. Parallel Inquiry Process: Student and Teacher Capacities

STUDENT	Inquiry and Learning Process	TEACHER
Documents learning and discovery	Joint Understanding of Standards, Learning Targets, and Criteria for Success	Documents planning and teaching
◄─────────────────►		
Asks questions and investigates through problem-solving	Ongoing Inquiry	Facilitates inquiry and problem-solving processes
◄─────────────────►		
Adjusts investigation and student work through ongoing feedback and reflection	Self and Peer Reflection	Adjusts teaching based on student evidence of learning
◄─────────────────►		
Demonstrates understanding in varied ways	Formative Assessment Through Varied Processes	Utilizes varied assessments to capture student learning progress
◄─────────────────►		
Curates evidence	Evidence of Learning	Curates evidence
◄─────────────────►		
Documents growth and shares progress	Documentation of Progress	Documents growth and shares progress

Students and teachers investigate, gather evidence, and document growth and progress, as outlined in Figure 1.2. Parallel inquiry and learning processes often happen simultaneously through complementary actions where teachers and students learn through inquiry, investigation, and self and peer reflection.

REFLECTIVE PRACTICE

Within the context of formative assessment, meaningful learning can be significantly enhanced if students are given an opportunity to personalize their learning through the feedback loop. This notion is far from new. After all, it is increasingly evident that the quality of life following a course of treatment is as important as improvement in more measurable outcomes. We want to consider the importance of student voice and agency. A means to achieve this is to have assessments that give students an opportunity to explore issues of particular significance to them (Kulasegaram & Rangachari, 2018).

Reflection and Personalized Learning

Building in structures for students to self-assess can be an exciting part of the feedback loop process. Students who can self-assess are poised to use self-regulation strategies to be their own best coaches as they learn (Brookhart, 2016). As students and teachers process information, they learn to make meaning and deepen their understanding of ideas and concepts while considering life implications. If reflective practice is incorporated in the classroom, students personalize learning and construct meaning for relevance and ownership. Reflection is a form of cognition that allows students to create and problem-solve and derive understanding through solo and group processes (Redmond, 2014).

Teaching students to be reflective practitioners encourages inquiry and the importance of continual self-reflection. Inquiry structures can be embedded in ongoing student practice so that they learn to expect to probe deeper. As Margaret Heritage (2013) points out, "The questioning techniques that teachers employ to stimulate students' reflection about their learning also provide a resource that can be gradually internalized by students" (p. 107).

If we embrace the need for personalized learning and reflective practice in the classroom, we can intentionally incorporate assessment methods that capture student cognition throughout the lesson or learning sequence. By engaging students in active, reflective processes, we ignite their interest and individualize learning allowing them to make connections, applications, and synthesize information rather than just memorize facts. In other words, authentic, classroom-based assessment is essential if we are to empower students to become self-directed, lifelong learners who exercise creativity, innovation, and agency.

Teacher Ownership and Agency

Learning doesn't have to stop in order to apply assessment strategies. In the words of teacher Joe Bower:

> We need to start trusting teachers. There is absolutely no substitute for what teacher's [sic] see and hear every single day they teach, and they work with children while they're still learning. Quite frankly, if you're telling me you need a test or a grade to find out what the kids are learning, my response or question

back to you is, what have you been doing? Have you not been working with them? Should you not have observed the learning while they were learning? (Bower, as cited in Brown-Martin, 2016)

Communicating clearly to students about intended outcomes and the evidence to be collected proves an effective strategy in building a thriving assessment culture of inquiry and reflection. While successful practices may vary by subject and style, good assessment requires a clear sense of what the lesson or unit is trying to accomplish and an accurate interpretation of students' responses to understand what students know at that moment (Strahan & Rogers, 2012). Sandra Sterrenberg, a veteran art teacher, shared her reflections about assessment:

I want my students to become thoughtful, skilled, knowledgeable, sensitive, and respectful human beings. I want them to feel connected to themselves, to each other, and to other times and places. . . . I have come to understand that it is important to be very clear about expectations and not to make assumptions about what students know, can do, or how they feel. . . . Ongoing review of content and project criteria is critical for reaching expected outcomes. (Sterrenberg, n.d.)

CREATIVE ASSESSMENT LINKED WITH THE ARTS

We would like to widen the lens of formative assessment now to consider how the arts might be a means for gathering critical evidence of what students know and are able to do. Creative approaches in assessment can become a welcomed part of daily classroom practice for you and your students and can transform your classroom. Creative assessment involves many opportunities for students to engage in and express understanding using the arts and other innovative measures. By inviting students to be active participants in the process of creation and reflection, we are inviting expressions of understanding through different modalities of learning. In fact, the use of arts integrated into the curriculum has a dual role. The arts learning itself can be embedded into any lesson as a means of collecting visible evidence of students' knowledge and understanding.

The Value of Feedback and Revision

Teachers can inspire creativity and innovation by incorporating ongoing reflection and metacognition opportunities within the learning sequence. Reflective processes allow students to think about their learning and investigate further. Reflection throughout the development of a creative work or project helps students to determine what is and what is not working and to share feedback with each other. As students learn from these reflections, they often view problems from different perspectives "Drafts and other first attempts at creation or production may be works in progress assessed by the student, his or her peers, or the teacher. These sketches and drafts or preliminary recordings and videos may be housed in each student's working portfolio. Students might periodically select items or exhibits from their working or process portfolios to place in a presentation portfolio. Both types of portfolios are to be included in the assessment process" (Ontario Ministry of Education, 2009, p. 23).

In the video *Austin's Butterfly,* Models of Excellence curator Ron Berger (2013) shares a student project with elementary school students illuminating the power of critique and multiple drafts. He asks a series of questions that allow students to make critical observations that ultimately inform student practice and outcomes. Through analyzing together, a sequence of student work that evolved into a very exact replication of a butterfly, students experienced the power of revision and that critical feedback, when given without punitive judgment, can be valuable in increasing the quality of student work. It is a great example of oral reflection based on observation. Berger shares a progression of student work by a 1st-grade student from an early, more primitive sketch to a final drawing that shows significant progress. It speaks to the idea that sometimes "we often settle for low-quality work because we underestimate the capacity of students to create great work. With time, clarity, critique and support, students are capable of much more than we imagine" (Berger, 2013, n.p.).

Arts as a Way of Skill Development

As mentioned in the Introduction, the Four Cs (creativity, communication, collaboration, and critical thinking) are skills learned through engagement in the arts. For example, creativity and innovation emerge when students in the arts develop artistic literacy in the disciplines and try new forms of expression. In each of the disciplines of dance, media arts, music, theater, and visual arts students learn how to problem-solve, think deeply about text in a variety of formats, and determine ways to connect their learning through different creative expressions:

> To become proficient and skillful learners and innovators, students need to practice their thinking routines and processes multiple times with different content. They must internalize the thinking processes so that they can efficiently select the best process for a given situation. We maintain that these skills are best taught in and through the arts and acknowledge the importance of these

skills in building innovative, original thinkers when teaching all subjects. (Beers, 2011, p. 23)

When students create poetry, visual art, dances, music, sculptures, and so on, they are not only exploring and expressing understandings of subject matter, but also offering original texts that provide evidence for assessing their grasp of important concepts in the subject matter areas. Viewing the arts as an assessment tool may broaden the methods available to you as well as challenge some rather traditional notions of what constitutes a "lower" or "higher functioning" student. (Goldberg, 2016, p. 208).

An important caveat is that in arts integration the teacher connects the arts with other subject area content. Striking a balance is not always easy, but to maintain the integrity of the art form, it is important that the arts not serve as a handmaiden to other subjects. As noted in the Introduction, students should learn arts vocabulary, skills, and key content in conjunction with another subject area. In formative assessment, arts learning activities can be used as students learn through interdisciplinary curriculum and instruction. Arts, like other content areas, include a wide range of "practices and behaviors, inquiry methods, specialized language, and the global histories of fine arts, media arts, visual culture, design, and crafts— so that students can become competent creators" (Sickler-Voight, 2018, p. 1). And most beneficial is the idea that assessment is a natural part of the process, not an extra process that feels unrelated to the work. A California teacher shared:

I have learned that student awareness and retention lie in events and experiences they have seen or heard through artistic media, i.e., music, TV, movies, etc. Creating a form of learning that taps into the students' automatic way of learning provides them with a greater passion and success rate for learning material they would otherwise memorize, and later forget. I believe the students' strengths/interests consist of creating, teaching one another information they have learned, and applying the information through creative art forms and personal experiences. (Russell, n.d.)

Discrete learning in each of the different art forms, as well as arts integrated learning, offer many benefits for students. Through the collaborative processes inherent in the arts disciplines, students are able to build artistic literacy that yields many positive results. Arts integration provides a means to connect and express new knowledge and skills through authentic engagement and collaboration. Through the arts, students express their learning with others and find relevant connections that often impact their lives in very meaningful ways.

INSTRUCTIONAL DESIGN

By intentionally designing creative structures to collect feedback so that students demonstrate understanding in a variety of ways, including the arts, teachers learn from student feedback to inform instructional decisions and interventions. This process can be carried out within the teaching environment day-to-day. Through documentation of conversations, discussions, creative processes, and showcasing teacher and student work, teachers make visible varied formative mechanisms to collect students' feedback and identify the gap between what students understand and what they need to know. By weaving in culturally and linguistically responsive learning opportunities, students start to see themselves as important to the learning community and, through ongoing work, begin to feel accepted and valued. The collaborative exchange through group problem solving is vital to ongoing learning and improvement.

While there is no one way to design instruction, we will focus on a process that will demonstrate how classroom evidence can be created, collected, curated, and documented. In this book we will explore multiple measures of collecting evidence throughout the learning cycle. As we do, we will move toward the creation of learning stories that capture the sequence of learning that then becomes a useful tool for educators, as they share results with their students and others in their community. In this process, both the teacher and learner curate evidence through a variety of media. It is important to weave into the learning sequence a variety of learning modalities. The following prompts can help with the instructional design process as you develop your lessons:

- Allow students to make their thinking visible. What does that look like? Do you use charts, thought maps, or murals to capture visual representations of students thinking?
- Build in creative opportunities for students to express themselves. Do your students have opportunities to self-assess?
- Ask questions so that students can make discoveries along the way. What questions can be answered through dance, media arts, music, theater, poetry, and spoken word?
- Provide multiple ways for students to demonstrate their understanding. Will students need time to make sense of content or apply a set of skills in order to do a task?

Throughout the lesson planning process, it is important to consider the academic, personal, and emotional needs of your students, and design varied ways they can dig deeper into content. Consider creating your own list of actions that will help you track and guide your lesson design and implementation.

The Time Factor

If you are like most of us, you are reeling with multiple tasks, commitments, schedules, deadlines, and requests for your time. While it is difficult to carve out time to observe what is happening with students and to check their learning and understanding in the lesson sequence you are teaching, we hope that you will see yourself in this cycle as you begin to unpack the components of the feedback loop (refer to Figure 1.1) and dive deeper to consider multiple ways to gather evidence. You might ask, "Does this involve more work?" The answer is yes. But the time invested in this process will be worth the extra work and you will find transformative results. Teachers who have taken risks and set forth on a journey to authentically approach their classrooms with formative learning strategies and inquiry realize that they are not just helping their students in different ways, they are learning much more about their own instructional practice.

The Hero's Journey

Using creative formative assessment instructional design in the classroom is really like going on the hero's journey. You set out oriented for your destination, elicit help from colleagues, students, and other resources, and travel sometimes into the unknown. You take risks and confront certain fears and setbacks as you design and implement learning sequences rich with opportunities for student expression and feedback. Undeniably, challenges and setbacks may deter you from your destination—but you continue! You work for those surprise understandings, the aha moments, and the meaning-making that elevates it all. As you persevere, things start to get exciting as you and your students together nurture their curiosities, explore possibilities, enact your understandings of content, and collaborate for new results. And what is the reward as you end your journey? Student achievement and understanding. And this can all be captured in a story, a learning story that shows where you have been and what you have accomplished and how you are different for having gone on the journey. The Elixir? . . . Well, that is the learning that students take with them for the rest of their lives so that they can go on their own hero's journey.

WE ARE THE CHANGE

The ideas in this book emerge from issues articulated by teachers and administrators from various parts of the country. Continually, we have bumped up against the idea that assessment is something from the outside imposed on teachers. Sometimes that is clearly the case. However, the more we have investigated, we have uncovered many new insights that really put teachers at the center of change in the classroom. An underlying question emerges: "How does change happen?" We tend to think that change doesn't necessarily happen in one place. Some think that change can only happen from the top. Others think that someone needs to dictate the possibilities for change through policy. Still others believe that it is through grassroots efforts that teachers become better equipped for change. One thing is for certain: teachers know more about the students they serve than anyone else. Perhaps there is a hybrid of change that happens when leaders from all levels find synergy and intersections when determining the policies that impact students.

Years ago, I (Lisa) was the executive director of the Alliance for Arts Education in Massachusetts, presenting across the state on new research. I made five visits to schools and community centers across the state and they went like this. I'd introduce the research and for about 10–15 minutes people would respond to its significance and the potential for the field. And then the conversation shifted, and a repeating theme ensued: "Someone needs to_____." Fill in the blank: Someone needs to give us more funding; someone needs to respect the arts more fully; and someone needs to give us time to coplan. Someone needs to allow us more flexibility, give us more say, address the issues in education, and so on. By the time I had arrived in Cape Cod, I stopped the conversation midway and asked, "Who's the someone?" The someone is us. If we are waiting for change from above, we are throwing our energy to the wind. Change is initiated most often by individuals working in their own sphere of influence. Our "sphere of influence" is our relationships, our work in curriculum development and assessment, and our teacher leadership. I firmly believe that change happens at the local level—in the classroom. As Mahatma Gandhi said, "Be the change you want to see in the world."

History bears out the fact that change is sparked by individual effort. For example, in one of Lisa's courses in New Hampshire, teachers in a curriculum course watched four videos that documented educational trends over time and presented their understandings of these issues and changes. Several key ideas surfaced in discussion from group after group, including the idea that many of the changes we are hoping for today are embedded in seeds of the past. Some of the topics that surfaced were the importance of educating the whole child, valuing creative education strategies, and embracing constructivist learning practices that have long been advocated by a variety of educational activists. We suspect you could add to the list of many challenges evident in your education landscape.

Many of the larger issues that emerge in this era of assessment and accountability are multilayered and multidimensional. Although we teachers can all contribute to systems change on a larger scale, ultimately, where we can be most effective, is in the sphere of our own influence—with our students, colleagues, and community members. Change that sticks emerges from individual efforts. This perhaps is most striking. The process we're about to take you through is grounded in the idea of change—the kind of change that can happen at the local level—in your classroom. If you accept the idea that you—yes, you—could be both a "hero" and "an agent of change," we invite you to read on.

CHAPTER 2

Culturally Relevant Arts Teaching, Learning, and Assessment

The arts also call on students to draw from and contribute their cultural
knowledge and linguistic background as they enhance their communication
skills. (Wager et al., 2017, p. 15)

This chapter will explore the need for educators to value the diverse (cultural, linguistic, social, and socioeconomic) backgrounds of our students and provide ways to foster connections between students' cultural traditions and school learning. We will discuss considerations for deep work in culturally responsive integrated learning. Included in this chapter will be guidelines to build positive learning environments with students and the greater community to empower students to explore, question, make meaning, and observe the world through multiple perspectives. This will set the stage for signature work in creative assessment through the arts.

Changing demographics in the United States show that over half of K–12 students are non-White. Data indicate that U.S. classrooms are becoming increasingly diverse. The U.S. Department of Education's Office of Planning, Evaluation and Policy Development, Policy and Program Studies Service released a report *The State of Racial Diversity in the Educator Workforce* (2016) that notes:

Research shows that diversity in schools, including racial diversity among teachers, can provide significant benefits to students. While students of color are expected to make up 56 percent of the student population by 2024, the elementary and secondary educator workforce is still overwhelmingly white. In fact, the most recent U.S. Department of Education Schools and Staffing Survey (SASS), a nationally representative survey of teachers and principals, showed that 82 percent of public school teachers identified as white. This figure has hardly changed in more than 15 years; data from a similar survey conducted by the Department in 2000 found that 84 percent of teachers identified as white. (p. 1)

Promoting diversity and equity is a goal shared by many American educators in pre-K through post-secondary classrooms, but achieving this goal in day-to-day classroom practice is often difficult to do. Every child—from every culture, geographic region, and socioeconomic level—deserves a quality education. That sounds good—it looks good on paper. As some have said, "equity has become the new kale" as the word becomes popularized in educational systems at all levels. Educators often say the words but don't always support their claims in concrete, visible educational policies, and instructional practices. To get to a deeper understanding of how to best meet the learning needs of diverse students in their classrooms, teachers need a clear vision and some signposts to guide their work.

WHAT IS CULTURALLY RELEVANT TEACHING?

Gloria Ladson-Billings (1994) defines culturally responsive teaching as "a pedagogy that empowers students intellectually, socially, emotionally, and politically by using cultural referents to impart knowledge, skills, and attitudes" (p. 382). We recognize that most instruction is culturally responsive to some degree, but yet may not be responsive to the cultures and traditions of the diverse students that we teach.

Teachers need to ensure that their curriculum and pedagogy are relevant to the students they serve. Culturally and linguistically responsive teaching is an approach to teaching that embraces the reality that exists in our classrooms across the United States. Culturally responsive teaching is about helping all students reach deeper levels of learning in the classroom.

Hammond defines culturally responsive teaching in the following way: "An educator's ability to recognize students' cultural displays of learning and meaning making and respond positively and constructively with teaching moves that use cultural knowledge as a scaffold to connect what the student knows to new concepts and content in order to promote effective information processing" (Hammond, 2015, p. 15).

We are a diverse country with a rich tapestry of cultures, languages, and backgrounds that comprise a very complex student population. All students have a right to high-quality learning opportunities in which their cultures, languages, and experiences are valued and used to guide their learning. Rather than approaching our diversity as a challenge, it is important to recognize that each student with their own significant background and culture is an asset. It is often difficult to construct the bridge between learning in the classroom and the learning that takes place in authentic family and community settings; this learning grows out of strong traditions and cultural knowledge passed from one generation to the next.

Teacher-researchers Gonzáles, Moll, and Amanti share insights gleaned from educator interviews of families uncovering the real world knowledge students bring to school. The findings suggest that teachers need a more sociocultural approach to education, understanding whom they are teaching and valuing the deep "funds of knowledge" and family networks that students bring to school (Gonzáles et al., 2005). All the children and their families bring knowledge networks that should be honored and integrated into the curriculum. Moll's work situates diversity as difference not deficit. Teachers can work to integrate life experiences more fully with academic engagement that promotes individual expression and student voice.

Moving Toward Being a Culturally Responsive Educator

As you think about the instructional practices expounded in this book, we want you to keep in the forefront the knowledge that in honoring your students' cultural assets, you will continue to work toward creating equitable, authentic, relevant, and engaging practices in the classroom that assist them in reaching their full potential. From this assets-based approach, the goal is to be truly inclusive (not just give lip service to the term) so that you build equity in every aspect of curriculum and instruction. In addition to being attentive to the students whom you are teaching, it is also important to build strong relationships with each and every child, removing obstacles that may prevent your students from learning and empowering them to reach their potential.

Privilege is defined as "An unearned advantage that a dominant group has over marginalized groups" (see https://uca.edu/training/files/2017/11/Privilege-What-Does-It-Mean-Handout.pdf). With privilege comes power for some and oppression for others. The role of privilege in our society leaves many students with extra challenges for success. Sonia Nieto (2006) suggests that the achievement gap could instead be referred to as "the resource gap or the caring gap" because of the vast differences in resource allocations for students in different zip codes and differences in "support and care given to children based on their identities" (p. 3). This results in structural inequities affecting areas such as "funding, curriculum, class size, testing, tracking, and other matters of policy and practice [which] exacerbate rather than ease social class and race inequalities" (p. 3). Despite these inequalities, teachers can have a profound impact on our students, counteracting the impact of inequity on the students we teach, supporting student achievement, and making students feel valued and cared for. Because of this, Nieto notes that "teaching is political" (p. 3).

It seems clear that if we are ever to address the ethnic and racial disparities that continue to prevent equity, we must level the playing field for all learners through education. This requires that teachers move toward being culturally responsive. Becoming a culturally responsive teacher requires that you do the following:

- Establish desired learning goals, content, and assessment activities grounded in a diverse, multicultural context.
- Collaborate with others to build deeper understanding of the students you serve.
- Commit to designing learning that embraces each student and uncovers the language, history, and backgrounds of all cultures represented in your community.
- Create a culture of acceptance by incorporating empathy and understanding in the learning environment (the arts can help us create this culture). A crucial part of this work is being willing to investigate and understand our own practice.

Questioning Current Practice

Doug Fisher and Nancy Frey (2015) point out that "everything we do as educators, whether big or small, helps create a school environment that affects student hope and engagement" (p. 81). It is from this stance that we invite you to weave into curricular pedagogy an array of approaches that place the student at the center of any educational endeavor. One key to ensuring that every student is viewed and treated as an asset is self and institutional reflection. Often when learners struggle, teachers identify the issue as emanating from the students rather than engaging in the introspective work to assess their own practice and whether they are creating culturally responsive classrooms.

Is every student in your classroom, school, district viewed as an asset—a valuable treasure? Moving into practices that build on students' strengths requires an environmental scan to determine what mindsets, perceptions, and actions are inhibiting culturally responsive, inclusive practices. This internal assessment requires courageous conversations and evaluation of procedures that may at first glance not seem to be perpetuating inequity but do just that. Consider the questions below to build awareness of opportunities for equity and cultural and linguistic responsive teaching:

- Who are my students and how can I build on the rich cultural experiences they bring to the classroom to create new learning success?
- In what ways can I acknowledge that my students bring a wealth of positive attributes to the classroom?
- In what ways can I utilize community resources to deepen culturally and linguistically responsive arts learning?
- What are the biggest challenges to ensure equity, diversity, and inclusion of marginalized students?
- What practices do I employ to build relations and trust with marginalized students?

- Does my work with other institutions, organizations, or community groups improve representation of marginalized groups in practices and services?

As you begin to examine your current situation more closely, you may see opportunities surface as you assess the learning cycle and how you can best infuse intentional culturally and linguistically responsive strategies into the classroom that will provide a wealth of evidence as to how your students learn. It is from that place of assessment that you can orchestrate new, vibrant processes that open bright worlds for both teacher and student.

A FOCUS ON DIVERSE STUDENTS

Valuing What Students Know

By understanding and valuing the cultural and linguistic backgrounds of our students, we learn how to foster connections between students' background experience and school learning. What becomes so prevalent in most cultures are the artistic traditions that are a central part of family and community networks.

Zaretta Hammond, in her book *Culturally Responsive Teaching and the Brain* (2015), writes:

> Culturally responsive information processing techniques grow out of the learning traditions of oral cultures where knowledge is taught and processed through story, song, movement, repetitions, chants, rituals, and dialogic talk. Tapping into these traditions and honoring the collective knowledge of current and past familial storytelling enlivens classroom practice. Integrating the arts creates space for a variety of ways of knowing that can honor and value diverse cultural traditions. (p. 127)

Yvette Jackson, author of *The Pedagogy of Confidence* (2011), discusses how to make education relevant to students who have been underserved by our well-meaning attempt to help them overcome their weaknesses. "How can we help students fully realize their potential? Give them a pedagogy that builds on their confidence, their natural areas of high achievement, and a sense that what they learn in our schools is relevant to their lives" (p. 5). Creating a pedagogy of confidence means finding ways to honor how students learn and, by tapping into cultural knowledge and tradition, allowing students to express themselves and who they are in ways that honor their abilities and traditions. As you approach the complex work of increasing achievement for all students, consider integrating the following actions into your practice:

- Equipping the daily teaching repertoire with strategies and skills that assist students to share their voices and unleash their hopes, desires, cultures, and backgrounds
- Creating pathways to relevant learning so students can clearly make connections, find relationships to their own lives, and apply learning to real-life settings
- Breaking down barriers, processes, and structures that diminish opportunities for students
- Strategically opening doors for students to find their creative voices and expressions of their cultural traditions during all parts of the lesson planning and teaching process
- Joining with students as partners in the learning process so that reciprocal learning can take place
- Creating a culture where the classroom is a safe haven where everyone is valued and honored

Beyond Heroes and Holidays

As educators work toward equity for all children, they are often challenged by recognizing that "classrooms . . . must change in order to pursue ways of teaching that value and honor the humanity of each and every child— honoring them as social, cultural, and historical beings" (Souto-Manning, 2013, p. 16). Teachers need to move beyond the "heroes and holidays" approaches that often only honor the accomplishments of a handful of people from cultural groups, or that feature only a special event such as Cinco de Mayo. Token attention to culture in this way can only position these groups as "other" and the inclusion of their voices as "extra." Instead, educators can seek to transform their curriculum to center diverse voices as important to understanding the world. (Gorski, n.d.)

It is important to recognize the critical role educators play in establishing environments that build trust and relationships with students and the greater community. This may necessitate purposeful inclusion of a wide range of cultural traditions interwoven throughout the curriculum. A key component of this is asking students to share their own cultural traditions in ways that are honored and supported. With mindful attention to antiracist approaches, teachers can break down barriers to language and actions that cultivate deeper learning and community. Danielle Moss Lee (2012) writes, "Even well-intentioned teachers can perpetuate the structural racism built into the fabric of our education system if they are not conscious and do not take active steps to address their own biases, and recognize how those biases can affect practice and decision-making."

ARTS AND CULTURALLY RESPONSIVE TEACHING AND LEARNING

In our experience we have found that the arts can provide potential bridges
between the curriculum and students' needs, interests, and learning styles.
To this end, below we suggest themes that position the arts as critical for
culturally responsive teaching to consider, followed by examples of what
this might look like in a classroom setting.

The Arts Provide Strategies for Culturally Responsive Teaching

With the plethora of processes, curricula, and research on equitable access
for all students to a quality education, many teachers are still stumped on
how to incorporate these strategies and processes to help all their students
achieve. The arts can provide powerful strategies for culturally responsive
teaching. Deep engagement in the arts can provide students with a sense
of agency, choice, and voice. Students are invited to tap into their funds of
knowledge, valuing what they bring to the classroom.

The purpose of culturally responsive pedagogy is to help traditionally
marginalized and underserved students become empowered, independent
learners. But cultural responsiveness may be confused with simple multicul-
turalism to "honor diversity," rather than associated with building students'
thinking skills. Those educators who continue to confuse the purpose and
process of culturally responsive pedagogy will never realize its full potential
to create more equitable outcomes (Hammond, 2018).

The goal may be to avoid the common issues that are observed when
students of color, poverty, special needs, or from a different culture or language feel isolated and without a purpose in our educational system today.
Yet the reality is that so often these students do not have an opportunity
to truly express themselves or to share what they value. For the creative
classroom teachers who include interdisciplinary, arts-integrated approaches, there are a myriad of possibilities to mine the talents, backgrounds, and
cultures of all students while fostering creative expression and student sense
of self.

The Arts Promote More Inclusive Classrooms

Utilizing the arts is key to creating inclusive classrooms. The arts—dance,
media arts, music, theater, and visual arts—provide multiple ways for students to express themselves and their understanding of key content as well
as the world around them. The arts provide an open door for students to
share their authentic voice and their unique differences and contributions
to the learning community. Inclusive classrooms include language, images,
stories, and materials that reflect diversity and perspectives from groups
or cultures that have been historically underrepresented. As teachers and

students value the stories and perspectives of diverse cultures and languages, empathy and understanding become part of all learning. Creating opportunities for dialogue and inquiry to represent different points of view allows students to respect differences and to honor language and culture with more openness and acceptance. "The arts are our history and our vision. They record, are shaped by, and reflect culture, and in turn transform culture by providing a focus for reflection. Thus the arts are the means for communicating interculturally, the ways for teachers to learn, and the media through which students can teach" (Hanley & Noblit, 2009, p. 65).

The Arts Provide a Vehicle for Students to Share Backgrounds and Traditions

Through the arts, students are provided opportunities to learn new critical thinking and communication skills and ways of knowing that shed light on cultural traditions adding to their rich tapestry of learning. For example, students can be invited to share the traditions, upbringing. and experiences that have shaped their lives while working on English Language Arts skills through the creation of an "I am from" poem—a poem that allows them to creatively express information about their own background (Christensen, 2009). Another example is the production of a collaged image that shows societal influences in a specific time period. Through multimedia, students can express understanding of a section of text, a point in history, or a scientific concept.

Imagine a language learner who is learning about cellular division by designing a creative movement sequence to explore the processes within mitosis. Another example is the creation of an imaginary soundtrack of erosion. A teacher invites students to imagine the unseen processes of erosion at work, to create sounds that replicate the experience, and to create a composition that tells the story of erosion through sound. Students could then explore the impact of erosion on some cultures across the world. Demonstrating a scientific process through sound also allows students to have an experiential sense of learning rather than just reading about the forces involved in erosion. In this example students are engaging with content in many ways in and at the same time, making cultural and global connections.

By exploring content through artistic expressions that transcend language, students can translate ideas across symbolic systems honoring a variety of approaches of making meaning. Students may bring a piece of text to life by creating sounds of a habitat, weather, or historical moment within a specific culture or geographical location that connects students' lived experience, eliciting stories, memories, and visceral connections. In the chapters that follow, you will see how to create pathways to learning and assessment, opening the access points for children who may learn in different ways. Through these artistic translations—drawing, speaking, writing, reading, creating, sculpting, acting, and singing (the list could go on)—key benchmarks can be articulated. Showing understanding of concepts, traditions, and perspective provides evidence for the curation-minded teacher and opens new dimensions for teaching and learning. This kind of embodied, experiential learning can tap students' "funds of knowledge" and bring learning to a full body experience connecting with emotion, felt sense, and personal narrative. Valenzuela (2017) emphasizes that "when thinking about educational contexts, we must recognize that our lived experiences also include sonic and viscerally rich forms of making meaning. Yet, these are often absent or silent from traditional educational systems" (p. 33). When you ask students to share their backgrounds you are asking them to be vulnerable, to take risks. It's of paramount importance to think about how you can support students in feeling a sense of safety in sharing about their lives. Homa Tavangar (2017) calls this "'psychological safety,' a sense of confidence that members of a group will not be embarrassed, rejected," or ostracized for speaking their minds. This safety can be cultivated through the arts as students learn to collaborate with and accept others, even those who have different points of view from their own. The arts provide an opportunity to incorporate ways to build social acceptance and safety into the classroom environment and prepare students for the global workforce.

The Arts Create Opportunities for Developing Cultural Awareness of Others

As our society becomes more global, finding creative approaches to understanding a myriad of cultures promotes universal values of tolerance, equality, and inclusion. Through the arts, students explore conflicts from a global perspective that opens minds to the meaning of human rights and the deeper understanding of how to become more active, responsible citizens. Powerful learning takes place when students can view an issue through multiple points of view and reflect on their role in the world. As explained in the Introduction, the Universal Design for Learning (UDL) suggests that teachers can increase access to the curriculum for all learners by representing content using a variety of approaches, increasing engagement with curriculum by providing many ways for students to work with content, and inviting demonstration of understanding of content in diverse ways (CAST, n.d.). The arts provide alternate ways of translating, investigating, and making meaning that increase students' access to the curriculum. (Glass & Donovan, 2017; Glass et al., 2013). It is critical to see the arts not only as an avenue for aesthetic and creative exploration and expression, but also as a means of demonstrating student understanding and knowledge as well as social and emotional understandings.

Through dramatic exploration of characters in a text, children can explore multiple perspectives as they take on the roles of characters different from themselves and make meaning of stories from the inside out. Taking on a character in a dramatic scene allows students to locate their own identity, values, and perspective in relationship to that of others. During the dramatic role-play, you could invite students who are observing to stop the action and interview a student playing a character. Thus the students can explore vantage points different from their own.

Students bring diverse ideas about multiple literacies in their lives—including multilingual, multimodal, and digital ways of storytelling. Tapping into the lived experiences of our students using the contexts and literacies significant to them, you will draw upon cultural representation, memories, and varied ways young people make sense of the world (Jewitt, 2008).

This kind of student-centered teaching means that the experiences of students (and their families and communities) are brought to the forefront of the classroom, making learning active, interactive, relevant, and engaging (Nieto, 2010; Souto-Manning, 2013). In a TED talk, brain researcher Todd Rose (TEDx, 2013, 17:02) makes the point that education is often designed around the idea of an "average" student. In reality, he notes, "There is no average." Brain research shows that we are all variable learners.

As noted above, UDL allows increased access to the curriculum for all learners. As such, it is another strategy for culturally responsive teaching. In exploring the lens of Universal Design for Learning in a curriculum course I (Lisa) taught, one teacher noted that "designing curriculum with UDL in mind 'is a new way of thinking' that prompts focusing process leading to 'three dimensional' approaches to teaching, and developing 'textured,' well-rounded options" (Glass & Donovan, 2017, p. 46) . Reflecting on the framework provided by Universal Design for Learning, another educator remarked:

> This framework provided me with a very clear focus, and I was able to concentrate even more deeply on the needs of my diverse students. Even though I subconsciously acknowledged that my students were highly diverse, I did not fully grasp the totality of their differences until I was introduced to the research supported in UDL —how students gather facts, organize ideas, and engage in learning is uniquely individual. Upon reflection of what my assessments have been in the past, I realized that they are oftentimes an afterthought. They are not connected to essential understandings that I hope my students will carry with them for a lifetime but are merely focused on a resource or activity." (S. F., 2013, as cited in Glass & Donovan, 2017, p. 47)

In other words, using the tenets of UDL prompts educators to create more points of access to curriculum and to express what they have learned. This creates more culturally responsive approaches that honor the myriad ways in which our students learn.

REFLECTING ON PRACTICE

In *Culturally & Linguistically Responsive Arts Teaching and Learning in Action*, lead author Francisca Sánchez created a template used in 22 "strategies" for applying key pedagogical principles and practices (Sánchez et al., 2017, Figure 2, pp. 13–14). Educators from across California contributed to this resource which includes culturally and linguistically responsive strategies aligned to the visual and performing arts. The questions in Figure 2.1 are taken with minor changes from the Sánchez template and help identify some key ideas for strengthening instructional expertise with a culturally responsive lens. We adapted the questions slightly in Figure 2.1 to assist educators in reflection of their own classroom practices. As a next step in developing your own practice as a culturally responsive teacher, we invite you to reflect on the questions in Figure 2.1 as you think about the students you teach. This tool is meant to spark reflection, ideas, and next steps.

CREATING A POSITIVE ENVIRONMENT FOR LEARNING

On the way to becoming stronger culturally responsive teachers, Hammond (2017) emphasizes that "we have to remember that part of keeping hope alive is cultivating and expressing positive emotions like joy, love, gratitude, and awe." She notes that teachers can balance their focus on "what is wrong (oppression and trauma) with a focus on affirmation and joy." At the end of the day, this work is about building positive, authentic relationships with all our students and paying attention to what individual students need to be seen, valued, and successful. The arts can create deeply joyful experiences producing a positive environment for learning. Hanley (2002) calls for a greater understanding of the power of the arts in the curriculum:

> The arts tap into our need to understand and to create, to change the world in so many ways—intimate and social, tiny and enormous. The artist, whether wondering dabbler, serious student, or professional is engaged in perception, conceptualization, expression, and transformation of self, culture, and medium, all of which are at the core of making meaning of the world. Because the struggle of transformation and expression is so personal the work becomes relevant and ownership increases. One can see the impact on young people involved in arts-based work in the way they focus and participate. It's a wonderful thing we must acknowledge, educate people about, and demand room in the curriculum for. (n.p.)

There are many factors that influence a positive classroom environment and empower students to actualize their learning. As you review the examples in the chapters to come, we invite you to consider how the practices we detail may lend themselves to creating a space where students thrive. By

Figure 2.1. Questions for Reflection on Teaching Practices

Creating a Culturally and Linguistically Responsive Learning Environment *How will my instructional practice contribute to creating a culturally and linguistically responsive learning environment?*	Reflection *What specific practice in my teaching addresses, contributes to, and/or enacts one or more of these features of culturally and linguistically responsive learning environments?*
Language and Culture	
Assert the legitimacy of students' languages and dialects and use students' languages, cultures, experiences, and skills to create new successes?	
Build a broad array of language, literacy, cross-cultural and multimedia communication skills?	
Celebrate, respect, and appreciate language and cultural diversity?	
Take advantage of cultural traditions to help students process information more efficiently and effectively?	
Respond to the lives of our students and families?	
Learning Community	
Develop a sense of community, self-determination, trust, and democracy?	
Provide affirmation, mutual respect, and validation?	

Minimize social threats, and maximize opportunities to connect with others in the community?	
Create a safe learning environment and model high expectations for learning?	
Promote assets-based rather than deficit-focused perspectives and behaviors?	
Explicitly address the impact of the context in which students of color live and help them develop counter-narratives to resulting negative portrayals of them and their families?	
Student Agency, Voice, and Mindset	
Honor students' voices and create environments where student voice permeates the classroom instruction?	
Help students create a counter-narrative about their identity as learners?	
Provide students with language to talk about their learning and thinking (metacognition) and to review their progress?	
Support students in using their learning to create new knowledge, art, and understanding?	
Activate students' ability to direct their attention to their own learning?	

Provide a clear process for reflecting and acting on teacher and/or peer feedback?	
Stretching and Bridging	
Intentionally connect new learning to students' background knowledge and experiences; help students bridge from prior knowledge to new learning?	
Challenge students and provide opportunities for them to stretch, expanding their potential to do more complex thinking and learning?	

Note. Adapted from *Culturally and Linguistically Responsive Arts Teaching and Learning in Action* (pp. 13–14), by F. Sánchez et al., 2017, California County Superintendents Educational Services Association, Arts Initiative (https://ccsesaarts.org/wp-content/uploads/2019/08/Culturally-Responsive-Guide.pdf).

incorporating key concepts of the "pedagogy of confidence" mentioned earlier in this chapter, students can demonstrate high intellectual performance and achievement through practices that nurture student success both academically and personally (Jackson, 2011). Yvette Jackson developed some High Operational Practices (HOPs) for addressing the needs of all students. These practices include the following:

- Identifying and activating student strengths
- Building relationships
- Eliciting high intellectual performance
- Providing enrichment
- Integrating prerequisites for academic learning
- Situating learning in the lives of students
- Amplifying student voice (Jackson, n.d.)

When students engage in arts learning, they find inspiration, joy, and a love for learning. By integrating the arts into the classroom, students find voice and agency through creative expression. As we think about the needs in our education system, it is important to be mindful of the wealth of stories our students need to tell and the significance of those stories in shaping a better world.

CHAPTER 3

Teacher as Curator

Initially, curation will play a major role both in the way we "teach" and in the way we educate ourselves on any topic. When and where it will be adopted, it will deeply affect many key aspects of the educational ecosystem. (Good, 2016)

One overarching theme of this book is to investigate how curation is a key component of creative lesson design and formative assessment methodologies. As explained in the Introduction, the word *curator* often brings to mind the museum curator who oversees an exhibit. In fact, the word *curator* is "borrowed from Latin *cūrātor* [that means] 'one who looks after, superintendent, guardian,' from *cūrāre* 'to watch over, attend'" (Merriam Webster, n.d.). Although it is usually attributed to someone who is a keeper of cultural artifacts such as in a gallery, library, or museum, we will focus on the practice of curating learning. Curation in education is often linked to selection and critique of online resources. In this text, we invite you to think about curation more broadly.

THE ART OF CURATION

George Siemens (2008) describes a *curator* as "an expert learner." Robin Good (2016) predicts that "curation will directly affect the way competences [sic] are taught, how textbooks are put together, how students are going to learn about a subject, and more than anything, curation will affect the value that can be generated for '*others*' through a personal learning path" (emphases in original). Curation takes place throughout the processes of lesson planning, teaching, and assessment, and the curator's approach brings different benefits to each area of focus. Much has been written about online content curation (e.g., J. Gonzalez, 2017, 2018). Indeed, today the use of online tools and resources is an important part of most educators' educational practice. But beyond search and curation of online media, we recognize the multitude of possibilities when teachers seek to make meaning of the materials, resources, and methodologies they use.

This art of curation can be viewed through many lenses and involves ongoing learning both by teacher and learner. It also involves scrutiny. The potentials for curation are abundant, but it requires intentional, careful consideration. We will provide some of the insights into what we have gathered, but we encourage you to reflect on your own practice and seek to find the treasures that can be found in the process.

As John Spencer (2017) points out: "Teachers are already curators. We piece together resources, research, and ideas as we develop lessons. We curate the content that we teach. This isn't anything new or groundbreaking. It's what happens when we find a great book or video and share it with our students." While the curation process is not new, it does warrant deeper investigation to determine how best to curate and translate this into our instructional design process.

Content Curation

Information overload can inhibit our ability to process due to the breadth of resources available to us. "In fact, 90% of all the data in the world has been generated over the last two years. To put things in perspective, between the dawn of civilization through 2003, about 5 exabytes of information was created. Now, that much information is created every 2 days" (Briggs, n.d.). With the volume of information available to us, it makes sense that we need to be active, thoughtful curators and teach curative skills to our students. Strong curation skills are crucial for us to navigate information and to be intentional about what we bring into our teaching. Curation involves scanning, selecting, and evaluating online and printed information. It also involves review of many different teaching resources, research studies, curriculum, and artifacts. Many teachers have their own collections that they have gathered over the years. Do you have a pile of information you have collected? Part of the process of curation is the selection of key information that supports your curriculum. Engaging in lesson planning through the lens of a curator empowers you to select the information that supports your classroom content while not including "everything but the kitchen sink." Curation involves more than selecting; it requires a keen sense of the big ideas you want students to understand and the ability to manipulate information for critical teaching purposes. While selection is common, curation takes more intentional thinking, grouping, selecting, reflecting, and analysis (Casa-Todd, 2018).

We suggest that curation has a spectrum of possibilities in the classroom and that student work must be curated to invoke the results that make meaning in the lives of teachers and students. As we probe into this idea of curation, you might recognize many attributes of curation within your own instructional practices. You indeed are a curator!

Finding synergies between the content you select and the entryways for learning is an art. The standards help drive deeper understandings, but it takes orchestration of the many elements to create learning opportunities that are seasoned with a mix of resources, pedagogies, and curriculum. Beyond searching for content online or by other means, content curation involves organization of content. It often involves putting content into categories or themes. As John Spencer (2017) points out, "The best curators are able to find connections between seemingly opposite artists, ideas, or disciplines in ways that make you think, 'Man, I never considered that before.'" To become critical consumers of information is indeed important, and by allowing your students to also learn to curate, make decisions, organize content, and evaluate it (from a variety of perspectives), you can facilitate innovations, develop new understandings, and inspire aspirations with your students.

"Curated learning is not intended as a stand-alone pedagogical approach but should be combined with other constructivist approaches to teaching and learning. Understanding how to effectively curate learning may have significant ramifications for improving classroom pedagogy and [consequently] on student learning" (Cattlin, 2016). Curation is another way to elevate your teaching expertise and to guide your students to also be curators of the vast amounts of information we all encounter daily.

Curation Skills and Higher Order Thinking

Curation skills employ higher order thinking. According to Jennifer Gonzalez (2017),

> Curation projects have the potential to work at three levels of Bloom's Taxonomy:
> - Understand, where we exemplify and classify information
> - Analyze, where we distinguish relevant from irrelevant information and organize it in a way that makes sense
> - Evaluate, where we judge the quality of an item based on a set of criteria

Bloom's Taxonomy of Educational Objectives has had a long life in education. Published in 1956 by Benjamin Bloom et al., it was a means to classify outcomes and objectives and has been widely used in education across disciplines. Lorin Anderson and David Krathwohl revised Bloom's Taxonomy in 2001 to replace "synthesis" with "creation" as the highest level. The taxonomy has been used for curriculum and assessment design, classroom instruction, and in technology (Heick, 2020).

In the hierarchy shown in Figure 3.1, most levels involve selection, investigation, and/or analysis. In the upper part of the pyramid are the deeper learning skills that result when students manipulate and make sense of information

Figure 3.1. Bloom's Taxonomy

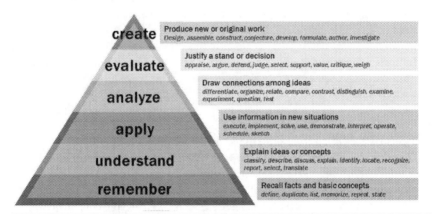

create — Produce new or original work
Design, assemble, construct, conjecture, develop, formulate, author, investigate

evaluate — Justify a stand or decision
appraise, argue, defend, judge, select, support, value, critique, weigh

analyze — Draw connections among ideas
differentiate, organize, relate, compare, contrast, distinguish, examine, experiment, question, test

apply — Use information in new situations
execute, implement, solve, use, demonstrate, interpret, operate, schedule, sketch

understand — Explain ideas or concepts
classify, describe, discuss, explain, identify, locate, recognize, report, select, translate

remember — Recall facts and basic concepts
define, duplicate, list, memorize, repeat, state

Note. From Vanderbilt University Center for Teaching (https://cft.vanderbilt.edu/guides-sub-pages/blooms-taxonomy/).

with actions such as organizing, supporting, weighing, comparing, critiquing, and investigating. That is, the upper half of the pyramid represents skills developed through curation. Curation involves investigating and sifting through content, artifacts, resources, and assessments including evidence.

Curation in Planning and Lesson Design

Most teachers have a set curriculum but are continually finding additional resources, activities, and teaching tools that support their curriculum and lesson design. Perhaps many who search for these resources have an internal lens as they peruse and sift through information to assist in their classroom planning and preparation. The decisions needed for this type of curation really center on student need, grade appropriateness, content, standards alignment, and functionality for classroom implementation. Most notably, with the expanse of online resources and libraries, educators need to be selective and prudent consumers.

Developing a set of criteria to assist in decision-making can be a valuable exercise. Curation of teaching strategies and approaches happens in the continual review, investigation, and decision-making focused on pedagogical content that is often aligned to state or national standards. Through an inquiry-based approach, developing key questions that guide your curation process may help as you plan and implement your classroom curriculum. When you are planning a unit of instruction, so many opportunities exist to collect evidence of learning. As we discuss further in Chapter 4, planning your lesson sequence with appropriate measures allows you to think about the different students in your classroom and what they need.

Once you have curated content and resources to bring to your lesson or unit, it is helpful to integrate content that aligns with your overarching goals. Selectivity is very important so that whatever resources you have curated deepen your students' learning. In Chapter 4 we guide you through the process of working through an evidence chart, unpacking evidence in your own words, and choosing the strategies you will use to collect the evidence. In this exercise in curation, you are setting the focus and outcomes in your plan, and this becomes your curator's frame for integrating content. Too often teachers let the lure of activities and resources lead lesson plan development. If you set your trajectory on getting to specific evidence that meets the standards, you are leading with the end in mind. This allows you to integrate the content in ways that support your end goals.

Curation in Assessment

Most teachers have a long list of assessment ideas and measures available to them. Some of these informal assessment measures are tailored to process-centered information gathering. Creating a rich grouping of assessments allows students to express understandings in diverse ways and through different modalities. Artistic work and processes can be blended in the assessment process to provide multiple means of expression and communication of student knowledge and understanding. Some teachers have shared with us that they get accustomed to a set of practices and sometimes push back on the idea of broadening their purview with other approaches, especially when their current methodologies have proven successful. That may be true for many of you, but reaching beyond the "tried and true" can yield exciting results. Curating methods that intentionally engage students may provide new insights and uncover approaches that you have not yet envisioned nor tried.

For example, in studying the ocean, your research and curation might produce new active learning approaches. Students might demonstrate their knowledge and skills in a variety of ways:

- Creating a mural of the elements of marine life reinforcing the elements of design
- Acting out the ecosystem while putting into practice theatrical conventions
- Enacting a commercial about visiting the ocean and what one needs to know before a trip by first curating different commercials and determining key strategies that are effective
- Creating a video on the endangered ocean ecosystem
- Collaborating on a group project which culminates in a performance task
- Creating a hypothetical scenario that would embody the learning

of a lesson or unit, allowing students to synthesize the vocabulary
and content they have learned and make learning visible

An example of a summative performance task is one where students
are asked to create a floor plan of a hypothetical museum of oceanography.
Students are invited to design each wing of the museum and determine what
information would need to be curated in the museum to showcase certain
aspects of marine life. Students then create a map of the museum and present this to the class, indicating which aspects they think are most important.
This action-oriented assessment pulls together many of the prior learning
activities in a final display of information. Students are asked to curate their
evidence of learning through this task, which could not be completed without their prior knowledge of the lesson or unit. An extended task would be
to have the students role-play as if they are museum designers sharing their
map with other "colleagues" (class members). The other class members can
be their audience and join in the role-playing. Throughout the process, the
teacher can collect, curate, and document evidence of learning as it unfolds.

In this example, notice that assessment is implemented through the
arts and is integral to the unit of instruction. Too often we remove assessment from the process of learning by asking students to prove what they
know with paper-and-pencil approaches only. Teachers benefit by providing
students with targeted learning opportunities that allow them to actively
express their learning. Through curation and embedding arts-integrated,
formative assessments in the unit of instruction, students begin to uncover
hidden meanings and deepen their understanding of content.

Inquiry in the Curation Process

Through inquiry, teachers can determine what processes and analyses are
needed as they curate content and create assessment opportunities. Two
questions you may ask yourself are: What elements inspire you to dig
deeper? What important information is surfacing as a result of your inquiry and review? Developing essential questions focused on the big ideas you
are introducing can help inform methodologies and results in the classroom.

These essential questions can first guide in the curation, but most important, inquiry used in the actual teaching and learning process can drive
student engagement. In *Quality Questioning* (2005), Jackie Walsh and Beth
Sattes note, "Questioning. Thinking. Understanding. These three processes
interact in a dynamic fashion to advance student learning, performance, and
achievement. Think of these classroom processes as action verbs that create
the energy for student work, the fuel for learning" (p. 1). Questions can help
you curate. Here are some that may be useful in classroom planning:

- What are my top 10 assessment measures that will induce audial, visual, and kinesthetic representations in student work?
- Of all the resources in a particular topic, what are the top three that would be most digestible and relevant to this lesson or unit on_____ [you fill in the blank]?
- When I taught this lesson or unit before, what roadblocks surfaced for students? What information could I curate that will help students overcome those roadblocks?
- In what ways can I curate content to develop real-life problem solving? Are there online resources that would allow students to explore and find relevant applications and connections?
- What arts or media best allow students to apply learning in visible ways? Of the possibilities available to me, what are the key art forms (dance, media arts, music, theater, visual arts) that will allow students to actualize content?
- What additional resources convey multiple perspectives and viewpoints? How can I help students to critically understand the value of comparing and contrasting different perspectives?
- What digital media are available that will support students in curating evidence and analyzing authenticity of artifacts and research?
- What resources and assessments relate to students and allow applications that reinforce cultural and linguistic relevance?

As you move through this text, you will see that we intentionally guide educators to really uncover the evidence they are seeking during the lesson process. The artistry of teaching can be personified as you thoughtfully consider the organic relationships that evolve as you deeply reflect on your practice and the students you serve.

BUILDING CURATION SKILLS

Curation skills are life skills. Teachers developing their own ability to curate information are learning essential life and workplace skills. To this end, they can make their curation processes visible to students and thereby build students' curation skills as well. As educators share how resources were curated and link to the goals of meeting the standards selected, they provide a platform for students to also engage in the same kind of careful selection, analysis, organization, and sharing of content in their assignments.

Siemens (2008) suggests that "instead of dispensing knowledge, [a teacher] creates spaces in which knowledge can be created, explored, and connected." The powerful model of curating together additional resources, research, artifacts, and so on, involves intentional practice. As a wealth of information is available to educators, perhaps we all need to rethink how we approach our pedagogy.

Through inquiry and investigation both teachers and students become more active learners. When teachers and students collect information regarding what went on in the classroom and take the time to analyze it from a distance, they can identify more than just what worked and what didn't. Educators and students will be able to look at the underlying principles and beliefs that define instructional practice. This kind of self-awareness is a powerful ally for a teacher, especially when so much of what and how they teach can change in the moment (Serra, 2015). Making this awareness visible to students can heighten students' understanding of the relationship between teaching practices and the way they learn.

A common theme in curation is the idea of bringing to the surface chosen materials from what often is a plethora of resources. Sifting through possible materials can be daunting, and once you find the resources you need, more work is needed to incorporate them into lesson planning and formative assessment. When you teach students to be surveyors of information and selective, inspective consumers, they come to understand that not all information is accurate nor necessarily "the best" for the learning at hand. As students research online and curate information from multiple sources, they need to learn how to determine what is authentic and what is not.

Similarly, finding patterns that emerge in the learning process, students can strengthen their investigative chops. The investigative skills are best learned through observation and inquiry. When students come to understandings based on their own processing, they begin to see that not all material, research, or information is equal. These skills are often developed through an inquiry process that allow students to wonder, ponder, and discuss. Developing criteria together (students and teacher) can be an effective means of coming to some agreements about what might be effective and what might not. For example, if high school students are asked to investigate a current court case that is in the public eye, the class might agree that it must be a case that involves a teenager and that it must not include violent crime. They could agree that the court case has to have occurred in the last 2 years, and that it has to have involved two compelling sides. As the criteria develop, the lens gets clearer on what to investigate. As students begin to find examples, this is when they curate the best examples of two conflicting points of view.

CURATION AS PART OF FORMATIVE ASSESSMENT

When you settle into this idea of curation, you can investigate and reflect on what is possible and what are the implications for your students. In other

words, understanding how your students process information will inform
the curation of resources you select and how you organize them. Ongoing
assessment of students' work guides your planning of next steps for teaching
and identifying content needs. As we have emphasized earlier, use of multiple measures in the classroom can produce positive ways for students to
express their knowledge, especially through the arts. Let's add some other
options to the list of what you may already use to assess student learning:

- Dramatizing a story, circumstance, news event, historical event, or
  concept
- Role-playing different perspectives, characters, or key historical
  characters
- Creating video that showcases several scientific experiments in
  action
- Constructing visual arts representation of key concepts by creating
  a collage, mural, poster, or storyboard using principles of design
- Dancing key concepts such as movement representing how the
  planets in the solar system function
- Creating musical phrases that represent a culture, story, or
  significant social movement

Each of the examples above employ a level of curation, selection, and
analysis. Think back to your experiences in school. What do you remember?
For us as students, the learning experiences that were profound involved a
high level of collaboration, investigation, and engagement. One experience
of Sarah's involved a project studying the Amish culture as part of a high
school sociology class. We students researched materials about the Amish
people and collected volumes of information about their values and beliefs,
settlements, and historical contributions. Through a process of collaborative investigation, problem solving, and curation, we created criteria for
what was to be selected based on a series of questions that helped drive
decision-making. With the end goal of a formal presentation to the class,
we curated content and worked on a learning story that was visually compelling. What was the significance? The power of this learning project was
the curation and choice-making based on criteria that resulted from collaboration. What was ultimately showcased was a collage of writing, artifacts,
visual images, and historical documents that together were woven into a
montage presentation. The teacher in this context was a facilitator of learning. She continued to probe and guide, but never led. What were the results?
We students were empowered. We were driven. We took ownership of our
learning journey and felt a sense of pride in our discoveries, achievements,
and ultimately our final curated product. This kind of learning sticks.

Much like a museum curator, the teacher joins together with students in
an evolving process of investigation, discovery, and analysis. It is important

to draw conclusions and be explicit about the new understandings that are emerging. Intentionality is critical here. Through curation, students and teachers together discover many new nuggets of insight that can be ultimately shared with a broader audience. The documentation process, as described in the Introduction, provides a vehicle for teachers and students to tell powerful learning stories that provide evidence of their own learning. Exhibiting the results of the curation becomes an essential component. So often this element is missing, leaving students void of celebratory opportunities to share their progress and achievements. Teachers need to take the time to draw conclusions and explicitly express that which comes to the surface as they consider so many factors throughout the lesson or unit. It is here that they begin selecting evidence that will be translated into the learning story. In Chapter 6 we will explore development of learning stories in more detail.

Curation and Visible Learning: An Example from Sarah

As a secondary teacher, I (Sarah) was part of a teacher research cohort with the University of California–Davis. As we investigated our own practice, we wanted to also listen to students. We would often purchase pizzas and gather students at lunch or after school and ask questions about their approaches to learning. One student shared, "If I know someone is going to exhibit or showcase my work, I work harder. If what I write or create merely stays in a teacher's folder, I find little motivation to work very hard." That became a game changer for many of the teachers in the cohort.

Through collaborative processes, we began to find multiple ways to curate and exhibit student work. This often took the form of poetry readings, collaborative art making, and investigations that crossed disciplinary boundaries. For example, when we were studying endangered species, we explored screen prints that Andy Warhol created in 1983 depicting endangered species from around the world.

Exhibiting student work became a theme with the teachers in the cohort, who represented science, visual arts, music, theater, and English language arts, and each worked with their students on a project involving research and curation. As students were studying endangered species in science, two of my colleagues, both veteran arts teachers, asked their students to research and curate different examples of Warhol's artwork, compare and contrast his work, and ultimately create masks of different animals using a style similar to Warhol's.

When students finished the mask making, they were asked how they thought the animals would move and interact with one another. They came to the theater where I taught classes. We met at lunch and after school and began to explore dramatic expressions using the masks. I asked students what kind of character their particular mask represented. We explored movements and sounds as they began to improvise with the masks. The music teacher got involved when we started asking, "What sounds could be attributed to the way the animals moved?" Soon science, visual arts, theater, and music students joined together in the process and helped each other. Musicians from the music department joined us in the theater and improvised different musical sounds to accompany each performer's movement and interaction and selected the specific instruments that best supported the masked animal characters' movements. All were researching to make informed decisions. Ultimately, we curated together to select what sounds, movements, and interactions could be created in a montage performance. Other students wrote poetry to contribute to the performance art. What started as a mere investigation emerged as a journey of learning that culminated in a performance and public forum at the Crocker Art Museum in Sacramento, CA. While a formalized performance was not the initial intent, the collaborative process that we teachers facilitated allowed for the interdisciplinary connections and provided a rich learning experience for the students—one that they talked about for months. The level to which students worked together and continued to edit, perfect, and develop their final performance was an example of how important it was to allow space for the investigation, research, curation, and discovery that culminated in an exhibit of student work.

Their collaborative work yielded something that eventually gained the program national attention and awards. In fact, when an evaluator visited our school to determine if our work warranted a national award, the teachers were ready to share what they had done to make this happen. The evaluator listened intently but then moved quickly to ask if he could talk to the students. It was then that the "gold" emerged. He heard students speaking intelligently about their journey, what they had learned and researched, and what further investigations were inspired by their work. It reinforced our learning that one boy, over pizza, had so eloquently shared. Creating forums for student interdisciplinary research, curation, and display impacted our practice significantly.

We discovered that as students engage in the curation process, they become more involved in independent learning processes. We supported students in discovery rather than imparting knowledge. This required shifting our approaches so that students own their learning. In so doing, we became facilitators of learning rather than "sages on the stage."

Curation of Evidence

In sum, curation involves review of teacher and student work, creations, and/or collections, which can also include work online. It is important to keep specific overarching goals or understandings of lessons or units in mind as you think about curating evidence that demonstrates student understanding.

By taking a formative approach, you can intentionally draw out evidence of learning through processes involving artistic expressions. The data you gather as your students are incubating ideas, brainstorming, and planning will be different than the information gathered from the editing, revising, and rehearsing or reworking process.

Like many teachers, you may collect evidence of learning as part of your regular practice. The question becomes, what do you do with it? Is it in piles on your desk or in the closet? Donning the role of curator of evidence provides an opportunity to select evidence and critically review and analyze it to learn more about teaching and the students' understanding of content. Selecting evidence can be a reciprocal process with students as they sharpen their skills of self-assessment and critique in ways that produce deeper understanding. Collecting this evidence can happen in online, digital student portfolios, in traditional student-made portfolios, or through other structures that allow you to review and analyze work. Finding the means for collection that works for you and your students may take time. Once students are familiar with the protocols, they will be able to hone their curation skills and become more adept at making valuable judgments about their work and the work of others. Beyond collecting work, the call to action is to manipulate and make meaning of the data that have been curated. Here are a few guiding questions to consider as you assess your current practices:

- What kinds of analysis do you incorporate in the classroom?
- Do you provide time for students to review and reflect on their work?
- Do you take time to distill information and/or identify patterns?
- Do you create a space to gather trends and unique insights?

The evidence may be pointing to trends, and you may begin to see new discoveries that students are finding as they progress through your lesson sequence. With deliberate practice, students can become expert curators of artifacts, research, resources, and new information. Carving out time to analyze student work in dialogue with students can build their curatorial capacity while helping you to identify what elements will be part of a learning story. When students actively participate in assessing their learning by interpreting their performance, they are better poised to recognize important moments of personal learning. This helps them identify their own strengths and needs and discover how to make "Where to next?" decisions.

Students should be educated in ways that build their curation and assessment capabilities, so they can take increasing ownership of their learning and, through this process, become more effective and independent learners. Students make progress when they develop the ability to monitor their own work. To do this well, they need to understand the following:

- What high-quality work looks like (by examining examples and models of quality work)
- What criteria define quality work (by participating in the development of learning goals and assessment criteria)
- How to compare and evaluate their own work against such criteria through peer assessment and self-assessment
- How to look for trends and emerging understandings and realize that quality often is the result of a process that involves revision, rethinking, re-envisioning, and growth over time.

For educators, the process of curating evidence provides valuable feedback that informs teaching practice. Teachers can see what worked, what needs more attention, and how students have translated their performance criteria into assignments. Evidence provides teachers with a road map for next steps in their teaching. For students, analyzing their work can provide a sense of proficiency and help them make critical judgments about where they are meeting the desired outcomes. Both perspectives are important and interconnected in the teaching–learning sequence. Making these processes and insights visible can create a dynamic classroom where students feel they are part of a larger process that they are helping to develop.

Simon Penny, media artist and theorist from the University of California–Irvine, described art as a culturally evolved strategy for human cognition related to complex problems. He explained, "Art and artistic ways of knowing are essential tools for learning about the world, and therefore indispensable in any form of education" (Penny, 2011, as cited in McDougall et al., 2012, p. 12). In applying this same approach in the curation of not only your teaching methodologies, but also in evidence of student learning, you too promote innovation in the classroom, transforming your environment into a research-driven, inquiry-saturated classroom alive with ongoing learning and meaning-making.

CHAPTER 4

Deepening the Lesson Plan

To begin with the end in mind means to start with a clear understanding of your destination. It means to know where you are going so that you better understand where you are now so that the steps you take are always in the right direction. (Covey, 1989, p. 98)

A *lesson plan* is a teacher's road map for planning a specific learning trajectory that has several components including key outcomes that students should accomplish along with assessments and experiential activities. The lesson plan, when carefully constructed, can be an important guide to help the teacher curate and map out content, formative assessments, and strategies for differentiated instruction. So, let's work to reclaim the lesson plan as a tool for you to document your expertise, scaffolding, and intentionality in your practice.

In this chapter, we move into developing lesson plans that provide opportunities to articulate specific learning outcomes through the arts and nonarts content and reflect on the unique role that the arts can play in assessing teaching and learning. We will demonstrate how you can make visible evidence of learning that emerges from the creative process. We will explore the process of making intentional design choices in the lesson plan and share some guidelines that can be used or adapted to customize lesson planning with a curator's lens. Through intentional planning, teachers develop a heightened sense of what choices they are making. The planning process helps teachers blend curricular ideas and concepts aligned to standards and determine what components best meet the needs of learners.

LESSON PLANNING

Moving Beyond the Outline

There is a tendency for lesson plans to be created as simple outlines. . . . As if we're in a rush. . . . As if they are for someone else rather than us. . . . As if we're not really going to put them to use. . . . And perhaps . . . as if . . . they don't matter. Lesson planning is an often-missed opportunity to show our skills as educators. Let's think about how you might design lesson plans that show your expertise as an educator and model how strong arts integration can lead to engaging cross-disciplinary explorations that are as interesting and engaging for our students as they are in developing skills that transfer across many areas. Think about lessons that can serve as a model and how assessment can serve as a feedback loop. What can you do to reinforce your own teaching practice? As emphasized throughout this book, arts integration offers new possibilities for assessment, providing opportunities to engage students in the creative process, yielding a rich pool of data. There is deep rigor in arts integration, and, more often than not, learning in, through, and with the arts goes deeper than more traditional approaches to teaching and learning.

Take a moment to scan one of the plans you teach most often. How would you rate your level of detail? If another teacher were to pick up your plan, could they replicate it? Does your plan show the complexity of teaching? Let's think about how you can develop some of your signature lessons to be infused with compelling documentation of the work that actually happens in the classroom, to capture student insights and reflections as well as your own.

Imagine a lesson plan that is richly developed and engaging to read. Our thinking is that the plan would not only describe the plan for teaching and learning in a nuanced, detailed way, but also it would map the places assessments would take place, including the kinds of questions asked by teachers to draw out evidence of learning. On the resource site at tcpress.com/teacher-as-curator-9780807764480, we invite you to download an editable version of Figure 4.1, which you can use as a planning tool.

Planning with Evidence in Mind

During the preplanning phase, be sure to identify points in your teaching where you will collect and curate evidence through project-based, performance assessment where students "show" their knowledge. A key element throughout the instructional process is the exchange of information between students and teacher. Students share their thinking (creative process) and produce artistic products expressing their learning in a variety of forms (i.e., exhibit, performances, and so on) signifying performance-based outcomes that exemplify target criteria and standards. To this end, consider how you might engage your learners in the curation of their work. How might you invite students to discuss the choices they have made about the work they present, the way they have organized material, and what they have learned from what they selected?

Let's be clear what we mean by "evidence." Merriam-Webster's online dictionary defines *evidence* as "an outward sign: indication; something that

Figure 4.1. Teacher as Curator: Evidence Chart Template

Standards	Specific Evidence of Learning Targets (Assessment Criteria)	Collection strategies (Formative Assessment & Summative Tasks)
Arts Standard(s): Select arts standards and non-arts standards that will work well to deepen learning in an integrated lesson or unit.	*Detail what students will know and be able to:* Consider varied evidence that allows students to demonstrate understanding of the subject area. • What criteria should be considered as you collect evidence? • What will you look for in the evidence? • What is able to be documented? • What will students be able to demonstrate?	*How will you collect evidence* (methods can include arts-based approaches)? How will you collect evidence? Consider varied methods to collect evidence that include arts-based approaches allowing students to demonstrate understanding.
Non-Arts Standard(s): Select non-arts standards and arts standards that will work well to deepen learning in an integrated lesson or unit.	*Students will know and be able to:* Consider varied evidence that allows students to demonstrate understanding of the subject area. • What criteria should be considered as you collect evidence? • What will you look for in the evidence? • What is able to be documented? • What will students be able to demonstrate?	*How will you collect evidence* (methods can include arts-based approaches)? Consider varied methods to collect evidence that include arts-based approaches allowing students to demonstrate understanding.

furnishes proof" (n.d.-b). Evidence-based teaching involves the use of evidence to: "(1) establish where students are in their learning; (2) decide on appropriate teaching strategies and interventions; and (3) monitor student progress and evaluate teaching effectiveness" (Masters, 2018).

There are different types of evidence gathered in formative assessment. The following instructional practices guide educators in gathering different kinds of evidence of learning during teaching and learning processes.

- Eliciting evidence through activating prior knowledge.
- Eliciting evidence through academic dialogue.
- Eliciting evidence through questioning.
- Eliciting evidence through observation and analysis of student work.
- Eliciting evidence through peer and self-assessment. (West Ed, n.d., p. 2)

Take time as you plan your lesson to identify where you might collect and document evidence from students' background knowledge. Design discussion prompts that illuminate students' thinking promoting metacognition. Designing questions in advance can intentionally link back to standards, support students' ability to identify connections, show their thinking, and share their ideas. Engage students in multiple ways of showing their understanding to get a 360-degree view of their thinking process. Also, remember that students can play an active role in documenting their learning along the way.

Utilizing a Curator's Checklist

Below is a list of ideas to get your curator's lens working. If this is a lesson you are designing for the first time, more research initially may be needed to tailor it to student needs. If it is a lesson that has already been taught, it is an opportunity to review and find points to either change or embellish.

- Establish your enduring understanding and/or your big ideas. This will guide your curation and help drive your lesson research and design.
- Select standards and essential understandings of what students should be able to know and do.
- Translate standards (both arts and other content areas) into specific evidence that can be collected to document learning and progress toward proficiency.
- Design assessment strategies that can be used to evaluate students' progress with special focus on arts processes and practices to generate and collect evidence of learning.
- Identify moments in the lesson when formative assessment activities can occur to inform you of adjustments that should be made based on students' needs.
- Create your top 10 list of resources that underscore and support the content that you are addressing (this can include curated lessons that help inform your design process, articles, teacher's

blogs, or artifacts such as images, songs, and videos from online or other sources). By determining some criteria that help you choose your top 10, you begin to hone in on the most important resources.

- Remember the cultures and backgrounds represented in your classroom.
- Determine which activities will help you curate instructional support and engage students.
- Think about what evidence you will collect in the sequence. By determining this early in the process, you can curate assessment measures that will meet the needs of your students. The evidence chart in Figure 4.1 will help you think this through.
- Create a list of artistic strategies and processes that could be used as part of your formative assessment plan. What ways of "knowing" can you weave into the lesson design process?

Beginning with the End in Mind

As we identified in the Introduction, Wiggins and McTighe (2008) suggest that teachers begin with the end in mind when planning lessons. Beginning with identifying the desired evidence for content standards that will demonstrate students' understanding helps to clearly plan learning and assessment experiences for classroom instruction. This may feel like a very different approach to planning lessons if you are used to going right into planning lessons and thinking about the activities you will use to engage students first. You will find that you are much more likely to meet your standards if you plan for evidence of success and assessment strategies right up front.

A useful metaphor is that of driving to a destination using a GPS. We know the destination of our journey and that doesn't change. There are, however, many options for getting there. It's true for teaching and learning as well. Being clear about our destination helps us align our efforts to ensure that we will get there. In the next chapter, we will provide a step-by-step progression to guide your thinking. The protocol we're about to guide you through builds on the backward design process with an arts integration and documentation lens. Fasten your seat belt and suspend your assumptions. We will guide you in a process that will give you a new lens on assessment and demonstrate how formative assessment incorporating the arts can deepen your teaching. Key features of this process include the following:

- Clarity about what evidence and criteria for student achievement you are seeking.
- Identification of creative, formative assessment tools and methods to collect evidence of learning throughout the process of teaching and learning

- Inclusion of arts-based strategies of assessment in your classroom
- Differentiated evidence using varied arts forms and processes
- Curation of evidence to guide instruction, make meaning, and provide documentation of student growth
- Development of learning stories that capture student progress

LESSON DESIGN

Revisiting Backward Design

Wiggins and McTighe's (2008) work in backward design has been a powerful method for curriculum design for educators. Here's a quick overview of the backward design process for those of you who may not be familiar with this design model. As explained above, you begin with your destination, identifying your desired results and the big ideas and skills you want to cover. This includes your standards—the enduring understandings you want students to take away. The second phase is moving into determining acceptable evidence that will show you have arrived successfully. That means thinking about all the standards you have identified. What evidence do you need to show what students know and will be able to do? Arriving at your destination means that you have achieved your goals and objectives. How will you know?

Here's where the backward-design approach feels quite different from traditional approaches to lesson design. Too often assessment is tacked on at the end of the lesson. Instead, backward design foregrounds assessment in planning at the beginning of curriculum design. By identifying the evidence of learning you are looking for before you design your activities, you are much more likely to get the outcomes you desire. Just these first steps will help you demonstrate later that you have successfully achieved your goals: (1) identifying where you are headed, and (2) determining what evidence you need to demonstrate that students have successfully achieved your goals. Then, and only then, do you plan the "how" you will get there. The third phase is your plan for teaching—planning your instructional strategies and activities. You identify where you are headed and what it looks like when you have arrived. The instructional activities you select should flow out of and be aligned with the evidence you need to collect.

By rethinking how they approach lesson planning and assessment, teachers can create profound results in the classroom that impact their school, community, and, on a larger scale, the field of education. If educators bring forward their expertise and insights and harness the power of assessment to shed light on student learning and the impact of educational approaches, then teachers' perspectives will play a larger role in shaping approaches to teaching practice. In other words, we believe that teachers can demonstrate their ideas and expertise in the way they write their lesson plans, in the way they articulate and document their own instructional practice, their learning, and the learning of their students. This will require rethinking how they develop lesson plans and document student progress. With the volumes written about assessment in education, it is easy to get numb to the "noise" of too much information and the plethora of pedagogies that address closing the achievement gap. Imagine using assessment to capture the evidence of learning not just to "prove" to someone outside the classroom that learning is happening, but rather, as a feedback loop for you and your students to understand the impact of your educational approaches in real time.

Focusing on Enduring Understandings: What Sticks?

In addition to essential questions, taking the time to write the enduring understandings—what you want to stay with students long after the lesson is completed—helps align the work to what is most important. What is the real purpose of the lesson? Note that it is less about definitions and simple skills but more about making meaning for life. What are the big ideas or concepts students should take away from your lesson?

In a blog post, Megan Davenport mulls over the question of lesson purpose, writing, "I have so much to cover—how do I see the forest through the trees? How do I capture the big picture of a unit without getting stuck on each individual standard? How do I create a rich context for the standards that will help my students truly retain and develop a lasting understanding of what I'm teaching?" She suggests considering the questions below to be sure that you are identifying the purpose of the lesson—that is, to focus on students' remembering ideas and concepts that matter over time:

- Why have I chosen to put these particular standards together?
- What is the common thread?
- What do I really want my students to remember at the end of this unit?
- Why should this information matter for my students today?
- Why should this information matter for my students ten years from now? (Davenport, n.d.)

Davenport makes the case that focusing on the enduring understandings you want students to leave with will help you avoid activity-driven assessment that pulls focus from the main purpose of the lesson.

Identifying Essential Questions

We recommend that you start by getting a provocative question in place, one that can drive curiosity and point to the connection of work in the classroom to the larger world. Wiggins and McTighe (2013) identify criteria of strong essential questions. They note that "a good essential question"

- Is *open-ended;* that is, it typically will not have a single, final, and correct answer.
- Is *thought-provoking* and *intellectually engaging,* often sparking discussion and debate.
- Calls for *higher-order thinking,* such as analysis, inference, evaluation, prediction. It cannot be effectively answered by recall alone.
- Points toward *important, transferable ideas* within (and sometimes across) disciplines.
- Raises *additional questions* and sparks further inquiry.
- Requires *support* and *justification,* not just an answer.
- *Recurs* over time; that is, the question can and should be revisited again and again. (p. 3)

Be sure to craft questions that engage students' thinking and determine if the arts can be woven into the lesson sequence. The point is to show equal rigor in both arts and nonarts content. For example, here are a couple of essential questions from the National Core Arts Standards (National Coalition for Core Arts Standards [NCCAS], 2014):

Under the Creating Strand in Media Arts:
Essential Question: What is required to produce a media artwork that conveys purpose, meaning, and artistic quality? How do media artists improve/refine their work?
Under the Performing Strand in Music:
Essential Question: How does understanding the structure and context of musical works inform performance?

Setting Clear Learning Targets to Drive Instruction

It is important to identify learning targets. The learning targets will be translated into specific evidence that will demonstrate the desired outcomes. Subject matter standards will help set clear learning targets based on key underlying concepts and themes. By setting clear targets as destination points, the necessary steps to meet those targets can be taken. This is about aligning your work—setting a clear trajectory to stay on course.

A *learning target* should identify for students (in understandable language) what they will learn from a lesson and should be clear about what the student will do, say, or write in a lesson. Students should understand what the target looks like, how to get there, and how to generate evidence that shows how well they exemplified the learning. Moss and Brookhart (2012) describe learning targets as "student-friendly descriptions—via words, pictures, actions, or some combination of the three—of what you intend students to learn or accomplish in a given lesson. When shared meaningfully, they become actual targets that students can see and direct their efforts toward" (p. 9). Adults also can use these established targets to monitor success and improve their teaching and the opportunities that they construct for their students.

Selecting Your Standards Intentionally

Teachers tend to create lesson plans that are often overloaded with standards. It's common to see 10–15 standards at the beginning, and sometimes these appear as just a laundry list of standard numbers; not even the full standard language is included. Often teachers front-load so many standards that they never return to them in the learning plan or assess them. It often becomes a false claim that all the standards are addressed. Choose carefully those standards that will be addressed in your lesson or unit. Here's the thing: *Your standards are your north star.*

For the purpose of this guided exploration, pick just one standard for the arts and one for other content so you can dive deeply into the enduring understandings you want students to explore. This will prevent you from designing a plan that is "an inch deep and a mile wide."

Finding the "Elegant Fit"

As you are selecting your standards, consider the relationship between the arts and other content areas with which you are integrating. Is learning in the arts deeper because of integration? Is learning in the other disciplines deeper as a result of the arts integration? This is what Burnaford et al. (2001) describe as finding the "elegant fit." This means that the integration of arts and other content makes sense. Both disciplines benefit from the presence of the other. They are taught at the same time, with investigation, creative work, and assessment in both areas while illuminating an enduring understanding.

Establishing Equal Rigor

Arts integration by definition positions the arts with equal rigor through interdisciplinary learning with other content standards. This means that both the arts and nonarts standard should be visible within the lesson. It also means that arts standards will be taught and assessed (vocabulary, history, technique, and so on) with the same care and emphasis in your teaching as the other subject area that you are integrating.

In the example below, taken from her unpublished lesson plan of November, 2018, visual arts educator Theresa Cerceo, from St. Agatha, Maine, specified her Enduring Understanding and Essential Questions:

> *The Enduring Understanding for this unit was:*
> Artists and designers experiment with forms, structures, materials, concepts, media, and art-making approaches.

The Essential Questions explored in this unit included:
How do artists work? How do artists and designers determine whether a particular direction in their work is effective? How do artists and designers learn from trial and error? (from National Core Arts Standards [NCCAS, 2014]).

Theresa provides a rationale describing the "elegant fit" in a lesson that integrates bookmaking and the exploration of the digestive system and writes about how bookmaking can provide the visual representations of scientific content:

> Books are containers for information. Students experience books in a variety of ways, from personal, beloved, favorite picture books to textbooks used in class. Bookmaking allows students to expand on this personal relationship with books. They are able to expand on their experience from being the receiver of the information to now becoming the owners of it. As creators of the book, they have ownership in the delivery of information, not only the content but in the visual stimuli (through their choices of paper, paint, and other media, they supply the viewer with textures, colors, and patterns). The student bookmakers influence how their viewer or reader will receive the information. In so doing, the reader can reflect on the ways in which they receive information. In addition, acting as an illustrator of information allows the student to learn about and act as a medical illustrator. This addresses careers in the arts as well as teaches the students multiple functions of visual arts in our society. The book pages can be altered to show the intricacies of digestion by the inclusion of layers (overlays), shape, color, texture. This will provide students with a creative challenge to share information in a form that can reveal a variety of aspects.
>
> Having more scientific knowledge, students will have more information to influence their artistic choices. They will be able to independently consider materials (such as paper textures or line types), and the work therefore functions equally as a book and as an artwork. (T. Cerceo, unpublished lesson plan, November 2018)

Determining Desired Evidence of Learning

Early in the planning process, as we noted earlier, you need to define clearly what evidence of learning will help students demonstrate their understanding and synthesis of content. Taking time to determine the evidence that will show that students achieve proficiency in target outcomes is a critical (and frequently missed) step. Often determining key criteria can be done collaboratively with students.

If you know what you are looking for and can communicate this clearly to students, the process of documenting that evidence becomes a joint process with teacher and student. Once you pinpoint the evidence that will demonstrate that students have met the standard, you can identify strategies (including arts-based performance tasks that are embedded in the progression of work). Open your mind to think about possibilities of how students will demonstrate their understanding. So often teachers think about how students remember facts and key concepts but don't think about how to connect this learning to real-life applications.

The evidence chart: unpacking the standards. Now that you have identified your standards and decided how you might want to show your students' learning, let's work to determine what the evidence of success might look like for the investigations you have planned in your classroom. We have designed an evidence chart to help describe the picture of what it is— *exactly* what it is—you want to see in the evidence (refer to Figure 4.1, column 2). This will help you and your students see the destination where you are headed. Too often teachers are not clear about what they're looking for but have the sense of "I'll know it when I see it." This isn't good enough. You need to be able to communicate to students what you are looking for in advance.

If you spend time in advance identifying the specific details of the evidence that you intend to collect, everyone will benefit. Teach to get the results that you want by determining early on what it is that students will do to unpack the enduring understanding and the content that it embodies. Working through the specific details of what you want students to know and be able to do in concrete, documentable terms will create clear criteria for students to align their work in order to achieve success. And if the work falls short, it provides a guide for you and your students to understand what is lacking and what needs more focus. In essence, you are curating the standards and expected evidence for the "elegant fit."

Sometimes teachers rely on "canned" assessment tools. Why not create your own, with clear descriptions of exactly what you will be looking for? When you collect student work, and you sit down to grade and find that they've missed the mark, and think, "How could this happen? I thought I was crystal clear!" Often what teachers perceive to be student gaps in understanding is actually the lack of clarity about the expected evidence. You want to be clear and detailed enough so students understand exactly what you are looking for in their work. The clearer you are, the easier it will be for your students to demonstrate learning that mirrors what the standard is addressing. There is no shortcut for this important work. It takes time to think through what specific evidence you seek. The thinking that goes into the evidence chart becomes the platform for everything to follow. Some standards are either quite broad or very dense. A standard that is broad can be generic, lacking detail. In this case, the standard may not provide guidance in terms of what evidence you are looking for. Conversely, some standards can be overloaded with multiple parts. This can be overwhelming if you intend to address only one of the parts. In both cases, it's important to translate standards into the actual evidence you will be collecting.

The evidence chart will provide a map for you (and your students) to follow in the teaching and learning sequence. The chart will also allow you to reframe the standard in terms of your language and the outcomes you are planning for. We suggest taking time to tailor your evidence to the direction that you know you are going. Bringing forward your expertise, voice, and intention starts here—in how you unpack your standards and identify the evidence you will be looking for in students' work. In determining evidence, think about how students will demonstrate understanding. While formalized assessment measures are important, we encourage you to also incorporate formative assessment that highlights learning in the process of student engagement as part of creative exploration.

Measurable evidence linked to standards. We're inviting you to translate the standard into concrete, measurable evidence that links to the work you know you will be doing in your classroom. Be specific with your language. If you are going to ask that students use the elements of the art form they are working in to discuss their artistic choices (and we hope you are), then list each element so it's visible in column 2 of Figure 4.1. You are creating clarity for your students by identifying key criteria you will use to assess their work, and for you by creating a clear trajectory that defines the direction you are headed in scaffolding your teaching.

Taking time to be intentional about what it is you want students to know and be able to do and distilling the specific evidence that demonstrates proficiency will be very helpful as you plan your instructional sequence. Take a moment to work with the standards you have selected, using the following actions:

- Underline verbs and important nouns.
- Consider the content you plan to cover.
- Pin down an accurate description of the specific evidence that you expect students to produce.
- Specify how students will document their understanding of key content (including the specific vocabulary, concepts, and so on).

Keep in mind that if you can describe what it is you are looking for, you can document it. As you define indicators of success (the evidence that you are looking for), be sure that it's meaningful to you as an educator. Indicators will lead you to the evidence you intend to curate and collect.

Describe this evidence in concrete, specific language that your students will understand. Define your terms. If you want students to know the definition of *erosion*, for example, specify the key elements you will expect to see included. This invites you to project forward, imagining what proficiency will look like and considering what you would want to see evidence of along the way. The more specific you are, the clearer the criteria you are creating for assessing evidence of learning. Your description in column 2 of Figure 4.1 is not only the evidence you will be looking for, but also can serve as criteria for a rubric or checklist.

Consider the following example in which Lisa worked with a teacher who had designed a lesson for students integrating science and dance. The standard looked at Interrelationships in Earth/Space Systems. The standard identified that the student will investigate and understand the organization of the solar system and the relationships among the various bodies that comprise it. The evidence the teacher listed in the chart was that students would create a dance that depicted the movement of the planets around the sun. Here's the dialogue that ensued while working with the evidence chart:

> **Lisa:** So, if I am moving fluidly around an object we've identified as the sun, do I get an A?
> **Teacher:** No, students have to show they understand the distance between the planet and the sun.
> **Lisa:** Okay, so if I demonstrate by standing on a grid that shows how far away I am from the sun, do I get an A?
> **Teacher:** No, you have to show the revolution and rotation.

And so it continued with size and the role of gravity as well as with the understanding demonstrated in dance—including use of the elements of dance; use of body, energy, space, and time; and qualities of movement. When pressed, this educator actually knew very specifically what she needed to see in students' work—the criteria for success— but did not explicitly identify it in advance. The chart asks for specificity in evidence because the more concrete and detailed you are about what you are looking for, the more likely you are to integrate these ideas deeply in your teaching, and the more likely you are to get this from your students. See Figure 4.2 for a richly detailed example of an evidence chart focused on integrating science and theater.

The evidence you detail is proof you have met the standard. Generating clear criteria for what you expect the evidence to look like or contain provides students with a picture of what you are asking them to do. Creating your description of criteria in user friendly language for your students will be more precise than using premade rubrics. It also allows you to be deeply familiar with what you are asking students to produce.

Be wary of naming the method of collection rather than the evidence itself. Often when asked about the evidence they are looking for in a lesson or unit, teachers will respond by describing their collection plan rather

Figure 4.2. A Completed Evidence Chart

Subject Area Standards	Identify Desired Outcomes with Acceptable Evidence	Collection Strategies
2.Earth & Space Science 2-2. Map the shapes and types of landforms and bodies of water in an area.	*Students will be able to:* in small groups accurately depict different types of landforms found in the United States through tableaux. Landforms covered include: plateau (found on map in Colorado, Utah, Arizona, New Mexico) volcano (found on map in Washington, Alaska, Hawaii) plains (found on map in Kansas, Nebraska, North Dakota, South Dakota) mountains (found on map in Kentucky, Tennessee, Virginia, North Carolina, and so on). Students will be able to: Identify bodies of water that may be found around landforms (rivers, oceans, lakes) Students will be able to: "Map the shapes" with their body gestures in creating the tableaux. Each tableau pose should clearly show the landform's defining characteristics: plateau = body positions that emulate a tabletop; sloping sides, flat top volcano = body positions that indicate slope (like a mountain) and opening at top for lava plains = low, flat body positions mountains = sharp, angular body poses to evoke rocks and sense of height Students will be able to: Point out on a U.S. map the location(s) where the landform(s) is found.	Tableau Photographs Documentation on maps Student discussion of artistic choices Teacher observation Photographs Peer review
Pre-K–4 Theater: Acting 1.4. Create characters through physical movement, gesture, sound and/or speech, and facial expression.	*Students will be able to:* collaborate in small groups to effectively develop their characters (inanimate objects, landforms) which they'll convey through a frozen physical pose in a tableau. *Students will be able to:* use gestures and facial expressions to show the characteristics of a landform such as volcano, plateau, mountains, or plains. (For example, students make sharp, angular poses to illustrate Rocky Mountains. See other details above.)	Teacher observation Tableau Photographs Peer discussion Student reflection

than specific proof of learning. Consider this scenario: When asked how she will assess learning, a teacher responded, "I will observe." What exactly is she observing? She is identifying *how* she will collect rather than *what* she will collect. It's important to see the difference, because often assessment is glossed over.

Identifying Assessment Strategies for Collecting Evidence

The final column of the chart (refer to Figures 4.1 and 4.2) identifies *how* you will collect the evidence. Taking the time to isolate the clearly identified evidence of learning by naming the criteria for your assessment and identifying how and when you will collect the evidence, will make assessment a core element. Note that in the chart, we separate the evidence from how it will be collected. The evidence is different from the collection mechanism.

As you identify your collection strategies, we encourage you to select diverse methods for collecting evidence that allow students to demonstrate learning in a variety of ways (the arts do this well). Note that your collection strategies can include performance tasks—where students can apply the skills and knowledge they have gained to demonstrate understanding by synthesizing and connecting information.

The evidence chart was designed as a planning tool that provides alignment for your lesson plan. Using it in your lesson planning will allow you to revisit the frame for your lesson as you are teaching. It was developed in a curriculum design course where teachers struggled to pinpoint the exact evidence they were seeking. Separating the desired outcomes and acceptable evidence from the method of collection helped keep a clear focus on defining the evidence of learning that would demonstrate that standards were met.

The purpose of the chart is to serve as a road map to guide your thinking. It prompts you to crystallize your thinking about the kinds of evidence that will be most meaningful and helps you to determine whether you have achieved your desired outcomes.

In the planning, you set the outcomes. You define the evidence. In the next chapter, you will see how the chart continues to be valuable during the process of implementing the lesson. It can provide an opportunity to be iterative—to return to your lesson throughout the process of teaching to add notes, adjust, and capture your observations.

As you move through the main categories of the lesson plan feel free to adapt as needed to the format you feel most comfortable using. We understand that the plan will change in implementation, but having a clear trajectory at the beginning is critical. Review your plan and deepen it by making visible your educational thinking, such as scaffolding, accommodations, interdisciplinary connections, applications, and so on. Think about this plan as the foundation for a "learning story" you can continue to build upon as you implement the lesson (see Chapter 6).

EIGHT CURATORIAL LENSES
FOR REVIEWING AND DEEPENING A LESSON PLAN

In this section, which is organized by a teacher's curatorial lenses, we invite you to revisit your lesson plan with an eye toward showing your expertise and making the nuance of the teaching–learning process visible. Show how you will introduce key concepts, including examples and talking points. Articulate how you will guide your students throughout the learning process. Give your lesson "connective tissue" so that it reads like a map as opposed to an outline. As you read through the lesson lenses below, review a plan you are currently working with and see how the content can be deepened.

Lesson Lens 1: Make Your Expertise Visible

Earlier in this chapter we asked you to think about one of your lesson plans. Please think again about that plan. Does it reveal the nuance and complexity of your work? We suggest that you move beyond a lesson outline to a robust documentation of your thinking and curation as a teacher.

You know the thousands of decisions you make daily, so make the complexity of your planning and teaching visible by adding detail to your chart and your plan. As you develop your plan and include details of evidence, you are showing your expertise as a teacher. Through this process you are identifying the junctures at which you will collect and assess evidence, how and where you involve your students, and how you are scaffolding your teaching.

Here is a reflection about the process and how it shifted the teacher's perspective on lesson plan development. Fourth-grade teacher Jason Roberts from Richmond, Virginia, describes his decision-making and the importance of documentation:

> As teachers we are constantly making decisions and choices based on what we know our students need. The challenging aspect of this is getting what is in our brains down on paper in a way that others may be able to utilize our experiences and see how our work benefits students. The process of making these conscious decisions and documenting the benefits and strategies used is almost as crucial as the delivery of the lesson itself. (J. Roberts, personal communication, November 2019)

As you plan lessons, it is important to include a step-by-step, detailed progression. Here are some suggested steps to consider:

- Activate the map of your lesson by developing your plan showing a detailed step-by-step progression.
- Include your talking points—detail how you will introduce concepts, vocabulary, techniques.
- Articulate how you will set up and guide investigations and learning experiences.
- Provide enough details that someone else could take the lesson and picture how the work would unfold.
- Include documentation on exemplars you will curate, including handouts, rubrics, and so on; images of your examples help tell the story of teaching.
- As you list materials needed and resources used, provide full bibliographic citations with links, if available, for curated resources. This list helps others access resources that will be helpful, positioning you to share or publish your work later. Full citations are a great resource for other educators who may wish to replicate your work. The materials and resources you identify will be helpful to other educators if you share your work now, and will be useful to you if you publish your work later.

Example. To help you understand the process outlined above, consider how teaching artist Aijung Kim documents an arts-integrated lesson linking visual arts exploration creating a zine with developing writing skills and communicating a personal story. In this example, she is working with a class of 6th- and 7th-grade English language learners in a middle school in Virginia. Her students are to share stories of how they came to the United States.

A *zine* may be defined as follows: "A zine is a self- published, noncommercial print-work that is typically produced in small, limited batches. Zines are created and bound in many DIY ways, but traditionally editions are easily reproduced—often by crafting an original 'master flat,' and then photocopying, folding, and/or stapling the pages into simple pamphlets. Zines may also be sewn, taped, glued—or even exist in unbound, sculptural, and other non-folio formats" (Milwaukee Zine Fest, n.d.).

In her lesson plan, Aijung carefully curates the content she'll share with students. Some of what she will share includes materials she has created herself (sample zines, guide sheets, checklists, and so on). She includes an image of an exemplar she has created. She guides students to notice composition elements in preparation for supporting them in creating a page of their zines. She uses bullets to detail steps, but there is enough detail that someone else reading her lesson plan can use it to guide their

Figure 4.3. Composition Exemplar

Using the same text drawn from her own parents' immigration story, Aijung created different versions of a page to show the process of arranging found and hand-drawn imagery and developed a finished composition. She also wanted to highlight the choice of using typed or hand-drawn text.

teaching. She has preplanned debriefing questions she will ask to draw out evidence of learning.

Culturally responsive connections. In this lesson, the teaching artist invites students to write personal narratives about their lives drawing upon their experiences and prior knowledge. This honors students' "funds of knowledge" and values the experiences they bring to the classroom (N. González et al., 2005). Wager et al. (2017) advocate the use of multiple literacies to value students' multiple identities:

> For students who are in the process of learning a new language in a new land, while still holding on to their native language, the ability to investigate, reflect and share this knowledge through rich multimodal literacies (i.e., through textual, gestural, visual, spatial, audio, and digital ways) that are not oral language dependent, is crucial (Franks, 2008). (p. 15)

The arts can help anchor learning by creating a personal connection, increasing personal relevance to the content, and providing students with many languages to express their understanding.

Demonstration of creating a final zine page. Teaching artist Aijung outlines the following instructions in her lesson plan:

- Ask students to play with collage images precut on the final zine
  page by showing [weak] examples first.
- Ask students what they think and why the image doesn't work.
  For example, explain that just "jeepney" (a kind of Filipino bus)
  with words on the bottom looks a bit boring. Also, in looking
  at all the images crammed together, it makes it too hard to
  understand.
- Show students an example of the way I chose to finalize my zine
  page and point out the use of text and images together. Point out
  that I decided to hand letter my text and design specific words [see
  Figure 4.3].
- Ask students to take their first page of writing and follow the
  same method:
  » Underline or write words and concepts of EMPHASIS
  » Draw thumbnail sketches or collect imagery
  » Star best thumbnail idea
  » Start composing on page

The steps above demonstrate how students were able to make a connection with text through images. The step-by-step process helped students to
gradually make meaning through analysis and reflection.

Lesson Lens 2: Teach About the Integrated Art Form

As you write your plan be clear about *what* and *how* you teach students
about the art form you are integrating. What specific techniques will you
introduce? How will you introduce and discuss the vocabulary and elements
of the art form?

For each step of your plan include direct instruction about the art form
using the elements and techniques of the discipline. Without this, it looks
like the arts can be taught as an add-on, and it reduces the importance
of the art. The arts have a rich history, specific vocabulary, and processes
that should be taught with the same level of thoughtfulness and detail as
you teach about science, social studies, math, or reading. In your plan, if
you say, "I will teach students the process of tableau" (a drama strategy
explained in Chapter 7), explain how you will approach this. How will
you introduce the vocabulary word *tableau* as a building block of drama
that means a frozen picture? How might you engage students in the process
of creating a compelling stage picture using levels, space, a sense of frozen
action? In being specific, you are also embedding ideas about how you will
introduce the criteria in assessing student work. Can students engage in peer
review of each other's tableaux by critiquing students' use of levels, space,

and communicated sense of action through their frozen image? How might you give specific instructions to guide students' thinking? What exemplars might you curate? How will you discuss them?

It's important to teach about content in ways that students will be able to demonstrate their understanding in documentable evidence. In arts integration, students will learn as much about the art form that is explored as they will about the nonarts content. Showing the deep progression of work in your lesson plan reveals how you guide students through each process. How will you model key concepts and skills? What examples from the field will you use to inspire and instruct?

Lesson Lens 3: Make Moments of Formative Assessment Visible

Now that you know what evidence you will collect and how you will collect it, it's important to identify key checkpoints in your lesson plan when you will gather and curate evidence of learning and assess student progress and understanding. Make the moments of assessment richly detailed. If you are observing, specify clearly the evidence you are seeking to gather from the students. What are the specific knowledge, skills, and indicators you expect students to demonstrate?

If you are facilitating a discussion, take time to craft the exact questions you will pose so you can link intentionally back to the standards and the specific evidence you are looking for. If you will ask students to give feedback on the work of others, what parameters will you offer them to guide their review?

Consider places in your plan where you can invite your students to collaborate in assessment processes. As active participants, students begin to know the value of assessment. You can create a culture of gathering and curating evidence, where you model for and engage with students in the idea that assessment is an important part of the feedback loop for learning.

Formative assessments can be integrated throughout the plan to help monitor students' learning. These assessments allow you to plan for next steps, to see what individual students need on the way to proficiency, and to provide continuous feedback to the students and to you as the teacher. These are low-stakes assessments that can help students target areas that need support. Formative assessment prepares students for summative assessment at the conclusion of their lesson or unit to evaluate their learning. These tend to be high-stakes assessments that measure how students address standards. Both are critical to teaching and learning. As you seek to pinpoint specific moments of assessment throughout your plan, consider the following questions:

- How will you design and embed your debriefing or discussion questions?
- How will you engage students in the assessment process?

- How and when will you make sense of the evidence you have collected?

It is important to create a set of checkpoints and evaluation for dialogue with students to make meaning of their own learning. The questions above represent specific opportunities for student and teacher feedback. In your plan you should also identify your creative assessment strategies.

Lesson Lens 4: Identify Moments of Decision-Making Throughout the Creative Process

In her book *Art Matters* (2002), Eileen Prince talks about the decision-making processes embedded in art making. She notes that art "requires constant decision making, no matter how subconscious those decisions might be. It requires superior observation skills, the ability to process information and then apply it in unique ways and, perhaps most importantly, something of substance to communicate" (p. 3). If teachers make these elements visible, they will show the complexity of creative, arts-integrated work. How might you make the decision-making aspects of arts-integrated learning visible in the development of your lesson plan?

As students move through arts-integrated lessons, there will be multiple points to collect evidence of decision-making. The evidence you collect and curate at different points in the journey will take on different characteristics. This is where formative assessment can reveal the complexity of the learning journey. Collecting evidence of learning in the beginning of the process is going to look very different from that of the middle or final stages of the process. Be intentional in your lesson plan about when and how you will collect evidence of decision-making, so that information can be part of a feedback loop.

Lesson Lens 5: Triangulate—Collect Evidence from Different Perspectives and Methods

When making sense of a phenomenon (in this case, learning), researchers ensure that they are collecting data from a variety of sources through different methods (Patton, 1999). This is called *triangulation*, which means that you collect and curate at least three sources or different methods of collecting evidence representing a variety of perspectives. This cross-check ensures that you are getting a clear understanding of what is happening and why. You will glean a stronger understanding of student progress if you collect data from different sources.

What does this mean for assessment? It means that you will gain a more comprehensive picture of learning if you collect data from more than one source and from more than one perspective. If the only approach to assessment listed is teacher observation or teacher review, you have one perspective—yours. You will be happily surprised by the nuanced information you will get from collecting data also from student and peer perspectives. The intersection of these data points provides a more holistic picture of learning.

Think about how you might triangulate your data through formative assessment processes. Make assessment visible and an integral, celebrated part of your lesson and assist students in seeing how they can understand their own learning from this curated mosaic of evidence.

Lesson Lens 6: Increase Points of Access for Diverse Learners

Brain researcher Todd Rose notes that every student is a variable learner and yet teachers tend to design curriculum for the "average" student. He suggests that there is no average student. In fact, we are all variable learners. A high school dropout himself, Rose (TEDx, 2013, 17:02) explains:

> I've been to the very bottom of our educational system. I've been to the very top. I'm here to tell you that we are wasting so much talent at every single level. And the thing is, . . . for every person like me, there are millions who worked as hard, who had the ability, but who were unable to overcome the drag of an educational environment designed on average. And their talent is forever lost to us.

Arts integration provides multiple, flexible options for student learning, assessment, and student voice. The arts provide multiple means for students to connect curricular ideas across the curriculum and demonstrate their understanding in ways that lead to deep learning.

Another useful thinking frame to apply to your lesson plan design is Universal Design for Learning (UDL). UDL is an approach to teaching and learning that increases students' access to curriculum, offering "flexibility in the ways students access material, engage with it and show what they know" (Morin, n.d.). The concepts of UDL connect what is known about neuroscience research and the brain with the intentional curriculum and instruction elements that build greater accessibility for all kinds of learners, including special needs students and students from other cultures. UDL invites educators to consider how they can diversify teaching strategies in three ways.

As explained in the Introduction, the Universal Design for Learning (UDL) suggests that teachers can increase access to the curriculum for all learners by (1) representing content using a variety of approaches; (2) increasing engagement with curriculum by providing many ways for students to work with content; and (3) inviting demonstration of understanding of content in diverse ways. (CAST, n.d.). The arts provide alternate ways of translating, investigating, and making meaning that increase access to and relevance for students (Glass & Donovan, 2017; Glass et al., 2013). It is critical to see the arts not only as an avenue for aesthetic and creative exploration and expression, but also as a means of demonstrating student understanding and knowledge as well as social and emotional understandings.

Review your lesson to consider how you are creating a variety of access points for your diverse learners. The more ways you give students to share what and how they know, the more complex and holistic picture of learning you will get.

Lesson Lens 7: Identify Creative Assessment Strategies

Designing and employing arts-based, creative strategies within the lesson allows students the opportunity to provide feedback. Creative strategies allow for formative assessment through arts-integrated choice-making. Students translate ideas into new forms through problem solving, critical thinking, and collaboration. Creative expression becomes a key hallmark of the demonstration of learning. By curating concrete, creative opportunities, for students to show their knowledge, you can gain revealing insights into students' diverse ways of learning and their unique skills as well as their ability to innovate and create. Review your plan for moments of assessment and design the specifics of your assessment tools.

Lesson Lens 8: Design Your Debriefing Questions

Design your debriefing questions to draw out specific evidence to show that you are meeting the standards. Use the criteria from your evidence chart to design checklists, or rubrics. Take the time now to design what your assessment tools will look like in order to curate targeted evidence. Continuing to develop your assessment approaches will keep your destination at the forefront of your planning. Consider the difference between asking "What did you enjoy most about this work?" versus "What artistic choices did you make in depicting the content?" What you ask will determine what evidence you elicit from students reflecting on the work, but also how students understand the content.

RECLAIMING LESSON PLANS

One of the issues identified in this work is the idea that lesson plans are often abbreviated for a variety of reasons. A common sentiment articulated by teachers is that lesson planning takes too much time and is difficult to do within the school day. Some teachers have said that they think that the lesson plan is not for themselves, but part of an expectation from their supervisor. Others articulate that there are too many requirements for the lesson plan, making it cumbersome and difficult to develop. Some teachers believe they don't need to map out every part of what happens in the classroom. One teacher remarked as she was reflecting on how foreign it felt to embed thoughts and reflections in her lesson plan, "We tend to 'haiku' it" (meaning that the lesson plans were often written in a deliberately brief form like a haiku poem). (C. Lucas, Richmond, VA, personal communication, 11/5/18)

Another teacher took on the challenge of writing things down because he noted that he was "constantly making decisions in the moment and shifting things to move through the process of teaching." He said it was an intuitive process. We want to invite teachers to tune into the intricate web of choices they make while teaching and to attend to what's happening for them as well as for their students. An elementary music teacher from Raymond, New Hampshire, wrote this reflection in a curriculum design course:

> As I look back on the process of creating this unit, I have found I have undergone a large mindset shift. I have always integrated math, science, and social studies into my music classroom, but I now realize what it takes to truly dive deep into a lesson, seeing it from different angles and bringing enduring understandings to my students that are meaningful and essential to their learning. . . . Now, I see assessment in a new light and I feel comfortable and confident with the assessments I have created for this unit. These assessments will be positive and will promote growth and learning because they will not reflect talent but will instead reflect understanding. I see assessment not only as a way to promote growth, but as a way to guide my teaching and ensure that what I am teaching is meaningful and specific to my goals. This [process] has changed my perception of assessment, and I look forward to implementing meaningful and structured assessment into my curriculum. (A.S., unpublished course reflection, 2018)

In the next chapter we will move into documenting evidence in a "curation map" that tracks and annotates the insights, connections, and course corrections that unfold in the implementation of your lesson. You will find that documentation of the work in process captures student insights and reflections as well as your own. Mapping the process of learning in your plan will create an important archive of evidence and reflection as well as ideas for next steps, which will deepen your practice as an educator and uncover fresh insights about your students.

CHAPTER 5

Curation Maps
Tracing the Journey

> Documenting means more than being organized or supporting learning by providing evidence. It involves accessing and reflecting on one's own learning processes and articulating what is taking place throughout a learning journey. (Tolisano & Hale, 2018, p. 4)

Once the lesson is in the implementation phase, you can flip from planning to mapping the journey. Documenting what actually takes place can create important opportunities for reflection and key insights. This can include capturing opportunities to adjust your teaching and the marking of important learning moments. Documenting these reflections in the lesson plan becomes what we are calling a "curation map"—documenting choices, selection and analysis of specific moments, evidence, students' observations and insights as well as your own. This curation map can create an archive of key features of what unfolded that can inform your practice the next time you revisit the lesson. Later, it can be crafted into a learning story that can be shared.

This *curation map* is your lesson plan embedded with your reflections, notes, images, and rich documentation that shows what strategies and resources you have incorporated, thus providing a means of notating student and teacher evidence as it unfolds. Mapping in this way captures your insights during and after a lesson and illuminates key evidence through many different measures of assessment. Central to the curation map is choice. Paying close attention to teacher choice and student choice within a learning sequence can provide profound learning that often lingers below the surface of the daily teaching experience.

Teachers are constantly running an internal critique of what's unfolding and how their instruction can be adjusted to be more effective, but if they don't record their thoughts, they are not likely to be remembered. Capturing ideas in the moment preserves them so you can constantly improve and deepen your practice. Embedding evidence and reflection directly into a written lesson plan makes it a curation map. This action keeps you close to your intentions and invites you to critique and develop as you move forward, evaluating signature moments in teaching and learning. You can engage your students in the collection and review process as well, if you wish.

ACTIVATING THE CURATION AND MAPPING PROCESS

Complex processes are interwoven in the lesson plan and implementation phrase. This chapter will explore how you move from lesson plan into a curation map that will ultimately reveal many new insights as you curate student and teacher evidence and document the progress made in a lesson or unit. We invite you to consider how curating student learning through formative processes can culminate in a learning story that can be created by both students and teachers to mark progress and celebrate learning and achievement (see Chapter 6).

The curation process described in the previous chapter continues in the implementation of the lesson as you tune into your own observations and insights, and analyze and reflect on students' learning and on the documentation and analysis of student evidence through formative assessment measures. Taking time for curation, reflection, and documentation will unearth endless insights about your teaching and your students, and will inform next steps in the process.

Curation maps are used for annotating lessons you will teach again and again or they will be part of a lesson or unit you wish to share. Many teachers who have entered this process find multiple ways to create and share stories that ultimately provide rich documentation giving significance to the multiple layers created in the sequence of learning and spotlighting your work and the work of your students. Engagement in the mapping process will allow for deep reflection on your practice and promote meaningful formative assessment.

The Reflective Curator

In earlier chapters, we have discussed the significance of being a reflective practitioner. We have made the case for the deep links between reflective processes and intention in lesson plan design. And now, as you embark on implementing the lessons you have crafted, we invite you to become a reflective curator.

In Figure 5.1 you see that there are five columns that represent components of the curation process that can be applied to your curriculum development and documentation. Below is a description of each column represented in Figure 5.1.

Figure 5.1. The Curation Process

Collect	Analyze	Select	Organize and Discuss	Share
Collect all evidence you've targeted. You won't know it's useful until you've analyzed what you have.	Look for patterns, connections, and discrepancies. What does the evidence tell you about your teaching strategies? About student learning?	Identify major pieces of evidence that provide important information about: What's working? What needs altering? Where to go next for you and your strategy?	Embed selected evidence into your lesson plan and add your reflections. Consider involving students in this process.	Create your learning story and share with key stakeholders.

Collect: By intentionally collecting evidence based on your learning targets throughout the sequence of a lesson you will find many different types of expressions of students' understanding. Think about the tools you may have for capturing student evidence, such as your phone or a video camera. Portfolios are another helpful tool in capturing not only product-oriented evidence, but also process-oriented evidence. For example, you may choose evidence from direct observation and collect this via your phone or video camera or by taking notes. Observation evidence may also be the result of an interaction with a student or students in groups. Other evidence may be in the form of artifacts of student work which could include thought maps, projects, assignments, and products.

Analyze: Take time to review the evidence to look for patterns, connections, and discrepancies. Include students in the evidence analysis as often they will uncover new insights or understandings. The analysis often will reveal what learning targets students understand clearly and what areas may need more attention.

Select: From the evidence, select key pieces that you think are most significant. You may consider your overarching understandings, essential questions, and standards to help identify evidence and its importance. By including students in the selection process, they learn to be critical observers, contributors, and curators. The selection process may help you determine what is next for your students.

Organize and Discuss: Determine ahead of time what might be organizing features for the evidence you discuss. Ask students to reflect on why and how the selected evidence proves an argument or demonstrates understanding. Organize evidence focused on key themes supporting your enduring understandings. Determine together what evidence is most compelling and what it might mean for reaching any conclusions. Allow time for students to process their evidence and facilitate ways to discuss and group the evidence.

Share: Create unique ways to share the evidence of learning. Consider developing a learning story that may illuminate your process and discovery in a lesson or unit. Incorporate your findings and the evidence you have curated. Think about innovative ways to showcase, exhibit, or perform your findings.

Reflection During the Process Versus Reflection After the Process

As you curate the evidence and review learning moments, remember that reflection is at the heart of the formative assessment process. Dewey (1934) notes that without reflection, there is no learning. You and your learners can gain new knowledge as a result of reflection. As such, we invite you to move into the creation of your curation map, paying attention to reflecting along the way.

Donald Schön in his classic book *The Reflective Practitioner* (1983) distinguished between "reflection-on-action" and "reflection-in-action." Reflection-in-action is thinking about your practice in the moment as the work is unfolding. Reflection-on-action occurs after the experience is done. Schön explains that practitioners can allow themselves to experience the emotions of a unique situation (i.e., "surprise, puzzlement, or confusion"). The practitioner reflects on the phenomena, taking into account prior knowledge, and "carries out an experiment which serves to generate both a new understanding of the phenomenon and a change in the situation" (p. 68).

For Schön, reflection-in-action is the core of "professional artistry" (as cited in Finlay, 2008). Reviewing experiences thoughtfully and critically brings new insights that can improve practice. Finlay (2008) notes:

> Professional practice is complex, unpredictable and messy. In order to cope, professionals have to be able to do more than follow set procedures. They draw on both practical experience and theory as they think on their feet and improvise. They act both intuitively and creatively. Both reflection-in and on -action [sic] allows them to revise, modify and refine their expertise. (pp. 3–4)

There are different levels of reflection—"rapid reflection" that is undertaken in the moment, "repair" where teachers correct course based on information from students, "review" when teachers focus reflection on a particular element of their teaching, "research" when teachers systematically review work over time drawing upon collected data or reading research, and "retheorizing and reformulating" when teachers examine practice critically through the lens of theory (Zeichner & Liston, 1996). Including all these forms of reflections in your annotations will give a variety of checkpoints to deepen your teaching and assessment practice.

Finding time for reflection (even 5 minutes during or at the end of a lesson) is worthwhile. Creating opportunities to sit and review specific evidence in formative assessment processes will yield insights that can be noted in the curation map to annotate the way the lesson unfolds. Teachers who have engaged in creating curation maps have noted significant insights. One teacher in Maine (personal communication, March 3, 2017) said, "Collecting and analyzing evidence throughout the process provides ongoing reflection." Sitting and reviewing evidence brings many important insights to teachers' approaches. Through this critical observation and documentation process, you will be able to create a curated map of the lesson journey.

While teachers will benefit from embedding reflection into their practice, there are also varied opportunities for students to develop critical reflection skills as well. Students can reflect before, during, and after learning. Through reflection, students come to understand their own process of learning, analyze the relevance and meaning of what they are learning, gain awareness into areas in which they are doing well and also areas that need more focus, and identify strategies for success as they apply their learning (Alrubail, 2015).

Embedding places in your lesson where students' reflections are documented (reflections on content, purpose, and process) will build students' metacognition skills as they become aware of their own thinking processes. This will also provide you with documentation of student work that can be included in your curation map to add different perspectives on the work. Creating a culture of reflection in the classroom will increase the critical thinking process for both teachers and their students.

UNDERSTANDING THE CURATION MAP

Key Features of the Curation Map

As you move into implementation, change your frame of reference to that of researcher–curator–documentarian. You can now integrate documentation as you go forward. Don't overwhelm yourself by thinking you need to document everything. Look for significant learning moments—for yourself and for your students:

- What moments are worth documenting for further reflection, as evidence of connection, as indications of disconnections?
- What key elements warrant attention?
- What might be tweaked?
- What are you learning as you collect, curate, and reflect on evidence of learning?

Below we describe four features of the curation map—learning moments, reflection, review of evidence, notes for teaching the lesson next time—that will document your reflections, insights, questions, and ideas about course correction in the moment or in the future. There is no set order for applying these curation features.

Curation of important learning moments. Selecting and reflecting on learning moments that have significance can illuminate important occurrences in teaching and learning. Junctures where this might occur are planned for during the lesson planning process, but there will be unexpected moments as well. Both are important for documentation and reflection. A significant moment for documentation might occur when a student makes a connection that cracks open a new investigation, or when things go off course. Sometimes what feels like a misstep can breed great insights. Mining something that feels like a failure can turn into a pivotal moment for taking a new course to achieve your goal. The reflection by teacher or student can identify a missing element or suggest next steps to address a misconception or missed opportunity. Much can be gleaned by focusing in on specific moments. Training yourself to isolate signature moments can help save time and allow you to reflect deeply on a particular instance.

Curation of reflection. Salient learning moments are investigated through reflection. This happens when evidence is collected and reviewed rigorously or when something happens in the classroom that has enough importance that it is critically analyzed for insights and realizations. Engaging in consistent and ongoing reflection provides endless moments of learning from which to select. Consider documenting samples of student reflections (in writing or spoken word) that shed light on a connection or an area where more focus may be needed. Embedding these ideas into your plan as you go creates a rich map of what unfolded and informs what's next in your progression. These reflections may inspire you to tighten the plan to address student needs more effectively.

Curation of evidence. Collecting evidence of learning from multiple perspectives gives a 360-degree view of learning. Moving beyond teacher observation as the sole way of assessing learning can produce new avenues for gauging student progress. For example, students might express understanding through visual, aural, or written approaches. Consider creating opportunities for guiding students in self-review and peer critique. The more we engage students as active stakeholders in the process of assessment, the more assessment assumes the critical role at the center of teaching and learning. Once you have a rich pool of evidence, you can move into curating the evidence you choose to analyze. Selecting a few key pieces of evidence or learning moments allows you to focus in on areas that are ripe for reflection.

Notes for teaching the lesson next time. At the end of the lesson, take 5 minutes and jot down ideas about things you would adjust the next time the lesson is taught. This can include a spectrum of details such as logistics, teaching choices, student reactions to content, differentiation, scaffolding, and so on. Here are a few examples of notes from a recent workshop led by Lisa. She notes for the next time:

- Be sure to download the music before we begin so it's ready to play in the background as students are working on their movement phrases.
- Find additional exemplars from diverse artists so that I'm broadening students' perspectives on who gets to be an artist.
- Build in time for more structured peer review.

Annotating your lesson plan with notes as it unfolds catalogues your insights that inform the curation map. This prompts you to consider the implications of the evidence. What are you learning about moments of connection or disconnection? What insights are you gaining about your teaching? This curation map traces the journey of implementation. This documentation has proven transformative for teachers who have engaged deeply with the process and is well worth doing.

Moving Beyond the Written Word

The curation map provides new opportunities to reflect upon your work as an educator and to engage students in reflecting on their work and the process of their learning. This is an opportunity to consider different forms of reflection including visual approaches.

Many different forms of reflection can be useful in the classroom. While some standard forms of reflection rely on language to communicate, other means include visual reflections and tactile expressions that can communicate meaning metaphorically. For example, "within the field of art teacher education, visual reflection methods, such as collage and bricolage (McDermott, 2002), visual journaling (Hofsess, 2015), and mapping (Bertling, 2017), have been used to engage preservice teachers individually in contemplating their teaching contexts and practices, teacher identities, and teacher education experiences" (Bertling, 2019, Para. 2).

Teachers can ask students to select an image, photograph, or visual object to provide opportunities for interpretation, connections, and discussion. By adding a visual context, teachers and students can discuss topics from various entry points. The visual images help anchor meaning and help students express varying points of view. Turner and Wilson write that "images enable us to have different opinions about the situation, what it means, and what then we can know about the children in it, about who children are. We find this a very powerful way for people to focus on a topic and bring different perspectives to a conversation" (Turner & Wilson, 2009, p. 7).

The Significance of Documentation

The innovative use of documentation in education has been modeled nowhere as effectively as in the preschools of Reggio Emilia, Italy. In the Reggio Emilia approach visual documentation and reflection take center stage as students and teachers explore multiple means of reflection throughout the teaching and learning process. Reggio Emilia scholar Carlina Rinaldi writes, "We can continuously return to an experience and look for new pathways of inquiry that we may not have seen before" (Rinaldi, as cited in Turner & Wilson, 2009, p. 10). Carlina Rinaldi describes documentation as "visible listening, as the construction of traces (through notes, slides, videos and so on) that not only testify to the children's learning paths and processes, but also make them possible because they are visible" (Rinaldi, 2001, as cited in Gandini & Kaminsky, 2004, p. 5). Reggio Emilia's approach to documentation of early childhood learning has important implications for students of all ages. Loris Malaguzzi, founder of the Reggio Emilia approach, reflected on documentation, noting:

> We are like archaeologists who come home in the evening with their finds and look over their sketches, notes, and writings. Not only do we seek to position the subject or object in a time, a place, a culture, but we seek to position our relationship with that subject or object, and bring together our destiny with that of the subject/object. (Filippini & Castagnetti, 2006, p. 1)

Rich documentation holds rewards for those who look. Gianna Rodari urges us to consider that "everyday things hide secrets for those who know how to see and hear them" (Rodari, as cited in Turner & Wilson, 2009, p. 6).

As you move into teaching and collecting evidence of learning, begin to think about multiple modes of evidence and how you might curate key examples. Beyond more traditional evidence collection measures, consider other potential forms of evidence such as images, photos, quotations, performance pieces, written or verbal reflections, group murals or thought maps, and visible expressions that document student understanding and ways of knowing.

We often make these mental notes, reflections, and adjustments as a natural part of our instruction; however, having an actual way to document our work in this way invites a triangulation of evidence and analysis. The key to this mapping process is capturing your own insights and those of your students in a variety of ways that ultimately inform your teaching and guide student growth and engagement. Mapping will generate rich documentation that can later be excerpted and developed into a learning story (as discussed in Chapter 6).

Making Evidence Visible During the Process of Learning

Throughout this book, we have made the case that assessment rich with artistic processes can yield insights and provide multiple means for student expression and representation. Through these artistic processes, teachers uncover the gold mine of riches that students bring to the classroom every day and the ways that these strengths are drawn out and valued. Taking the time to thoughtfully proceed through a mapping process will provide avenues for you to document the complexity, rigor, and depth of your teaching practice and choices as well as areas that you can improve upon. Teachers have shared that this mapping has provided professional growth and awareness of student needs, proficiencies, and most of all, a better understanding of strategies and approaches that either work or don't work. Dana Schildkraut, Arts Integration Specialist with the Berkshire Regional Arts Integration Network, reflects on the evolution of her work:

> As my ability to write clear lesson plans increases, my teaching skills advance, and vice versa—as my teaching improves, my lesson plans grow more concrete. I write a lesson plan, lead it with students, and then I go back to the plan again to clarify, annotate, and edit, being careful to make notes about what worked well, how students reacted, and the places where I could see evidence of student growth and learning. The reflection process allows me to ask myself valuable questions: Why did I decide to add more time to the introductory activity? How exactly did students show their knowledge during the drama warm-up? What do I need to go back and reteach because of gaps in understanding? I am harnessing the power of reflection and channeling it into more clear-cut, valuable lesson plans. With the conversion of my lesson plan into a curation map I now see the whole document as a meaningful resource to be proudly shared with other teachers, administrators, or as a tool for my own learning. (D. Schildkraut, personal communication, December 2019)

It isn't as if you don't do this already. For some, it happens somewhat intuitively when you are going through your routines of the day, but how do you move that reflection to an expression of your processes and the story of the progression of learning?

CREATING CURATION MAPS

As we have emphasized earlier, take time during implementation of a lesson to make notes, document reflections, and embed examples of student process and products along the way. This will prompt reflection and allow you to capture thinking for ways to improve your work and to identify next steps for students. Think about the mechanism that will let you do this efficiently. Beth Lambert, Director of Innovative Teaching and Learning, Maine Department of Education, identifies the power of mapping the journey:

> Educators know there is more learning happening than a lesson plan or summative assessment can document. The curation and documentation of evidence paired with critical reflection gave our educators important methods to capture the true stories of the learning, both of their students and themselves, while valuing their practice and their creativity. (B. Lambert, personal communication, 2019)

Use your lesson plan as a tool for documentation, embedding sample evidence and reflections from you and your students that reveal signature moments in teaching and learning. You can review evidence that has emerged from the lesson progression with your students. Here is a sampling of evidence that students and teachers will be able to collect to help develop your curation map:

- Photos and images creating a visual map (documenting moments in the process)
- Quotations from students at specific junctures in the learning sequence—for example, students share an aha moment or reflect on a learning moment
- Segments of dialogue from in-class discussions
- Student work samples (written work, artwork, creations)
- Videos of movement and theatrical representations

What follows are some examples that show how teachers across content areas have used different means of documentation while using creative practices to elicit student responses. Their examples demonstrate how they have used curation and documentation processes in their classrooms. Included in each example are teacher reflections in their own words that demonstrate how and what they are learning from documentation in their classroom. We

Figure 5.2. Children in Listening Exercise

Students listened closely to musical excerpts and identified sensory connections (sounds, images, emotions, sensations) as they prepared to create their own soundscapes.

hope these excerpts will invoke some ideas about how you might be able to apply some of these practices in your own classroom.

MAP 1: SOUNDSCAPE FOR ORIGIN MYTHS

In this example of curation mapping, 3rd-grade teacher Denise Chesbro introduces the idea of creating a soundscape for an origin myth to bring the story to life and create sensory and emotional connections throughout the plot much as music serves to do in a film. At this point in the lesson she asked students to imagine a soundtrack for this myth. She asked them to imagine the story in image and sound and let them discuss their answers. After discussion, the teacher had the children lie on the floor and close their eyes (see Figure 5.2). Then she invited them to think about how composers of music make choices. She played audio clips of a variety of classical music pieces, each of which conveyed a different mood (sad, ominous, cheerful, energetic, playful). After each clip, she asked students to think about what they visualized in their minds, determine what mood or feeling the composer was trying to communicate through music, and describe how they felt while listening to each musical piece. The teacher prompted students to explain their thoughts referring to the tempo, pitch, volume, and instruments of the music. Students identified what images and emotions were evoked in listening to the music (see Figure 5.3). After this discussion, the teacher informed students that composers of musical scores make choices about tempo, pitch, and volume, and determine which instruments they want to play in order to meet their purpose. She referred to the students' observations to reinforce this concept. She questioned students to think about what might happen if a piece was played with higher or lower pitch, louder or softer volume, faster or slower tempo, and with different instruments. As the lesson plan was implemented, she documented moments in her curation map which noted places where students made astute learning connections that deepened comprehension of the plot points in the text.

> *Teacher reflection.* Denise then captured her own reflections:
> I had students lie on the floor with heads in the center. I instructed
> them to lie quietly and listen as I played audio clips of different music.
> After each, I asked them these question prompts:
>   » What did you visualize while you heard this music?
>   » What shades of colors did you see and why?
>   » What do you think the composer was trying to communicate
>   and why?
> I found that they were more interested in naming TV shows
> or movies that they have seen than in describing the music, so I
> had to redirect them to discuss their feelings, what they imagined
> happening, and what mood the composer was trying to convey. I
> charted their responses. Their descriptions lacked musical terms, so
> I had to do direct instruction about volume (loud, soft), pitch (high,
> low), tempo (fast, slow), and teach the names of instruments. This
> moment "popped out for me" because I was surprised at their lack of
> knowledge when it came to instrument names and what they sounded
> like. Most of the pieces were performed by organ, violin, and other
> string instruments. Next time, I think I need to incorporate more
> examples that include woodwinds and brass instruments, and perhaps
> find more examples of different music. I determined that I needed
> to [adjust the lesson] to include music that evoked a wide range of
> emotions. As students understood the role of a composer in creating
> music, they saw how music and sounds could amplify, punctuate, and
> create sensory connections that inform the plot of a story. They then
> were able to apply these ideas in the creation of a soundscape for the
> origin myth being explored.
> Also, it was important to make the connections with the sound
> and images to continue working on students' reading comprehension.
> I found that the time that I devoted to the sensory and audial elements
> had profound impact on students' understanding of the myth itself.
> (D. Chesbro, personal communication, November 2019)

Figure 5.3. Photo of Chart Documenting Student Observations

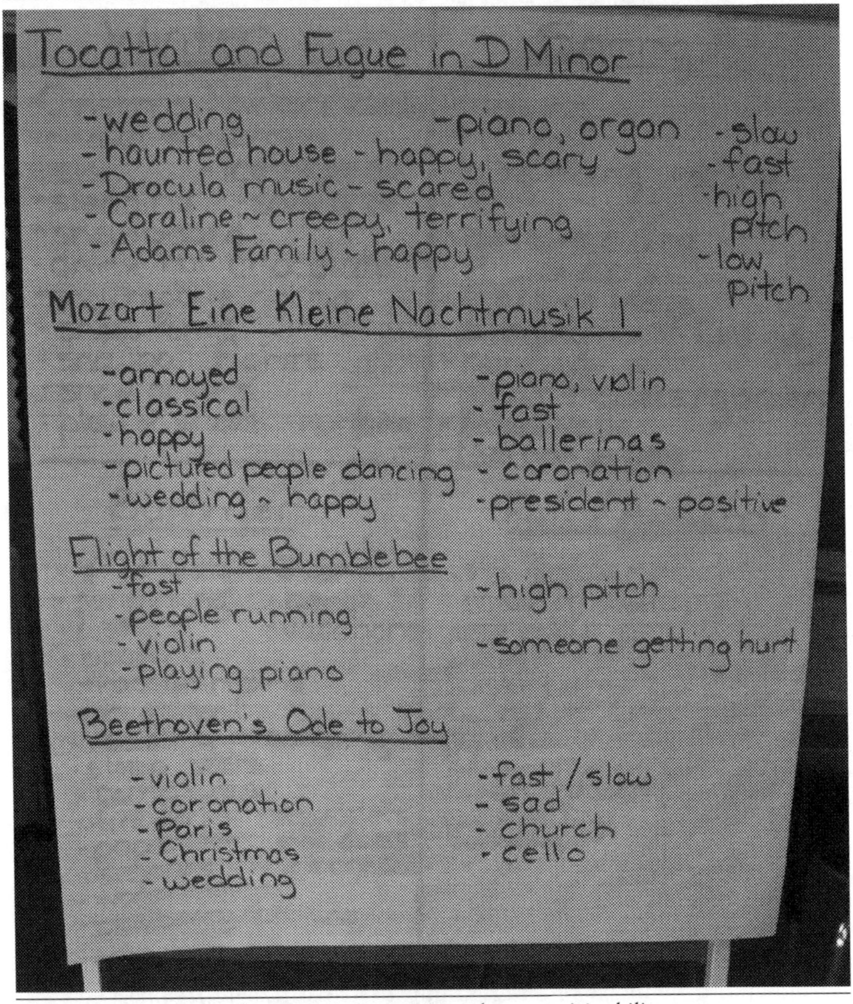

The teacher documented students' observations about music's ability to convey narrative.

Evidence in real time. Different sources of evidence yield many rewards for the teacher, no matter what the grade level. The evidence allows the teacher and student to pinpoint key milestones, benchmarks, and aha moments that emerge and curate them in the process of learning to inform teacher practice and student growth. The exercise of highlighting moments where shifts of thinking and practice occurred (in forming a new understanding) generates next steps for the teacher and also for the learner.

Once you have your documentation embedded in your curation map you can revise it to be shared with others. You will likely notice that key moments stand out for you. Focus in on a few enlightened moments versus trying to document everything. Note how these moments give you insights about the progression of the work. What observations emerge about the individual needs of your students? As you create moments of reflection, take time to analyze and capture your thinking.

Teacher reflection. Denise supplements the evidence (in this case, an anchor chart that details the plot points of the myth linked to sound ideas to be used in a soundscape; see Figure 5.4) with her own reflections. Here she reflects on the introduction of plotting out the story map with students:

> This portion went much more smoothly than I had anticipated as I was not completely confident in my own understanding of each of the six plot points in relation to the origin myth that we used. It was quite evident that some students could solidly retell the entire story with many key words and phrases, as well as many details. As I charted the plot points they shared, I had to encourage them to give the general events without all of the details. It was reassuring to me that so many students remembered so much of the story. One thing I need to think about for future implementation is how to ensure that all students share a retelling of the story. Some students sat quietly and were not engaged for various reasons (tired, uninterested, upset). I didn't necessarily want this to be another written assignment, as we had already analyzed the story and answered comprehension questions about it in reading class. I decided that as students explored creating sounds for the soundscape, I could check in with each student and have them retell the story to me orally to assess their understanding of the text. (D. Chesbro, personal communication, November 2019)

Capturing significant moments. Collect, document, and reflect on significant moments that occur within the lesson sequence. As you move through your lesson plan, tune in to what's happening and what you are noticing. You make constant decisions in the moment, such as redirecting your methods based on students' connections and disconnections. Often your teaching flow is interrupted to make space for an important learning moment, or a flash of insight about what you might do differently or more deeply next time. Turning up the volume on these moments makes learning visible, for you and your students.

Figure 5.4. Photo Image of Chart Linking Plot Points with Sound Ideas

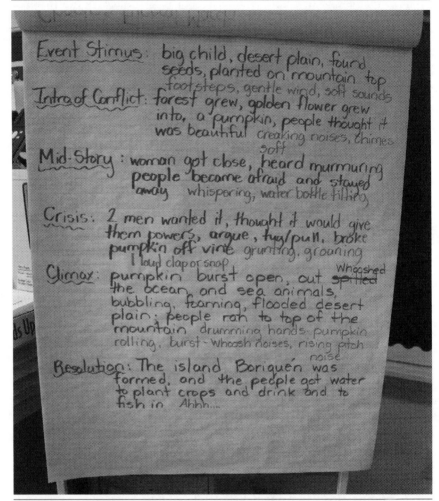

The educator mapped an original story with students by identifying specific plot points and documenting students' ideas for telling the story through sound.

MAP 2: GRAPHIC DESIGN AND ENGLISH LANGUAGE ARTS INTEGRATION

The development of the curation map can provide a lens on the complexity of teaching. Here's an example of an educator from Maine, Tess Hitchcock, who was integrating graphic design with English Language Arts standards for communicating effectively with an audience. She gave her 9th-grade graphic design students an assignment to design a magazine cover to demonstrate knowledge of the principles of design and the ability to communicate effectively with an audience. What follows are some of her lesson components:

Enduring Understandings:

- Designers use the principles of design to create compositions that communicate ideas to audiences.
- Words and images work together to communicate meaning.

Essential Question:

- How can design influence the way ideas are communicated?

Observations of this mapping process. For English Language Arts, Tess was asking students to demonstrate integration of knowledge and ideas. Students were asked to "integrate and evaluate content presented in diverse media and formats, including visually and quantitatively, as well as in words" (Common Core State Standards Initiative, 2010). She isolated two covers, one that she considered a proficient example of her assignment, and another cover that she felt was not as successful (see Figure 5.5). While spending time reviewing student work examples and applying her assessment criteria, she found students met the outcomes she set. In other words, she realized that some students were meeting the criteria in her lesson but not hitting the mark of proficiency.

Her selection, curation, and reflection of student work provided her samples on the evidence of her lesson. As she reflected on her student evidence, she began to find insights on what was working and what was missing in her lesson plan and approach. After careful analysis she realized that students needed better criteria to increase student proficiency and to guide the design of better products. This prompted her to adapt and revise her approach to planning and how she taught the lesson.

Teacher reflection: Analysis of student work. Reviewing the evidence during the curation process led to this reflection about the tension between her view of success and the assessment criteria: "Here's the catch—they both met the criteria that I set for the class. They both had five headlines and a title, they both had an appropriate image relating to their magazine, and they both switched up their fonts and used different alignments to make their magazine interesting to look at." She continued to reflect:

It's interesting how the students both met the criteria set but achieved dramatically different results. The "Gum" magazine cover was not yet proficient for the following reasons:

Figure 5.5. Photo of Student Work

Representations of student magazine covers

> » The headlines were all over the place and didn't have a readable flow, making the order quite hard to read and quite confusing.
> » There were too many fonts that were not readable, either because they were overlapped by something else or the background was too busy.
> » The headlines, while original, were about gum in general, not about different brands.

The "Gum" student used all the elements required for the lesson, but still missed the mark in meeting the proficiency level. It made me wonder how I could set more criteria or increase motivation to get the results I was looking for. (T. Hitchcock, personal reflection, November 2018)

Teacher reflection: New realizations. This teacher then revisited her process and revised it for the next time the lesson would be taught. In addition, Tess took the time to unpack each standard in more detail and used a variety of strategies to collect the evidence of learning. She reflected:

> I began reflecting on what was missing on my end; what I could change to increase student engagement in this project to get a different result. I still have the magazine cover as a warm-up, but I introduced a few new questions and a different final project. I

now have the students create a final design about an issue that is important or valuable to them. I also introduced peer critiquing midway through this project. While I gave all the suggestions that I expected to see, I wanted the students to learn how to give and receive constructive criticism. This also allowed me to tie in the standards in planning revisions for a work of art and also in identifying the message conveyed. By linking these standards, I can now have students ask the question, "What are you getting from my design? What meaning do you think I'm trying to communicate?" and reflect on the answers they get. By having them be critiqued on how well their message is communicated, it automatically made them clean up their design because their peers were asking for cleaner layouts in order to understand the message better. (T. Hitchcock, personal communication, 2018)

This type of aha moment is exactly the kind of commentary you might record in your own curation map. By putting a rich reflection like this in writing, the teacher has now decreased her chances of taking this same kind of approach in the future. How often does a teacher pull out a lesson plan from a previous year, teach it, trip over an obstacle, and then say, "Oh yeah, the same exact hiccup happened with the students last year; I wished I had remembered to make a note of that somewhere."

In this example, the learning moment selected marked the teacher's realization when she reviewed students' work and came to the realization that through the feedback loop, she needed to adapt her methodology to elicit different results (refer above to "Curation of Evidence"). Selecting just two covers to analyze helped her to focus in on a specific dilemma ("Curation of Reflection"). Through reflection, teachers can not only get a closer understanding of what evidence they have selected but also gain an understanding about what is working and what is not. This evidence can provide meaningful insights on how to revise teaching practices to get stronger results ("Curation of Notes for Teaching the Lesson Next Time").

MAP 3: ART AND HISTORY INTEGRATION

In this example, first-year teacher, Nick Bergheimer, in an Honors History class at Binford Middle School in Richmond, Virginia, documented student work samples as part of his curation map. He reflected on the evidence and what it suggested about where students were in their learning as they investigated how political cartoons communicated about the Progressive Era. He tells his learning story in Chapter 6.

A number of students produced strong work that demonstrated proficiency based on Nick's criteria. Below he shares observations from his review of student work, noting teaching areas that he could develop more fully to get to stronger levels of proficiency. In reading these excerpts, notice that through his critique of his own work in the classroom, he reveals his deep expertise as an educator and reflective practitioner.

Teacher reflection. Nick reflects on student understanding of symbolism:

> Students had a hard time creating higher level symbolism with their images and describing how they would use metaphors or humor to illustrate the content. The scaffold asked students to relate their images to the content directly, but there was difficulty in doing so in an abstract way. Many students went for a more "outrageous" sketch draft that simply portrayed the workplace as somewhere a worker gets gruesomely hurt. As I walked around checking for understanding, I pushed the students to think beyond the simple gruesome (yet appealing for middle schoolers) imagery that they were illustrating. I reviewed almost all of the students' work before they were finished with their sketch drafts and also offered assistance in brainstorming some ideas to push their thinking into a more abstract position on the content. I would refer back to the cartoons and how the images, such as the booze barrels or the shading of the sky in the prohibition cartoon, were simple, yet effective ways of creating symbolism and meaning. At this stage I think I helped most students go beyond their initial creative urges, but some still wanted to create a simple representation of a Progressive Era work scene gone wrong with no deeper meaning behind it. (N. Bergheimer, unpublished lesson plan, November 2019).

Assessment of learning: Determining next steps. Nick's reflections make a map for next steps to deepen his teaching practice and help students achieve proficiency:

> I realized that the evidence criteria that was listed in the beginning in the form of the rubric set the expectations too high for students. I realized that the process of creating the cartoons and having future students reflect on their successes and challenges when making the cartoons would be helpful. In future lessons, I determined that I would redesign the rubric and evidence criteria to reflect the process as the main source of assessment rather than the final product. . . .
> While many students were successful in creating a piece of visual art, many students had the most room for improvement in the areas of symbolism, metaphor, and satire. The content standards were executed in a proficient way and I was satisfied with those standards. In the future, I will simplify the criteria for evidence in the visual art

standard on a first attempt in creating this project. If I were to do this project numerous times in the school year, I would lift the visual art expectation each time we created a political cartoon.

In another moment along the journey, Nick notes the potential power of the peer review, but identifies the need to provide models of peer feedback:

Students were eager to see what their peers had created and to compare their work to others. The final piece of the graphic organizer that was designed to scaffold their learning independently as well as collaboratively, was finished. Reflecting back, the peer review section itself could have been modeled better. I did not model it for students beyond offering suggestions during the draft process. I found that many of the peer reviews were glowing and they did not offer many constructive suggestions to help their peers out. The few that did offer keen suggestions, the illustrator chose not to use their feedback. If this would have been directly modeled in the format I used, I think the students would have had more direction and received the feedback more openly. (N. Bergheimer, unpublished lesson plan, November 2019)

Interestingly, we learn more about Nick's skills as an educator in his critique than in his success. It's worth noting that Nick was selected as teacher of the year in his first year of teaching.

MAP 4: CREATING ZINES TO SHARE IMMIGRATION STORIES IN TEXT AND IMAGE

In Chapter 4 we introduced teaching artist Aijung Kim working with 6th- and 7th-grade English language learners in a middle school in Virginia. Excerpts from her curation map below show Aijung's reflection on specific moments in teaching a lesson on integrating visual elements to accompany stories about students' immigration experiences in the creation of a zine—an easy-to-make booklet using folded paper. Notice in this example how she embeds several features of the curation-mapping process including teacher reflection on specific learning moments and review of student evidence, notes for "next time" to adjust and improve the lesson to meet students' needs.

Excerpts from Aijung Kim's curation map. Students were shown examples of words cut out from magazines (see Figure 5.6). She asked students to compare and contrast the pairs of words and how they were presented visually by identifying line, shape, color, and mood. She asked students, "How are they different?"

Figure 5.6. Photo of Teaching Artist's Exemplar of Word Art

This word design example includes words cut out from magazines to demonstrate different choices in lettering design to enhance the mood and meaning of a word.

Next Aijung showed examples from her sketchbook of the word *Eat* drawn in different ways (see Figure 5.7). Students were then asked to bring a different word to life by hand-drawing the letters and visually depicting its meaning. She reflects on this phase of the lesson:

> Students were very engaged in the Word Design discussion. They laughed at some of my drawings —in particular the man with the word "Eat" in his belly. I ended up only asking them to draw the word "Playful" since they really got into it. They seemed unsure at first, but I reminded them there was no right or wrong way to do it. The students enjoyed the exercise and were very creative. One student drew several different words without being prompted. Many students volunteered to project their work onto the wall for the class to see. (A. Kim, unpublished student paper, November 2019)

Figure 5.7. Teaching Artist's Exemplar of Word Design

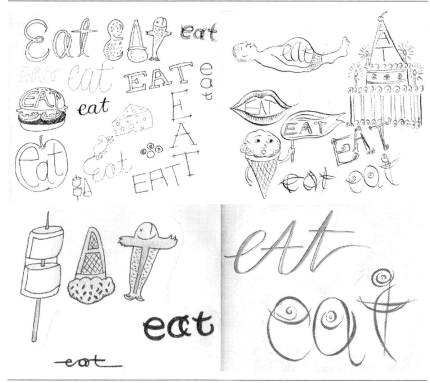

Hand-drawn examples of word variations by teaching artist Aijung Kim.

Aijung also asked students to create thumbnail sketches to brainstorm approaches to creating compositions (see Figure 5.8):

- Explain that *thumbnail sketches* are small drawings used to work out different compositions and help with planning. Note that students don't *always* have to plan or draw a thumbnail sketch if they want to experiment with collage imagery first. Collage lends itself better to experimentation than sketching a plan.
- Discuss the process of *brainstorming* —coming up with several ideas. Ask them for ideas and draw out some thumbnail sketches. Think about where words will go on the page —draw these as groups of lines representing text. Some ideas:
  - » Visual border of people, motorcycles, jeepneys, palm trees, and so on
  - » Illustration scene with the drawing on top and words on bottom

Figure 5.8. Teaching Artist's Exemplar of Thumbnail Sketches

These thumbnail sketches demonstrated the brainstorming process. Aijung Kim drew from the same written content to devise different images and compositions, demonstrating that each artist must make aesthetic and contextual choices for their page design.

>> Automobiles and words scattered around
>> Ask a volunteer to demonstrate drawing several thumbnail sketch ideas and put a star by the favorite sketch to develop into a more finished composition. (A. Kim, unpublished lesson plan, November 2019)

Aijung created and shared strong exemplars for composition (see Figure 5.9) but realized that designing additional examples and providing more guidance would help students understand the purpose and most useful approach to creating thumbnail sketches. Difficulties in comprehending the English language also played a factor in the students' understanding.

Teacher reflection: what to do next time. Aijung shares her reflections on her integrated art lesson:

There was a lot to do in one visit, and I would break it up so that Composition is its own lesson. Students need more help with their thumbnail sketches. I would make sure the students' writing is typed and printed first before commencing this lesson. For the Word Design exercise, I would have them finish the lesson by taking one sentence

Figure 5.9. Teaching Artist's Exemplar of Composition Principles

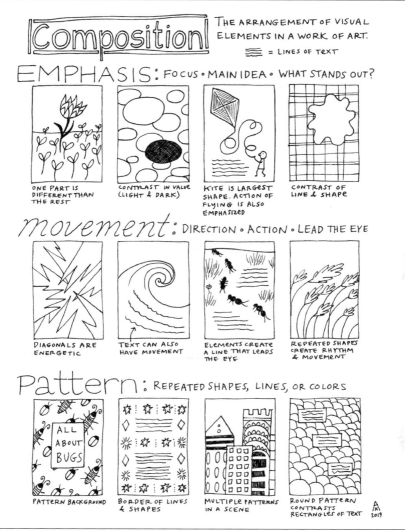

Aijung Kim created this handout to visually display a few elements of design and talk about the importance of composition to convey meaning in illustration.

from their story and designing it. Next time, I will create a graphic organizer to help them understand finding emphasis in their writing and creating thumbnail sketches. I will also have them do each step with me in turn, instead of demonstrating the entire process at once. I will show a clearer example of a thumbnail sketch and how it translates into the final image. (A. Kim, unpublished learning story, November 2019)

These insights, captured through reflection in action, were in response to the feedback and clues from the students and allowed Aijung to identify places to strengthen the lesson for next time.

CURATION LEADS TO INSIGHT

Creating a curation map captures the journey of the lesson or unit, and this can be incredibly useful as teachers analyze their practice and illuminate students' points of connection and next steps. Teachers using the curation mapping process have shared significant epiphanies. One teacher reflected:

> Analyzing [and] recording evidence either of the students' growth progress or reflections has empowered my teaching. . . . [This process] helped to rekindle some of the passion that I had when I first started out so many years ago! It forced me to become more focused on student learning, not simply on the creative process of the final project. Kids are smart, and they have a lot to share. I think they appreciate the transparency of what each day in my class is going to look like and exactly what I'm looking for them to take away at the end. (C. K., personal communication, March 2017)

Here are some other comments from teachers responding to the curation process:

- The "curating process . . . helped me isolate the real value of my lessons" (Maine educator, workshop reflection, March 9, 2017).
- Another teacher reflected on the importance of remaining flexible in the writing process. "It's important to be willing to adapt and modify your lesson and its assessments based on student work and evidence" (Maine educator, lesson plan reflection, March 9, 2017).
- One teacher said, "I have always thought of myself as a reflective teacher, but this process took me to a whole deeper level" (M. Valentine, personal communication, November 15, 2019).
- Another educator noted that "reflection is inherent in best practice in teaching. . . . Asking my students to demonstrate what they have learned can take several forms—visual, verbal, written. This practice deepens student learning" (Maine educator, lesson plan reflection, March 9, 2017).
- Another teacher noted that the curation map gets "my lesson reflections out of my head and onto paper and in an organized way" (Maine educator, lesson plan reflection, March 9, 2017).

Teachers are often surprised at the gaps they uncover in their work. These learnings led to important adjustments in their instructional approaches.

Our experience has been that teachers are excited about the ways that formative assessment can provide ongoing information that can guide decision-making. Curating evidence and reviewing how well students meet their objectives reveals many new insights that would not have been realized without taking the time to deeply understand what the evidence taught them about their teaching methodologies. One teacher commented:

> An important learning moment for me was learning to differentiate between the value of the process versus the product and therefore the difference between the evidence found in the final versus the understanding [as the lesson progressed]. It has greatly impacted and influenced my instructional practice as well as my approach in the classroom with each new lesson or unit. It has tied into many other aspects of assessment we have been learning as a district. As a new teacher, I have found this really defining for me. (Maine educator, lesson plan reflection, March 9, 2017)

Theresa Cerceo reflected that this process can be deeply creative as well as reflective:

> Curating my lessons in this way has allowed me to engage in the work of lesson design as a creative process. It complements and supports the flexibility teachers need in their classroom and it reinforces the process of reflective teaching while assisting meeting students as individuals. (T. Cerceo, Maine, personal communication, March 9, 2017)

There are multiple ways of curating evidence and reflecting on the work of the classroom. Teachers approach curation from a variety of angles and processes. One thing is clear, taking the time to curate and review student evidence through a process of reflection and analysis sets in motion a cycle of ongoing improvement.

CHAPTER 6

Learning Stories
Voices from the Field

> I can't express enough, the impact this journey has had on my teaching. In regard to assessment and classroom practices, it has opened a whole world to me. (T. Cerceo, personal communication, December 2018)

This chapter will explore the power of learning stories. We will highlight exemplars of several case stories from the field demonstrating the use of different art forms, content areas, and grade levels. As part of our work across arts-based professional learning projects, we have had the opportunity to pilot these ideas with teachers in different states including California, Connecticut, Maine, Massachusetts, New Hampshire, and Virginia. Participating teachers have benefited from the processes involved in moving from lesson plan to learning story.

THE LEARNING STORY

What Is a Learning Story?

Learning stories serve to share examples of the complex processes teachers use in their classrooms—what they plan, what actually took place, and why the information is noteworthy. Sharing the story of learning with others can provide new understanding of and appreciation for the dynamic methods and skills required of educators. These stories can also reveal the rigor and relevance arts integration brings to learning.

Much has been written about the creation of learning stories in early childhood classrooms to document students' learning. Traditionally, these "may be as short as one paragraph or one page or longer. A story is usually focused on a specific incident or episode but it may also be a snapshot of a child's activities over a specific amount of time" (Alexander, n.d.). In this text, we have considered how this type of documentation can be applied to all grade levels. Let's explore how the process of creating a learning story can be tied to the lesson plan development in order to prompt reflection but also showcase educators' expertise.

We have covered how teachers' learning stories really help focus on deeper reflection and documentation. One aspect that warrants exploration is the role that students can play in learning stories. Students can create powerful learning stories in a variety of formats that document what they are learning and also their journey in investigating topics and issues connected to whatever subject they are exploring. Picken (2012) suggests that "learning stories permit and even compel students to include their experiences of doing the work as well as the work itself. Learning stories, then, relate process and product. They help students to understand how they did what they did as well as what this means for themselves as learners" (p. 20). As such, the learning story can be a useful tool for summarizing and memorializing the learning of a lesson or unit. By highlighting the benchmarks of learning through the process and spotlighting key areas of investigation, the students are able to remember their learning journey. Learning stories "can be used to support the development of conceptual understandings in conjunction with a reflective class culture, strong community relationships, clarity of planning for and sharing conceptual understandings, and support for students to critically reflect" (p. ii).

This opportunity to "gather and analyze evidence can support the development of understanding of teaching and learning" (Donahue & Stuart, 2010, p. 61). Picken also explores the idea that learning stories can serve as a tool "that could authentically support learning for all and provide rich information about that learning" (Wolf et al., 1991, as cited in Picken, 2012, p. 25). Because learning stories tend to be student-centered, they can honor what students bring to the learning process. They can provide connections with family and empower students to become part of the assessment process, fostering a sense of connection and control (Picken, 2012).

Drawing Insights from the Curation Map

Once you have made annotations to your lesson creating your curation map, consider developing and sharing a story of learning; that is, transforming your richly documented curation map into a learning story. The curation map can be edited and polished so that it can be shared with other educators or developed into an article. Or, you can excerpt it to be a shorter version to be shared with parents, administrators, and so on.

University of Richmond's Partners in the Arts Director Rob McAdams summarizes the benefits of "reclaiming the lesson plan as a strategy for documentation." He says,

We are leaving the record of all the learning that is happening in a creative classroom on the table by not capturing and naming what is going on in between the "SWBAT" (an acronym used in lesson planning that identifies what Students Will Be Able To know and be able to do), content standards bullets, and performance tasks. By turning a lesson plan into a learning story, rich with documentation through images and reflection of student work and our own teaching practice, we bring to light the foundational and intrinsic processes we all use in developing the learning skills and processes of critical thinking, creativity, collaboration, and communication. (R. McAdams, personal communication, December 2019)

The learning story can be a powerful tool in the classroom. These stories can be incredibly compelling because both the teacher and student are able to show how they learned, what they learned, and why it matters. The teacher and students utilize higher order thinking skills to synthesize information and describe highlights of the learning journey. As teachers think about the diverse learners in their classrooms, they want to find ways that show how these students have progressed. Allowing students to work collaboratively to showcase the evidence through story can be a means of creating a level, common ground where everyone succeeds. The story can foster an increased understanding of students' different backgrounds and cultures and ways of learning. For teachers, creating a story based on the curated evidence provides opportunities to review a sequence of instruction and reflect on adjustments made in an effort to share some of the findings with others. Stories speak to the heart of teaching. "Assessment in a learning story is not fragmented. It flows through the process of noticing, recognizing, and responding. Teachers are able to communicate learning in the context of the whole child. It is about celebrating the competent child!" (Goodsir, 2017).

You can draw evidence and excerpts from your curation map to create a learning story that communicates a summary of the learning. As you select evidence for your story, think about what evidence captures key moments of learning. As you curate the most essential evidence, try to include a wide range representing different modalities of learning. You will likely see how the arts provide multiple means of expression and can play a critical role in the formulation and sharing of your stories.

The learning story can function in multiple ways. It can provide a more encompassing representation of your decisions as a teacher and the learners' milestones. In the process of developing the story, you find new insights about your students and the way they learn. Teachers report that they have reached new understandings of differentiated approaches and representation for meeting the needs of their students. The story can serve as a mechanism for addressing the cultural and linguistic needs of your students. At the heart of the story is the assets-based mindset in which students are honored and uplifted, even when they learn in different ways and achieve at different levels. The story can be a very positive summary that contributes to a cultural change in your classroom. Teachers who have incorporated the learning story into their classroom practice have found this to be a key instrument for professional growth.

Using the Learning Story to Communicate with Stakeholders

Increasingly it's clear that the idea of the "arts" is often loaded with assumptions. Support for the arts in education comes with the limiting attitude that they are "nice to have but not necessary." Documentation of what occurs in the creative process can demonstrate that the arts are not icing on the cake . . . they can be the cake itself. Students are engaged, deeply drawn into the work, and motivated. Think about how you can develop some of your signature lessons into learning stories. Consider developing your plan, creating a curation map, and documenting work that actually happens in the classroom as well as capturing student insights and reflections along with your own.

The learning story is a vital means of synthesis that brings to light the evidence you have curated by both formative and summative assessment measures. This may take many different forms (e.g., video, written, audio) and can be in various lengths, depending on the medium you choose. We aren't suggesting that a learning story will be needed for every lesson. However, building compelling stories can provide many new discoveries for both students and teachers. A learning story can be as simple as adding evidence and reflection to your existing lesson plan. The map of your lesson with rich detail can take the form of a short narrative or can further develop into an article or story. Learning stories can capture the context of the environment that appears to be enabling or constraining learning. They can be used like a case study to spark discussion or reflection, raise a question, or make a point. It is important to make the distinction that learning stories are not the same as case studies or running records about children—they are narratives, and they need to tell a good tale.

Providing actual exemplars of evidence as well as reflections on the process offers a lens for the reader to translate the evidence and cull out and share strategies that worked and the learning that took place. There are many ways to maximize the use of the learning story:

- Students can reflect, celebrate, and document their learning progression(s).
- Parents can be invited into the process of learning about specific content their children have encountered.
- Principals can glean insights about a lesson during the review process and discover whether or not students are making gains.
- Community members can be invited to explore what's happening in schools.

One teacher shared her learning story with her principal as part of the teacher-evaluation process. Her principal had this to say:

> As I sat down and listened to Kathy share her unit "Follow the Drinking Gourd" song and its historical significance to the Underground Railroad, I was so impressed. . . . Kathy goes above and beyond, and she certainly did so in this unit. . . . I was so pleased to see what knowledge she had gained from using this process and the impact it had on her students. The evidence and documentation along with student comments, pictures, recordings, etc. showed a diverse and well-thought out collection of meaningful learning goals. Kathy enriches her classes daily by sharing her "Stories." (D. Spencer, personal communication, 2018)

The process of preparing a learning story is valuable as it prompts reflection, ongoing review of evidence, and application of insights to next steps in teaching and learning. Theresa Cerceo, visual arts educator, reflects on the process of curation:

> Curating my lessons in this way has allowed me to engage in the work of lesson design as a creative process. It complements and supports the flexibility teachers need in their classroom and it reinforces the process of reflective teaching while assisting meeting students as individuals. (T. Cerceo, personal communication, 2018)

This work not only benefits teaching and learning but is itself a creative practice.

STORY EXAMPLES FROM TEACHERS

The story excerpts below represent different subject areas and grade levels. Look for the shifts in classroom practice that the teachers considered as they were documenting the evidence from students and reflecting on the possibilities for revision and refinement. Also, notice how they incorporated the feedback loop as a means for curating evidence from their students.

Story 1: Political Cartoons in the Progressive Era

The learning story in this section was written by Nick Bergheimer, whom we introduced in Chapter 4. His learning story builds on his experience with developing his curation map.

Context. My name is Nick Bergheimer. I teach middle school in Richmond, Virginia, at Binford Middle School, a Turnaround Arts School that is part of the Richmond Public School System. This learning story is a portion of a lesson I introduced from U.S. history. My students are part of an honors U.S. History II class that is comprised of approximately 50% White and 50% African American students. I am a first-year teacher working on integrating the arts in my lesson. What follows is a short snapshot of what I taught and how I assessed the lesson.

The first lesson required students to perform a tableau to represent a painting of a workers' strike (Robert Koehler's painting, *The Strike*, 1886) that was shown to students in advance. This was used to set the context of the Progressive Era in which we were going to analyze political cartoons and how they represented working conditions and the negative effects of industrialization. The tableaux gave students the opportunity to try and re-create the images explored in the painting. When re-creating the image, students were asked to demonstrate the emotion of the characters in the image to provide the audience with the impression given by the painting. In return, this would provide the students performing the perspective of characters in the painting.

The overall goal was to integrate visual and performing arts as methods for students to demonstrate their learning of the content. Students analyzed various literary and visual art techniques used in political cartoons, such as irony, symbolism, humor, line, space, and character exaggeration. After observing the political cartoons from the Progressive Era, students were then asked to use some of the techniques they observed in the analysis to create their own political cartoons that would demonstrate their knowledge of the content studied.

The intention of the lesson was to blend learning in visual arts and theater to foster understanding of how political cartoons make people think about political, societal, or governmental issues that generally emphasize one side of an issue. Often political ads use humor and drawings to make a point and play an important part in telling the history of a given period of time.

Enduring understandings. In the planning for this part of my lesson I wanted to identify three big ideas that could serve as enduring understandings students would remember over time:

- People gain insights into meanings of artworks by engaging in the process of close observation and analysis of theme, symbolism, metaphor.
- Art can be political.
- People develop ideas and understandings of society, culture, and history through their interactions with and analysis of art.

Essential questions.

- How does art help us understand the lives of people of different times, places, and cultures?
- How is art used to impact the views of a society? How does art preserve aspects of history? (adapted from National Core Arts Standards, [NCCAS, 2014])
- How does political propaganda influence change?

Overview. In this lesson students participated in an artistic process toward creating a well-thought-out political cartoon that incorporates historical topics from the Progressive Era. Students observed and analyzed political cartoons from the Progressive Era and then created their own political cartoons using the content information from their notes communicating their understanding of the negative effects of industrialization and how they led to reforms during the Progressive Era using symbolism and metaphor that conveyed a message through image and text. Students learned about the process of cartoon development from the perspective of a *New York Times* political cartoonist and used the elements of visual art and principles of design to design effective cartoons.

Rationale. The objective of this project was to expose students to the symbolism, themes, and topics of a historical time period through visual art, such as political cartoons and paintings, and then allow them to create their own pieces with the knowledge they learned, observed, and analyzed in our classwork. Students observed the process of a professional cartoonist and adapted his techniques and suggestions in order to create an authentic political cartoon that demonstrated their knowledge of the essential understanding and learning standards both in art and history. Both historians and artists created political cartoons, making this project a truly authentic assignment integrating art and history.

Students explored political cartoons from the Progressive Era, analyzing historical themes from the political era. They drew out narratives from the cartoons based on the artists' use of symbolism, theme, and point of view. They learned about artistic techniques used to create political cartoons by reviewing a video of *NY Times* cartoonist, Patrick Chappatte (True Heroes Films, 2015), discussing his approach.

Students analyzed historical images, which provided a frame for facilitating discussion to mine key ideas pointing to the inequities in the workplace during the industrial age. The following are some of the images that the students analyzed: Robert Koehler's painting *The Strike* (1886), depicting a confrontation between a factory owner and his employees; political cartoons such as [Herbert Johnson's] cartoon *Child Labor* (circa 1912), Art Young's cartoon *Eleven Hours a Day* (1910), and Bernhard Gillam's *The*

Protectors of Our Industries (February 7, 1883). Students observed the process of professional cartoonist Patrick Chappatte (September 16, 2015).

I invited students to imagine they were a "muckraking" editorial cartoonist working for a large newspaper during the Progressive Era. Their assignment was to create a political cartoon that represents an important social issue of the Progressive Era. They could select from several topics outlining the negative effects of Industrialization including:

- Child labor, low wages, or poor working conditions
- Women's suffrage
- Temperance
- Prohibition

After selecting their topic, students used guided questions from the teacher to sort out their ideas and identify a clear point of view as they prepared to create their cartoons.

Reflections after curating and reviewing evidence. There were a couple of things I would do differently, such as model the peer review process more clearly [refer to Chapter 4, Map 3], and perhaps ask a professional cartoonist or illustrator It is important to make the distinction that learning to come in and work with the kids to help them move toward more abstract imagery and symbolism. I was happy with the process and the product, and the students had a great time showing them off in our quarterly art showcase (see Figure 6.1 for examples of student cartoons).

Story 2: Weather Forecasting

The learning story below is told by Denise Chesbro, whom we introduced in Chapter 5. Denise teaches 3rd grade in Gabriel Abbott Memorial Elementary School in Florida, Massachusetts. She entitled this lesson Seasonal Patterns and integrated science and drama and visual arts.

Overview. In this lesson, I invited students to take on the mantle of the expert. They prepared to be weather forecasters presenting data about weather patterns in a televised program. Students discovered that weather patterns change in different seasons in our region. They also discovered that seasonal weather patterns vary depending on the region of the world in which they occur. As part of their exploration, students reviewed graphs and tables of weather data and drew conclusions about the weather patterns for a given region, citing evidence. Students wrote dramatic scenes for brief drama presentations using props in which they demonstrated their understanding of weather-related vocabulary and concepts.

Figure 6.1. Photo Examples of Student Political Cartoons

These student examples of proficient works of political cartoons met both art and content standards. The students were successful in creating a political cartoon with imagery to relate a topic or theme. Students used those images to create symbolism with meaning that relates back to the content standards.

Figure 6.2. Photo of Students Brainstorming Seasonal Patterns

Students worked together to list seasonal weather patterns and activities related to seasons. This prewriting process was helpful as they wrote "I Am From" poems in partner groupings. It generated not only content, but excitement for the task.

Enduring understandings. Students will understand that:

- Different seasons present different weather and weather patterns.
- Seasonal weather patterns are different in different regions of the world.
- Artists must improve their work by planning, revising, and practicing (drama).
- Actors communicate ideas through drama.

Essential questions. Students considered:

- How do people adapt to seasonal weather patterns?
- How do actors and actresses communicate science ideas through drama and visual arts?
- How do weather patterns change across regions?

Highlights. Here are some highlights of our process: Students brainstormed ideas and observations for each season and created a poem for each season, documenting the weather characteristics of different times of the year (see Figure 6.2). Students explored how seasonal patterns in different

Figure 6.3. Photo of Students Reviewing Weather Patterns and Data

Students analyzed weather maps, tables, and charts for both local and foreign locations.

parts of the world vary to understand that location affects the type of weather that exists (see Figure 6.3). Students then created a weather forecast as a class for a specific area in Africa. I chose the countries of Kenya and Zimbabwe because a family member was planning a trip there for July 2019, and my class was very excited to create a long-range weather forecast to share with this family member. They even made suggestions about what types of clothing she should pack based on the climate and weather they had learned about. As part of this work students collected data about these two countries in Africa and then presented the information in a collaboratively dramatized weather report in which forecasters presented a long-range seasonal forecast for their given area.

Their forecast addressed precipitation and temperature. Students viewed video clips of real weather forecasters as examples. Students used simple costumes and props, created a script, and rehearsed their dramatization. Individuals took on various roles: holding the charts, writing the script, making costumes and props, and playing the role of the forecaster (see Figure 6.4).

Student reflections on forecasting the weather. The following student reflections capture the insights that emerged from this process:

- "The progress was moving quickly and nicely. The runner job was hard and fun, (and) all the ideas were very creative. Making it with everybody in 3rd grade was thrilling!" —Hayden

Figure 6.4. Photo of Filming a Student Weather Forecast

One student videorecorded another as she rehearsed presenting the weather forecast that the class wrote together. After each take, the class reviewed the clip, assessed lighting, location, and sound, as well as the performance of the forecaster. They critiqued and revised until they were satisfied with the results.

- "I was the light technician and I did have fun doing it. I liked researching—it was fun and hard to research. I hope I can do it again and make a different one [film]."—Ethan
- "I had to help pass the props and we couldn't make noise doing it. I think in all it was a hard and fun thing to do."—Vivian
- "I loved being the forecaster because there were some hard parts and easy parts. Some hard parts were having to read the cards and I started reading too fast, then too slow. And we had to study a lot to make the movie. . . . It was really fun and you should do it with the next [year's] 3rd-graders."—Avery
- "I liked researching the weather for the forecast because we got to work in groups, and I couldn't have done that all by myself because I don't work fast."—Jaelyn
- "Partnering up with Hayden was fun and he had really good ideas for the 'I am from' poem." —Hannah

Assessment reflections. Students' forecast work was formatively assessed by the students themselves as they worked, as I wanted them to be the experts in their roles. They were constantly analyzing the work they did, making adjustments when they realized that what they had tried wasn't working. Their decisions were guided by questions focused on the performance and filming. I gathered information as they responded and revised their performances. Some of the questions and prompts I posed included the following:

- How well can we hear the forecaster?
- Does she need to adjust her volume so it is louder or softer?
- Does the lighting allow viewers to see both the forecaster and the map clearly?
- What would happen if the lights were brighter or dimmer?
- How would closing the shades affect the lighting?
- Where would be the best place for the forecaster to stand and in which direction should she face?
- Should the forecaster stand still, or should she use her body to help focus viewers' attention somewhere?
- How can we support the forecaster with cue cards in a way that doesn't make it look like she is staring at one spot reading?
- How will the props be introduced and removed as the forecaster is speaking?

Additionally, I realized that there needed to be a summative assessment. We did view the final weather forecast and the students were thrilled with their presentation. I think adding a rubric that the children completed as they viewed or after they viewed the forecast would be insightful. I would design it to include each feature of filming with a range of met, partially met, and not yet met, as scores, and a place for comments where students might write an explanation for the score. For example, a student might choose partially met for adequate lighting, but comment that they could see the forecaster, but there was a glare from the light making it hard to see some parts of the map.

Reflections on the process. I added a written reflection piece for the students to complete. This was helpful in getting their perspectives on the lesson. The written pieces also showed students' engagement in the process and demonstrated students' awareness of the need for revision and that writing is not necessarily done when they hand something in. It showed how it helped them feel more comfortable participating, and even helped them develop appreciation for peers. I don't think I would have gotten the excitement about wanting to go back and make writing better if I hadn't done the "I am from" partner poems.

Reflections after curating and reviewing evidence. The activity of looking at graphs and/or tables was challenging. In the future, I need to think about how to better approach this. Perhaps closely observing one whole group first would be helpful. It was important to read labels, keys, and titles in order to really understand what they were looking at, but most students focused on the colors and picked out details without really understanding what they were looking at first. I felt like I was repeating myself a lot, and if I had presented this better, students would have been able to get to work more quickly.

The dramatization itself was quite a learning experience for both the students and me. The students were excited to learn about all the different roles involved in filmmaking, and when they chose their job, they took it seriously. Individual students added their input throughout the process, showing that they really felt that they were the expert in their area. The students wanted to try different lighting, positions, props, and more. When they ran into a problem, they referred to the expert and they gave options for others to consider.

The students were set on making the performance as perfect as possible. They did over 20 takes before they decided that it was just right! It took much longer than I had anticipated, but it was time well spent. I truly believe that the depth of learning in both the arts and the science content was much deeper than if I had simply asked students to research weather patterns in different areas of the world and assigned them a job for the filming of a weather forecast. This was a lesson that students will remember for a long time. They can't wait to do another filmmaking lesson.

Story 3: Printmaking and Creative Movement to Understand Landforms and Continents

Arts integration specialist Dana Schildkraut (introduced in Chapter 5) partnered with Patricia Winkle, Massachusetts elementary teacher, to deliver a series of lessons that integrated visual arts, creative movement, geography, and science.

Context. Patricia's 2nd-grade students, located in Egremont Elementary School in Pittsfield, Massachusetts, engaged in an extensive unit on geography and science, in which students worked toward identifying the central physical characteristics of each continent and ocean.

Enduring understandings.

- Texture can be implied, meaning that it appears in a visual artwork as simulated or invented in order to look like another object.
- Color can communicate a place or environment, especially when it is based on realism.

- Ideas can be translated into movements, and creative movement can help us express our understanding of a concept and generate additional ideas, too.
- Each continent has major physical characteristics, like mountain ranges, deserts, and plains.

Essential questions.

- How do artists use the elements of art (color, texture, shape) to communicate ideas?
- How do artistic ideas (texture) translate across disciplines?
- How do geographic characteristics affect people and animals?

Overview. A series of arts-integrated lessons took place in the middle of this unit. Students learned the process of making monoprints with gel plates. By producing a variety of prints, each student explored relevant colors and textures for the oceans, landforms, and biomes found on and around each of the continents (see Figure 6.5).

Students participated in a creative movement lesson to broaden their concept of textures found on the physical features within each continent (see Figure 6.6). Students translated the textures they had created in their artworks into movements, and also used creative movements to continue to brainstorm additional textures to incorporate into their artworks.

Rationale. The objectives of this series of lessons were to teach students the mono printing process with gel plates so that they could produce visual artworks of the oceans and continents that they had studied. Creative movement was used to show students how to translate the idea of texture from a visual concept into a kinesthetic concept, with the goal of improving students' understanding of texture and how it defines landforms and biomes, like mountains and rainforests. Because knowledge can be expressed in many ways, it was important to give the 2nd-graders several artistic avenues through which they could demonstrate their understanding of the content. Students had to look closely at and analyze reference images (of continents) to understand how to translate what they saw into their monoprints. Students needed to internalize the concept of "texture" and reflect it through creative movement. The creative movement activity was scaffolded as to allow students a chance to brainstorm through body movements and to express their knowledge of physical characteristics on continents (the defining landforms and biomes) through creative movement. Students who struggle with more academic tasks, like reading and writing, had artistic methods through which they could show their comprehensions.

Figure 6.5. Photo of Student Printmaking in Progress

This student created a monoprint of the ocean, including wave texture and stencils of
fish. One student shared her definition of texture by saying that texture has "patterns
you can feel—that pop up." Students were asked to make predictions of what an applied
stencil would do. One student predicted "the fish will cover the paint, preventing it from
going on the paper."

Reflections after curating and reviewing evidence. I intentionally scaffolded the lesson in a way that had students first creating visual art, secondly
engaging in creative movement, and then returning to visual art because I
wanted to see how the creative movement informed students' choices during
the art making.

I started the creative movement activity off with a prompt that all students could be successful at and one that didn't require a lot of risk-taking.
We generated movements to reflect the types of wavy textures that they

Figure 6.6. Photo of Students Depicting Geographic Characteristics Through Movement

Students explored texture through prints and creative movement. They created jagged rocks that protruded from the side (the knee jutting out) and pointed peaks stretched toward the sky (arms above head).

had produced in their ocean-themed monoprints. Indeed, I was able to collect evidence of learning because all students were able to show some type of wave motion with their bodies, and as students felt comfortable demonstrating their creativity, some more inventive wave interpretations emerged.

When we moved onto the next prompts, where we explored different landforms and biomes and generated creative movements to connect to textures found in those places, the activity allowed me to see students' background knowledge on the topic. This came out through their movements and the accompanying dialogue. The creative movement activity became a way for me to collect evidence of students' understanding of the topic. For example, one student had a very frenetic movement for the desert, and when I asked him to explain it, he told the class that it was a sandstorm. It was meaningful to learn that he knew what a sandstorm was, and this information likely would not have emerged had we not engaged in a creative movement activity.

When we generated movements for other landforms and biomes, the students (through their movements) brought up all kinds of related things, like animals who live there (i.e., horses in the grasslands) and historical sites (i.e., pyramids in the desert). Even though we had started to naturally move away from the concept of texture, it was still impactful to pursue the direction in which the students were taking the activity.

The creative movement activity allowed me to see students' gaps in knowledge. For example, when we generated movements for the rainforest, many students repeated conventional movements around rain falling. Seeing a lot of repetition informed me that students did not really know much about the types of flora and fauna in a rainforest or the textures that you might encounter in a rainforest.

Later all students did indeed include textures in their second round of monoprints (see Figures 6.7 and 6.8). Students were eager to show me what they had included—"Look! Here are zig-zag lines for mountains!" (D. Schildkraut, personal communication, November 5, 2019). See the full curation map on our resource page at tcpress.com/teacher-as-curator-9780807764480.

The following standards were addressed in this lesson (Massachusetts Department of Elementary and Secondary Education, n.d.):

- *Social studies.* "Geography and its effects on people: On a map of the world and on a globe, locate all the continents and some major physical characteristics on each continent (e.g., lakes, seas, bays, rivers and tributaries, mountains and mountain ranges, and peninsulas, deserts, plains)." (Massachusetts Curriculum Framework: History and Social Science, 2018, p. 46)
- *Earth science.* "Map the shapes and types of landforms and bodies of water in an area." (Massachusetts Curriculum Framework: Science and Technology/Engineering, 2016, p. 36)
- *Dance.* Creating—"Generate and conceptualize artistic ideas and work. Generate dance ideas that utilize levels (e.g., high, low), pathways (e.g., straight, curvy), shapes (e.g., symmetric and asymmetric) and directions (e.g., backward, diagonal)." (Massachusetts Curriculum Framework: Arts, 2019, p. 25).
- *Visual arts.* Creating—Refine and complete artistic work. Use different tools to experiment with artistic elements (e.g., using found objects to create texture).

Figure 6.7. Photo of Student Continent Print in Progress

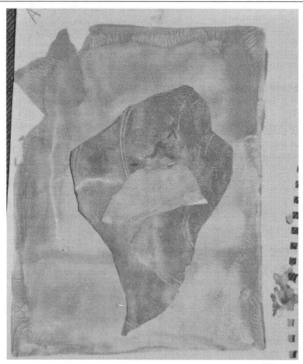

This student's work in progress showed the background as an ocean with a wavy texture. The South American continent included green for the rainforest. Later the student created textured prints of mountains and plains that were collaged on top of the image of South America to provide an overview of the continent's physical characteristics.

Figure 6.8. Photo of Monoprint Depicting Geographic Characteristics

This student example included a print of rocky, gray mountains. The zig-zag texture showed the craggy rocks.

Story 4: Ocean Currents

Context. In this lesson teaching artist and scientist Mary Brooks explores what factors can influence ocean waves and currents in two 8th-grade science classes in Waring Middle School, Beverly, Massachusetts, and Monument Valley Middle School, in Great Barrington, Massachusetts. In this science and arts-integrated lesson, students explore the many influences of ocean currents by creating 3-dimensional visual representations. She details what happens when students interact with these scientific elements.

Overview. As a scientist and an artist, I'm interested in the parallels between both fields. I believe that art and science share a common creative process. STEAM programs that focus on creative representation of science concepts invite students to engage and form a creative connection to their science learning. In this lesson students created a woven vessel that physically illustrates several (at least three) of the important attributes of ocean waves and currents. By creating a physical model, students understand more deeply what can influence ocean currents and interactions, and the etiology of ocean waves and currents. Students brainstormed ways that the listed causes of ocean currents can be translated into physical elements in the weaving. For example, temperature can be represented by "warm" and "cold" colors.

Enduring understandings. Students will understand that:

- Wind, water density, and tides affect ocean currents.
- Artists play a key role in creating models and illustrations to demonstrate scientific phenomenon

Essential questions.

- What are the links between the arts and science?
- How do artists make meaning of scientific phenomena?

The objective of this project was twofold: (1) asking students to represent the causes of ocean currents visually and (2) inviting students to consider how art materials and techniques can be used to represent a concrete scientific process. Students learned at least one bookmaking technique, and each created a STEAM notebook in which they recorded notes, observations, artistic choices, and sequential steps as they worked on their vessels. These vessels are not traditional models, but rather the students' individual interpretation of the scientific concept. This approach can be challenging for students—especially in the context of a science class where model making is more standard practice. However, once students understand that this approach is both art and science, they experience the freedom to express

**Figure 6.9. Photo of Student Artwork Representing Factors Influencing Ocean
Currents**

The student work above represents different stages of progress. The vessel in the upper
left panel was complete while the others required more work. Open areas represent less
dense layers of the ocean. The coiled yarn in the vessel in the upper left panel showed a
column of warm water rising through the cooler water.

Figure 6.10. Photo of Student Woven Forms Representing Dense Cold Water

These vessels demonstrate dense cold water. Students tightly packed yarns at the base of
the vessel demonstrating dense cold water. One student created a gradation of color that
reflected the more nuanced temperature variations that influence ocean currents (left
image). Another student showed sunlight around the rim of the vessel as well as rays of
light going below the surface (right image). Both images were captured at the midway
point in the project.

themselves and their understandings. There will be lots of questions as students grapple with what is being asked and how they can create their vessels. At these moments, guiding them toward which materials best reflect, for example, the quality of heat or density can be very effective. One important observation from this project is that students who were comfortable with arts projects became the leaders in this science lesson. In Figures 6.9 and 6.10, you will see representative works by students in this lesson.

Investigation of art and science connections. Each student created a physical model in the form of a woven vessel which represented how ocean waves and currents connect to the Coriolis effect. Students synthesized knowledge of ocean waves in poems and artistic works demonstrating underlying causes of ocean currents. (See poem below and Figure 6.11 for examples.) Students were asked to consider the following questions:

- Imagine that you are an artist and/or scientist creating a model through weaving to depict the elements that create currents and how they interact. How might you approach it?
- How might you use color to represent temperature, salinity, density, and so on?
- How might you use texture to represent temperature, salinity, density, and so on?
- Are you showing the relationship between *ocean waves* and *gravity* in your artwork? How? (Substitute any other two pertinent factors besides *ocean waves* and *gravity.)*
- Students were then asked to write a reflection about both the process of creating their vessels and how their design choices were tied to the science concepts. They had the choice of poetry, narrative story, or scientific protocol instruction. The following is a poem one student created:

Currents

the pointed edge of the
wire pricks my fingertip
as I twist,
curve,
manipulate,
and form it into
a circle.
slowly, a rim appears,
Then a base,
then outsides.
These early foundations

Figure 6.11. Photo of Student Woven Forms

This student demonstrated the importance of the moon on tidal currents. The wire was important to the structure and showed how waters are tied to the pull of the moon. The dark circle of yarn at the bottom of the image was used to indicate that tidal currents can run very deep. This vessel was at a midway point in the process.

> are the bare bones,
> the body of my sculpture
> In, out,
> over,
> under, I weave this dark green
> wire through itself tightly,
> not leaving gaps. It stacks neatly.

This weaving of wire
is the dense water in the oceans
Thick and heavy
sinking to the bottom.
Looser wire sits up top, representing
the light and thin waters of the
surface.
Thick to thin, basket to ocean

To summarize the learnings in this project, students

- Learned sequential steps of how to make a woven vessel and created a unique woven vessel using various materials
- Visually represented relationships and knowledge of ocean waves and currents through thoughtful artistic choices while weaving
- Reflected (through writing and poetry) on the creative process and justified all artistic choices in connection to scientific knowledge

The research journal and artistic work (book with text and illustrations, woven vessel depicting understanding of key elements that affect ocean waves) served as methods of collection for the evidence of learning identified above).

The similarities between artistic and scientific practice are demonstrated in Figure 6.12. In this chart the studio habits of mind (Hetland et al., 2007) are mapped to scientific habits of mind (National Science Teaching Association, 2014), and student outcomes are identified.

Shaping Your Own Learning Story

In Figure 6.13, you will find a simple structure for shaping your story. This is just one of multiple approaches you can use. Some stories are organized chronologically as teachers and students describe the sequence of learning. Other stories might be organized by essential questions or by identified learning targets. Beginning with the end in mind will help shape the key elements you would like to include as well as the artifacts that might be featured, such as photographs, student artwork, videos, and performances. Determining the audience for the story will also help you think about the essential elements to share. By curating evidence to find the salient discoveries or mastered content, you will find that "less is more" and that selectivity with criteria helps pare the story into a digestible length.

If you decide to ask students in pairs or small groups to create a learning story, you may intentionally document and collect evidence throughout the lesson or unit so that it can be folded into a performance task of creating a summative story.

Figure 6.12. Artistic and Scientific Habits of Mind

Studio Habits of Mind	Outcomes	Science and Engineering Practices
Develop Craft Learning to use tools, materials, artistic conventions; and learning to care for tools, materials, and space	*Students will*: Use fine motor skills, weaving techniques and illustration Depict scientific ideas about the Coriolis effect	Asking questions and defining problems Using mathematics and computational thinking
Engage and Persist Learning to embrace problems of relevance within the art world and/or of personal importance, to develop focus conducive to working and persevering at tasks	*Students will*: Explore and integrate their ideas about ocean currents into the creation of a woven vessel and a poem Iterate ideas to find what will communicate scientific and artistic ideas most clearly and in compelling ways	Asking questions and defining problems Planning and carrying out investigations
Envision Learning to picture mentally what cannot be directly observed and imagine possible next steps in making a piece	*Students will*: Identify key ideas about ocean currents (salinity, temperature, density, and gravity) and translate these ideas about ocean currents into visual form in weavings, image with explanatory text (artist statements, book captions, and poetry) Create a physical model which will represent how ocean waves and currents connect to the Coriolis effect Create representations of ideas that are not directly observed	Obtaining, evaluating, and communicating information Developing and using models

Figure 6.12. Continued

Studio Habits of Mind	Outcomes	Science and Engineering Practices
Express Learning to create works that convey an idea, a feeling, or a personal meaning	*Students will be able to:* Interpret how currents work through the creation of poetry and weaving Create illustration and text in a handmade book demonstrating understanding of how salinity and temperature affect water and currents using color, texture, and woven layers Describe artistic choices and convey scientific ideas in an artist statement and how scientific ideas inspired creative responses	Obtaining, evaluating, and communicating information Analyzing and interpreting data
Observe Learning to attend to visual contexts more closely than ordinary "looking" requires, and thereby to see things that otherwise might not be seen	*Students will:* Review their work and the work of their peers and identify how they used color, texture and form to represent temperature, salinity, density, gravity to create models Attend to visual characteristics of scientific ideas (real and imagined)	Engaging in argument from evidence
Reflect Learning to think and talk with others about an aspect of one's work or working process, and learning to judge one's own work and working process and the work of others	*Students will:* Reflect on how translating scientific ideas through the arts create compelling models for understanding scientific principles Consider how visual forms and creative writing can communicate ideas, construct explanations Identify and evaluate how ideas are presented in alternative ways	Obtaining, evaluating, and communicating information Constructing explanations and designing solutions
Stretch and explore Learning to reach beyond one's capacities, to explore playfully without a preconceived plan, and to embrace the opportunity to learn from mistakes	*Students will:* Explore a variety of means to communicate their understanding of ocean currents (through weaving, illustration, poetry, and descriptive writing) Interpret scientific ideas into creative work that provide alternative models for understanding scientific ideas	Obtaining, evaluating and communicating information Constructing explanations and designing solutions

Figure 6.12. Continued

Studio Habits of Mind	Outcomes	Science and Engineering Practices
Understand Art(s) Worlds Learning to interact as an artist with other artists in classrooms, in local arts organizations, and across the art field and within the broader society	*Students will:* Engage with a scientist who is also an artist Identify the intersections between scientific and artistic practice	Obtaining, evaluating, and communicating information

Note. Information in figure taken from Unpublished lesson plan chart], by Mary Brooks,and Lisa Donovan, 2020; Hetland, L., Winner, E., Veenema, S., & Sheridan, K. M. (2007), *Studio Thinking: The Real Benefits of Visual Arts Education*, Teachers College Press; and Science and Engineering Practices, by National Science Teaching Association, 2014 (https://ngss.nsta.org/PracticesFull.aspx).

FINAL THOUGHTS

Learning stories allow teachers to share unique highlights from their curation maps, excerpting and abstracting information to describe experiences in the classroom. As you can see from the stories above, teachers have accomplished this in a variety of ways. You can access more examples of learning stories that are embedded in arts lessons created by teachers from across California. In each lesson in the online compendium, the user can click on different tabs where the teacher provides an overview, information about themselves and their students, and reflections about their approaches through learning stories. These can be accessed at the California County Superintendents Educational Services Association (CCSESA) Arts Initiative website (https://ccsesaarts.org/arts-learning/lessons/). The point is that stories from the classroom deserve to be shared. It is important to tell the story of learning, to demonstrate the complexities and intricacies of the teaching and learning process, and to bring forward teacher and student voices that describe what works.

Arts-integrated practice brings students' interpretation of ideas to the fore, showing how ideas are translated, how students see the relevance of content to their own lives, and what deep learning looks like. As the stories in this chapter have shown, formative assessment, including arts integration, provides opportunities for students to construct meaning and to demonstrate their understanding. The learning story is a vehicle for capturing and curating learning moments that have significance and for summarizing student progress in ways that others can understand.

Figure 6.13. Sample Story Template

Synopsis

In just a few words, what's the key message or idea you want to convey? Why does it matter?

Message

Finish the sentences:
- This is a story about:
- It's important because:
- We have been learning about:
- Some of the questions we were trying to answer in this lesson were:

Setting

Give your audience a sense of place. Is your classroom located in an urban, rural, or suburban area?
- What important information can you provide to describe the setting of your classroom, school and district?
- Use descriptive language so others can imagine the place that you are describing.
- What is your unique context?

Key Characters

- Who's important to the story? What influencers (students, teachers, experts, authors, researchers) informed your learning story?
- What is your role in the story?
- As you think about your learning progression, what people helped inform your learning?

Plot

- What happened that's compelling for you?
- What are some learning moments that you found most interesting? Why?
- What did you find successful? Highlight as many of these key areas as apply to your "plot."

Helpful prompts to describe the learning process:

- We wanted to know about:
- We started looking at:
- Some of our questions were:
- We needed to learn more information about:
- The examples that best show how we learned are:
- We expressed this knowledge through:
- Some of our aha moments were:
- Some ways we found connections were:

Outcomes

- What work demonstrates what you learned?
- What did you do (give it a verb)?
- What would you like to learn more about?

Why It Matters

- What's the value of sharing this story? What do you want people to know about you and what you learned?
- Why does what you learned matter?

CHAPTER 7

Creative Assessment Strategies

> Innovative formative assessment examples are part of what defines any
> modern classroom. They provide crucial information about what students
> understand and what they don't. . . . When integrated into teaching and
> learning on an ongoing basis, students can constantly improve and excel. (Lee
> Watanabe-Crockett, 2019)

In this chapter we feature several flexible arts strategies as opportunities to assess learning in the classroom. As we have emphasized throughout this book, integration of the arts across curricular areas can provide rich evidence of learning through creative formative assessment approaches. Each strategy we present will demonstrate how different art forms can be incorporated into a lesson to elicit feedback from students and used to document evidence of learning. Each strategy includes opportunities for students to make artistic choices and to reflect, interpret, and demonstrate their understanding of content. For each strategy we will also provide an example of how the strategy can be used in the classroom. We'll explore insights and share some suggested ways that the strategy could be used in different curricular translations.

These strategies will be introduced with a step-by-step process to support teachers in integration of the arts into their assessment toolbox. The strategies can be easily adapted across content areas to be used in grade levels K–12 and in postsecondary classrooms.

While we will suggest some evidence you might gather when implementing the strategies, we hope many new ideas will be triggered that may go beyond our list of possible applications. As you incorporate these within your curriculum, you will find possibilities to make direct observations of social behaviors and problem-solving skills. Observations of oral and written academic responses, as well as individual and group reflection, provide many opportunities to observe student behavior and academic proficiency. While we examine formative processes in this chapter, we know that quizzes, worksheets, rubrics, and other formal assessments might also complement the processes we describe. At the end of this chapter is an assessment checklist that could be tailored to meet your teaching needs.

STRATEGY 1: ALTERED TEXT

Overview of the Strategy

In *altered text* strategy, students explore ways to manipulate text to find new meaning. The strategy can be used with various types of texts including but not limited to articles, excerpts from books, discarded periodicals, brochures, and/or other printed media. The purpose of the strategy is to allow students to connect with printed text to transform the meaning of words on a page (Bogard & Donovan, 2013). Students choose specific letters, words, or sentences, and are given other media, such as colors, markers, paint, and colored paper, to create a collection of chosen words or phrases that stand out to them. By altering the text, students can create a collage of words or poetry or add visual representations of what the text means to them. By adding artistic elements, they can also consider visual elements (color, texture, line, and so on) while also responding to and deepening their own meaning of the words to communicate messages. This can be a great way to introduce students to a specific literary work, such as Shakespeare. It is also a useful strategy to provide access to dense nonfiction texts with which students may struggle. Once students have manipulated words to create new meanings, they often want to go further to understand the author's original intent. This strategy is particularly helpful in allowing students to personalize learning by combining visual elements that often anchor understanding of words and phrases through creative expression.

Grade level(s). All

Space needed. Space for art making

Materials needed. Glue sticks or other adhesive, mixed visual materials such as photographs, magazine images and words, painted papers, origami paper, and so on

Subjects addressed in this strategy. Altered texts can be used in any curricular area. This strategy involves careful selection, editing, reconstruction of words, and the creation of new meanings. Text from different subject areas can be used. While this strategy can be used across the curriculum, different literary works are particularly well suited and can provide the impetus for additional creative writing.

Learning outcomes. Students will be able to:

- Derive meaning of a text by exploring word choice, extrapolating text, and juxtaposing ideas by creating new visual representations

- Select, curate, and manipulate text and visual images
- Create visual media using elements and principles of design
- Find connections, applications, and relationships by mining ideas, thoughts, and phrases from written text
- Create new meanings through creating visual representations of text
- Explore different points of view about the content explored
- Develop and embellish key concepts in the topic or theme
- Develop new content inspired by written text
- Compare and/or contrast ideas through written and visual representations
- Identify personal connections to content
- Engage in individual and/or group problem solving
- Reflect both individually and in a group
- Showcase their work either through spoken word or exhibiting their altered text

Steps for Facilitating This Strategy

Preparation. Familiarize yourself with the many techniques used in altering books by searching and curating images online that showcase altered books. Decide what type of printed media you will use and make sure you provide 1–2 pages of printed text for each student. Plan ahead to find your text pages. One resource is the local librarian who may be able to provide magazines, books, encyclopedias that are to be discarded. Another source of text is online media such as articles or blogs.

Depending on how you use this strategy, all students could receive the same pages of text, or if you would like to individualize the assignment, you can provide different text pages for each individual student. Another option would be to plan a long-term project where students alter text for an entire book over time. Be sure to check discarded books for appropriate content.

Procedure.

- Explain to students that they will have the opportunity to alter a portion of text and that they will be able to explore key words, phrases, or expressions that interest them. They will be given the opportunity to manipulate the text and transform or magnify it by creating a visual representation of some of the words that they find particularly interesting, intriguing, or provocative.
- Curate images of altered books from the Internet, and show students how altered books are showcased in museums. One particularly compelling artist who has worked with altered text is Tom Phillips (see his altered pages in a book he calls *A*

Humument). "*A Humument* is filled with pages where most of the text has been painted over, leaving only words that Phillips conceives of as a new narrative. He used a forgotten 19th-century novel titled *A Human Document*, written by W. H. Mallock. . . . The text of every original page has been painted or transformed in some way leaving only the words Phillips chose for his 'alteration'" (Larios, 2017).

- Have students select a page from a discarded book or provide a sheet of words copied from a text. Excerpts of students' writing can be used as well.
- Invite students to highlight or circle words and phrases that are interesting to them.
- Ask them to distill or transform the text to create new meaning. Note that the words do not need to be in order; you can create fresh meaning by drawing from words across the page.
- Invite students to use art materials (colored pencils, oil pastels, and so on) to add visuals to accompany the selected text. This can be as simple as adding color, shape, line to create patterns that highlight the text, or can include an illustration that amplifies or provides additional meaning to the text. The purpose here is to invite students to consider how image and text complement each other.
- Invite students to create thumbnail sketches on additional paper to test their ideas before adding their visuals to the page in its final form.
- Engage students in a peer review of work and invite individual student artists to discuss their work artistically and from the perspective of the theme explored. (Bogard & Donovan, 2013, p 229).
- Then, have students transform the pages through the inclusion of visual patterns and imagery.
- Engage students in a peer review of work and invite individual student artists to discuss their work artistically and from the perspective of the theme explored.

Culturally responsive learning. Working with altered text as a strategy can prompt culturally responsive teaching by providing opportunities for students to bring their voice, choice, and personal connections to a selected text. Teachers can mindfully select text that represents various cultures and traditions. In addition, Farkas (2019) makes the case that students often seem less intimidated in the process of deconstructing text "as opposed to composing new writing."

In *Culturally & Linguistically Responsive Arts Teaching and Learning in Action: Strategies that Increase Student Engagement and Achievement,* Sánchez et al. (2017) note the following about altered texts:

This activity allows participants to enter a text first, and make a deep connection with it personally, prior to having to engage in any other kind of analysis. . . . The important part of this is that it offers an anxiety-free opportunity to create a completed artwork. It also builds the capacity for participants to connect with the words of others. This is an important skill moving forward with making text-to-text connections, text-to-self connections, and text-to-world connections. For younger participants, this strategy allows them to engage in texts they may have thought were over their heads. (p. 24)

Teaching example. One art education student teacher, inspired by book artist Tom Phillips, created a lesson on altered text that focused on sentence structure. The lesson introduced an altering technique called "word blocking." Students were responsible for altering the original text found in their recycled books and creating new sentences. After reading over the text, the first step of the project was to select "interesting words—in order to form a new sentence." Students selected words and created new sentences focusing on sentence structure including "subject matter, an action, and additional descriptive words." Students continued by creating an illustration for the new sentence. Rationale: We use Shakespeare as an example in a different part of this chapter. The same student teacher noted in another lesson, "The project of creating an altered book really lends itself to the idea of a unit plan, because each page is a new opportunity for a lesson. If you treat each page like a blank canvas, the opportunities can be endless!"

Teachers who have used this strategy have reported that their students who have worked with particularly difficult text (or dense prose) find new meanings by manipulating words and creating visual images. Also, the teachers have reported that the exercise itself often has motivated students to really digest the text and understand its full meaning.

Assessment possibilities. Some of the possible formative assessment methods that could be incorporated in this strategy include the following: written and oral reflections, thought maps, writing samples, video- or audio-taped presentations, and other performance tasks. Students could write a piece based on the style of the text used. Students could also create a word or phrase log, develop a graphic organizer based on the text extracted and create a list of unique words that need further investigation or definition. Written reflections can be a tool to capture students' discovery and thought processes.

Debrief questions. The following questions are helpful for written and oral reflections:

- What theme did you explore in your page or book?
- What words or phrases stood out to you?
- How did you alter the meaning of a page?

- What choices did you make in designing the visual elements of your page?
- How did the role of being both author and artist affect the creation of your altered book?
- "What choices did you make in both roles? How were they similar and different?"
- "What new meaning did you give to the page or book?"
- "What artistic techniques produced the most interesting results?"
- "What is communicated by the composition of the pages?"
- "What did you learn during the process of creating your altered page or book?" (Bogard & Donovan, 2013, p. 230)

Extended learning. Some possible extended student activities include the following ideas:

- Create role-plays or dramatizations of critical meanings and themes found in the text explored.
- Write a group poem by putting together key phrases from their individual altered texts.
- Create a gallery walk of student work as students review each class member's altered text.
- Exchange the altered-text works with a partner and create headlines for the works. Each pair of students compare their headlines and then discuss if the headlines are true to the meaning of the altered text.
- Create a PowerPoint presentation that strings all the examples together. Students create a group mural or collage of the altered texts.

STRATEGY 2: COLLAGE

Overview of the Strategy

The strategy of collage refers to artwork that is made from an assemblage of a variety of visual materials with different textures, colors, and shapes creating a new work of art. A French term, meaning "to glue," *collage* is useful for exploring the meaning of vocabulary, concepts, ideas, and emotions. Collage promotes the translation of ideas into visual form through the use of elements of art and principles of design. This strategy invites students to explore their own ideas about content as they collect and create imagery from a variety of sources in investigation of a curricular concept.

Collage is a kind of visual storytelling that can reveal metaphoric and symbolic connections, personal interpretations, and documentation of learning. Gersh-Nesic (2019) points out:

The possibilities of using collage to address a variety of issues are endless. Quite often, the artist will leave clues within the elements of a piece to allude to anything from social and political to personal and global concerns. The message may not be blatant but can often be found within the context.

Collage can serve to open thinking processes, create new understanding, and invite meta-cognition (Simmons & Daley, 2013).

Grade level(s). All.

Space needed. Space for art making.

Materials needed. Glue sticks or other adhesive, mixed visual materials such as photographs, magazine images and words, painted papers, origami paper, and so on.

Subjects addressed in this strategy. Collage can be used across any content area as a means to explore text, reinforce key ideas, and consider applications of content. Students compose a piece that shares their insights and connections and evidence of understanding through varied media. The collage can also bring together unique ideas, events, and commentary through creative expressions of multimedia such as found objects, magazine pages, yarn, tissue, 3-dimensional objects, and/or objects of nature. Depending on the focus of the lesson, this strategy yields opportunities for student agency and expression as well as personal expression and feedback. Students can use collage to explore emotions and values, depict major ideas and trends of a historical moment, or share understanding of key themes, events, or characters from a story. "Rather than just a single image, collage provides an opportunity to include many images within one composition" (Panik, n.d.).

Types of content that could be incorporated into a collage include the following:

- Story elements or highlights
- Major contributions of a person or historical figure
- Themes, examples, symbols, photos, pictures
- Curated quotations or excerpts from text
- Suggested solutions to a specific problem
- Quotations
- Poetry or figurative speech
- Content vocabulary terms and meanings
- Important events or timelines
- Traditions, story elements

Learning Outcomes. Students will be able to:

- Create a point of view about the content explored
- Interpret and analyze content through visual representation
- Visually represent key concepts, vocabulary, or ideas
- Compare and contrast ideas through visual means
- Construct meaning through grouping and organizing materials and found objects
- Identify personal connections and meaning
- Use the language of the elements of visual arts and the principles of design to discuss their compositional and artistic choices
- Demonstrate understanding of visual arts elements and the techniques of collage
- Demonstrate the ability to apply principles of design
- Make informed judgments about student work and content explored

Steps for Facilitating This Strategy

Preparation. The teacher should gather materials and organize them so students will have access to different types of media, including but not limited to: magazines, paper of different colors and prints, yarn, found objects, glue, scissors, pastels, crayons, foam core, cardboard, fabrics, pipe cleaners, and so on. Think about lining tables or desks with plastic tablecloths or protective covers so that the sometimes-messy work of collage making doesn't damage furniture. Determine guidelines on how to manage students when gathering their materials, such as allowing a certain number of students to get their materials at one time. Also have in place space procedures so that students know the proper protocols for use of materials and how to clean up.

Procedure.

- Introduce the idea of collage as a strategy for creating a new work of art from an assemblage of images, textures, colors, shapes, and so on. Introduce the elements of visual art (line, shape, color, form, texture, value, and space) and the principles of design (balance, movement, repetition, gradation, proportion, emphasis, contrast, and variety).
- Share examples you have gathered to provide inspiration and ideas. These could include Picasso, Romare Bearden, Georges Braque, Radcliffe Bailey, Robert Rauschenberg, and so on.
- "Discuss the use of different materials and media to achieve various effects of line, form, color, and texture that could not be

achieved using only a single medium such as paint. Also consider the social and cultural meanings that the materials used in many collages might carry; these give multiple layers of meaning to an artist's work" (Herzog, 1990, n.p.).

- Invite students to conduct research on a topic, collect ideas for exploration, select images and symbols, and sketch or write down ideas that are relevant to the theme.
- Review material choices and explore a variety of compositions by juxtaposing images, drawings, words, colors, shapes and so on.
- Allow students to gather their materials.
- Set time limits and guidelines for collage production.
- Have students complete their work by gluing down the composition and manipulating materials, keeping in mind the elements and principles of design.
- Engage students in a peer review of work and invite individual student artists to discuss their work artistically and from the perspective of the theme explored.
- Conduct a discussion or debrief or ask students to write about the work they accomplished.

Culturally responsive learning. Because collage relies so much on personal choice and student voice, it can reflect the identity, interests and values of the student artist. Melanie Herzog (1990) explains that through this technique:

- Artists can express their cultural identity through styles and images that refer to their own cultural heritage.
- The subject of a work of art, and the way that the subject is portrayed, can tell us something about an artist's own life experiences and memories.
- Artists are influenced by a variety of artistic styles and concerns, and their art can reflect these influences.
- Students learn that photomontage can be an effective medium for conveying images of memories and tradition because it brings together fragments of photographs that have their own stories to tell.
- Teachers can stimulate imagination by providing examples created by artists from different cultures representing varied styles, traditions, and approaches.

Teaching example. Judith Dodge (2009) describes the unit collage as an assessment that shows another variation of the process described above:

A Unit Collage is a student-generated, ongoing, visual synthesis of a topic stud-ied in class. It includes on one page a group of eight to ten drawings, symbols, captions, and so forth that capture the essence of a unit of study. Creating individual unit collages allows students to process information more deeply through their own synthesis of ideas, both visual and linguistic. The benefits of completing a Unit Collage are many. Because the collages are open-ended, they appeal to learners of different strengths and intelligences. Along the way, these collages serve as a check for student understanding and an opportunity for informal assessment. These collages will later serve as effective study tools and triggers for student memory. Some students choose to save the collages for years, keeping a visual record of some of the most important ideas, principles, and key concepts that they have studied in a particular class. (p. 59)

Assessment possibilities. Some possibilities for assessment include a ru-bric for self, peer, or group review featuring the critical components of the information you are covering, including key elements and principles of de-sign. Students can provide written, oral, and group reflection with prompts the teacher prepares. Students can create a meaning statement that summa-rizes the meaning of the collage using the vocabulary covered in the lesson or in the new product. The teacher can create a gallery walk so that students can observe the other collages created and make observations about the meaning and content covered in the collages.

Debrief questions. The following questions are helpful for written and oral reflections:

- How did you use the principles of design to organize your composition?
- How did you incorporate the elements of visual art as you translated ideas from the topic into visual form?
- How does the collage communicate your interpretation of the content? How does your collage represent your unique interpretation of ideas on the topic?

Extended learning. Some possible extended student activities include the following:

- Write artist statements to discuss their artistic choices and their ideas linked to the topics explored, use of metaphors, and so on.
- Create an individual or collaborative poem that underscores the key themes of the collage.
- Connect their collages together to create a large mural.
- Add words and text as a headline or statement (with specific text from a story or other literary work).

STRATEGY 3: DIALOGUE POEM

Overview of the Strategy

A dialogue poem is a written or oral conversation between two persons or entities (such as giving voice to inanimate objects, processes or ideas) that represent different points of view. The purpose of the dialogue poem strategy is to provide students an opportunity to critically analyze the differences and similarities between two different perspectives by exploring a theme, issue, or topic. Using elements of poetry, such as mood, symbolism, meter, figurative language, repetition, imagery, voice or point of view, and word order, students can bring forward the essence of ideas in fresh language. Polly Collins (2008) notes, "In the content areas, poetry encourages interest, insight, and understanding. It is like no other form of written word in its ability to offer personal connections. Poetry reaches across all areas of life, and this universality invites teachers to embed it in instruction in all curricular areas" (p. 81). She goes on to say:

> When students create poems about topics of study, they enhance their comprehension through the connections they have made between the topic and their own lives, the topic and the world around them, and the poetry and content texts they have read. (p. 83)

In addition, the dialogue poem can serve as an important assessment strategy at the conclusion of the exploration (Regents of the University of Minnesota, 2006). This strategy invites students to work together to highlight different perspectives and ideas, as well as explore varied points of view, while co-creating and performing a poem. Depending on how the work is organized, it will require thinking together, collaboration, joint decisionmaking and consensus building for development of shared lines. Developing ground rules and skill building for collaborative work will help the flow of the writing and also create an atmosphere of respect for student presentations.

Compare and contrast is one of the most effective instructional strategies that teachers can use (Marzano, 2007). The strategy of constructing a dialogue poem works well when analyzing similarities and differences between related concepts or perspectives. Students are able to capture rhythm and experience contrasting views through the dialogue that is created and presented. The joint construction of a poem encourages "conversation about the content being explored and the ways to best translate ideas into poetic form. This collaborative work allows students to share what they know with their peers and to deepen learning" (Bogard & Donovan, 2013, p. 132). Constructing their poems also prompts students to better differentiate between two concepts being learned at the same time.

This strategy also invites reflection on the power of voice (internal and external). As Jefferys (2017) explains:

> "Voice" in a dialogue poem refers to how your speakers speak—particularly their word choices and the rhythms and structures of their sentences. The voice of each of your speakers should be distinct enough that a good reader could tell them apart without needing to be told which speaker is speaking.(n.p.)

Grade level(s). All.

Space needed. Space to write individually, in pairs, and to perform final poem for two voices.

Materials needed. Paper, pencil.

Subjects addressed in this strategy. Dialogue poems can be used in a variety of subject areas. Students use a dialogue poem to examine two sides of an issue, two opposing perspectives, or conflicting emotions. This is applicable for examining a relationship, conflicting views in a story or historical moment, or features of different scientific concepts (types of weather, earth science activity, such as volcanoes versus earthquakes, or chemical processes).

Learning outcomes. Students will be able to:

- Create representations of content through poetic language
- Portray people, characters, and historical figures to represent contrasting viewpoints
- Compare and contrast different ideas, concepts, and perspectives
- Identify similarities or differences of ideas in jointly read lines
- Create a clear sense of two different voices through word choice, rhythm, and emphasis
- Manipulate words and phrases to convey meaning
- Select, revise, and synthesize information
- Apply the elements of poetry
- Create and manipulate text using figurative language in their poems
- Explore performance choices to bring including articulation, inflection, emphasis, projection, and dramatic pause.

Steps for Facilitating This Strategy

Preparation. You can help students prepare through prewriting work to provide raw materials for their poems. Provide students with access to different perspectives. Examples might include examining historical figures who represent two sides of an issue, analyzing two contrasting characters in a story, or reviewing two opposing views outlined or implied in a newspaper article.

Procedure. Depending on age level, you can use this as a whole-group activity where the students work together with the teacher to determine the contrasting points of view and brainstorm words and phrases that characterize those perspectives that ultimately become a collaboratively developed poem. Another option would be to have students individually explore contrasting points of view by first mapping in two columns evidence from a story, play, or historical event that depicts differing perspectives. By charting words and phrases that contrast, students learn to differentiate and begin to shape information that could be used in the dialogue poem. Another translation of this strategy would be to break students into pairs and ask them to explore together different perspectives related to your topic before moving to create, edit, and perform a collaboratively created dialogue poem. In all of these scenarios, students generate lists of words, phrases, and vocabulary that provide a word bank to draw ideas and inspiration for the writing process. Here is a sequence that you might follow:

- Explain the term *dialogue poem* and provide examples that compare and contrast vantage points.
- Share a topic or issue that you wish students to explore.
- Read aloud an example poem and have students identify key ideas and features. What makes a good poem? What are the shared ideas? Contrasting ideas? What is learned by placing the similarities and differences side by side? What ideas might be useful as they develop their own work?
- Discuss vocabulary of poetry (mood, tone, symbolism, meter, rhyme, figurative language, connotation, denotation, repetition, alliteration, imagery, irony, voice or point of view, assonance, consonance, form, stanza, word order, and onomatopoeia).
- Organize students to work in pairs or individually.
- Research and generate lists of words, and prewrite. During this research phase students can generate lists of words and ideas for each perspective considering what the different vantage points are.
- Create a list of ideas to draw from, using a two-column chart.
- Identify contrasting ideas for each voice to explore.
- Identify similarities in each voice or perspective in the poem and create shared lines that can be read by both voices at key moments in the poem.
- Practice. "Each student will help the other practice performing his or her poem (dialogue poems are to be read by two voices).

Provide students time to practice performing their poems aloud in two voices" (Bogard & Donovan, 2013, p. 135).

- Have each pair perform their dialogue poems to the rest of the class.
- Each pair shares highlights of process and poetic choices.
- Invite individual and peer reflection.

Culturally responsive learning. This work develops critical literacy skills for all students. Since poetry is often taught in English Language Arts, different genres of literature can be the basis for the dialogue poem. Although dialogue poems can be used across the curriculum, Monreal (2017) makes the case for exploring perspectives in history:

> Dialogue poems challenge students to complicate moments, events, and perspectives by acknowledging multiple ways to analyze history. They also hold us accountable as educators. Does our curriculum include multiple voices and perspectives? Do students have the resources or guidance to complete such a task? Whose stories do we privilege?

Teaching example. One educator explored the well-known photograph of the Migrant Mother taken in 1936 by Dorothea Lang. Students were invited to compare the public view of the photograph with the perspective of the unknown mother who never received benefits from the photograph or its fame.

Assessment possibilities. Teachers and students can use formative assessment methods such as a dialogue chart, written reflection, Venn diagram, thought map, or graphic organizers in conjunction with this strategy. A video or audio recording of the dialogue poems can provide an artifact that can be used at a later time or in a peer review process. A rubric could be designed to highlight key components of the dialogue poem including content and performance criteria. Here is a list of possible criteria:

- Voices show contrast and comparison.
- Research on diverse perspectives is integrated.
- Word choice and rhythm differentiates different voices.
- Shared lines create unity in the poem.
- Two perspectives are clear.
- Contrast between voices is compelling.
- Figurative language is used.
- Students are able to identify clear poetic and content choices.

Debrief questions. The following questions can be used in debriefing the lesson:

- What topic, situation, or conflict did you explore through the dialogue poem?
- How did the poem bring different points of view to life?
- What did you notice about your poem delivery and/or the delivery of other poems?
- How do dialogue poems allow you to compare and contrast ideas?
- How did you use the elements of poetry to bring different perspectives to life?
- How would you interpret the statement, "There are always two sides to any situation"?

Extended learning. Some possible extended student activities include the following:

- Select a newspaper article about a controversial issue and explore the issue from two different perspectives.
- Explore different, competing points of view in a movie clip or video.
- Explore different types of weather or scientific processes.
- Create dialogue videos that compare and contrast different perspectives of significant historical figures.

STRATEGY 4: MOVEMENT PHRASE

Overview of the Strategy

Movement phrase, a dance strategy often used in arts integration, may be defined as follows: "Students create a series of movements to represent the parts of a process or concept. They perform this series of movements, linking each to the next, to illustrate a series of steps or components within a curricular concept. When students link ideas, they can better understand the relationships among concepts and form generalizations. As students create and build upon their movement ideas, they also develop the vocabulary of movement, such as directional words (pathways) and levels (high, medium, low)" (Bogard & Donovan, 2013, p. 25).

According to Stacey Skoning, "having a common movement vocabulary in the classroom benefits everyone because the common vocabulary makes it easier to discuss the movement phrases that are being created" (Skoning, 2008, p. 25).

The purpose of this strategy is to provide students an opportunity to create a sequence of movement depicting the essence of a concept or idea. Students will use movement to communicate ideas by integrating the elements of dance (body, energy, space, and time) and the qualities of movement (percussive, sustained, vibratory, suspension, collapse, swing) to form movement phrases that explore complex events or ideas. Ideas from curricular content are represented in movement connected by transitions that link ideas. The groups then work together to perform their movement phrases in sequential order. "Movement provides the cognitive loop between the idea, problem, or intent and the outcome or solution" (National Dance Education Organization, n.d.). Redman (2016) notes that "when using the body through dance and movement to explore academic concepts, students are given an opportunity and creative outlet to deepen their understanding of the content" (p. 30). Kinesthetic learning has been identified as one of the multiple intelligences that suggest that students learn differently (Gardner & Hatch, 1989).

Kinesthetic learners make meaning by active learning, movement, and hands-on exploration. Integrating dance across the curriculum creates new access points for students who learn best through physical exploration. Dance integration is an effective way to address this multisensory approach to teaching and to offer students' brains the best opportunity to learn. In his book *Learning with the Body in Mind*, Eric Jensen (2000) writes, "Movement activity, especially when it engages multiple brain systems, seems to accelerate learner maturation" (p. 47). He goes on to say, "There are many links between our brain and our body and activating one can activate another" (p. 48). (See also Appel, 2006, & Gilbert, 1997, for academic, and interpersonal benefits of engaging mind and body through movement.)

Grade level(s). All

Space needed. Open space that allows for freedom of movement and space to explore movement pathways.

Materials needed. Consider sharing exemplars of dance in action highlighting different dance styles and traditions.

Subjects addressed in this strategy. Movement phrases can be used in a variety of subject areas. Please see Chapter 6, story #3, to see how this was used to explore landforms through printmaking and movement.

Students can use movement to demonstrate properties of matter, explore force and motion, or chemical reactions in science. Movement can be used to demonstrate mathematical equations or bring to life nonfiction texts or plot points in a story in language arts, or cause and effect of historical moments in social studies.

Learning outcomes. Students will be able to:

- Translate concepts and ideas into movement and kinesthetic representation.

- Embody key ideas from the text.
- Discuss artistic choices using the elements of dance (body, energy, space, time).
- Identify the qualities of movement they have used (percussive, sustained, vibratory, suspension, collapse, swing).
- Create clear movements or gestures linked with intentional transitions.
- Improvise and explore the elements of dance.
- Select and assimilate movement concepts and skills to create meaning of content.
- Observe, analyze, and self-critique using dance terminology
- Identify and apply different dynamics to movement to create meaning.

Steps for Facilitating This Strategy

Preparation. The teacher should curate video examples that show how dance communicates different ideas and emotion. Find the text you would like students to explore through movement.

Procedure. Depending on age level, you can use this as a whole-group activity or break students into small groups and ask them to create their own movement phrases to share.

- Explain the term *movement phrase* and share video(s) of dance that communicates key ideas and emotions.
- Review dance terminology and terms as student explore different types of movement.
- Share an excerpt from a specific text that you wish students to explore and understand.
- "Ask students how ideas are linked in writing. Record responses on a chart for students to reference throughout the lesson. Talk about the importance of giving examples and connecting ideas. Explain to students that when we connect movements, we create movement phrases, and that such sequences can describe and represent the essence of a literary idea of story."
- "Divide students into small groups. Ask students to talk in their groups about how they could represent the sequence of the plot through creative movement. Remind students to think conceptually rather than creating a literal acting-out of ideas."
- "Have groups share their thinking with the class. Record their ideas to generate a class list of movement choices that can be used to create their movement phrases throughout the lesson" (Bogard & Donovan, 2013, p. 52).

- Review and discuss the six qualities of movement (percussive, sustained, vibratory, suspension, collapse, swing) with students. More than memorizing the list of terms, it is important to think about how the movement qualities are demonstrated and communicated in various ways. Have students physically explore each of the movement qualities. Here are how movement qualities might be expressed:
  » *Swinging:* Begin by swinging legs, arms, and then explore what it would be like to have the body swing.
  » *Collapsed:* Stretch high to the ceiling and then collapse into a small ball.
  » *Sustained:* Move evenly, gradually, and in slow motion to pick up an imaginary object.
  » *Percussive:* Hop up quickly or begin stomping your feet in a steady rhythm showing force.
  » *Suspended:* Raise your body up by standing on your toes or balance on one foot.
  » *Vibratory:* Start to wiggle by shaking arms, fingers, legs, or begin a vibration that starts in your toes and moves up to your legs, through your torso, to your shoulders, and your arms until it finally escapes through your hands.
- Allow time for students to explore additional variations of these movement qualities.
- Ask students to consider how they might go further to show how the qualities of movement could be identified in a person's movement. For example, they might say that an acrobat at the circus might be an example of swinging, or that a member of a marching band might use percussive marching steps, or they might describe how a person stretches in the morning to greet the day as an example of sustained movement. The students benefit from communicating movement qualities and exploring different combinations for movements that they demonstrate. Ask students to explore a variety of combinations of movements before they settle on final choices. Ask students to create intentional choices for how they will use creative movement to transition between ideas.
- Allow time for students to explore and rehearse movement phrases in preparation to share their work with the class.
- "Have groups present their movement phrase compositions. Ask students to begin and end in stillness in order to heighten the awareness of the movements."
- "Have viewers observe the movement presentations closely and identify the ideas being portrayed as well as the movement choices that were most compelling" (Bogard & Donovan, 2013, p. 53).

Culturally responsive learning. Creating opportunities for students to share dance movements derived from their cultural traditions, you build community and respect for your students' diverse backgrounds. This must be done carefully to honor the historical roots of the traditions that surface. It is important to research and curate other types of dance in order to provide students with the skills needed to understand, explore, and respect different cultural expressions of dance.

Learning through movement transcends language, engages students in active learning, and builds nonverbal communication skills allowing students to learn in varied ways. Movement anchors learning in physical memory. "Because imagery, memory, and elaboration are skills involved in both reading and dance, dance techniques designed to facilitate the steps involved in language art acquisition have the potential to improve reading skills" (McMahon et al., 2003, p. 108).

Teaching example. One educator used the definition of *transpiration* as raw material for the creation of a movement strategy. Nonfiction texts are often dense and challenging for students to deconstruct for understanding. Using movement can foster the development of a mind–body link. The teacher facilitated breaking down the description of this biological process for plants into key chunks of information. Students shared ideas for portraying the function through movement and gestures. A movement was selected by the group for each idea and performed as a group. The group then worked on intentional transitions to connect ideas. Once the movement phrase was complete, music was added and the movement phrase was performed with text read out loud as the movement was presented, followed by the performance of the phrase with music alone.

Assessment possibilities. As a formative assessment strategy, students demonstrate their understanding through dance movements and physicalization of concepts. Possible formative measures include the use of movement journals that link content to movement representations, symbol charts detailing a chain of movements, and graphic organizers prior to improvisation of dance movements. The teacher can curate video recordings of students' movement phrases in order to reflect on content and to define more clearly the qualities of movement that the students used. Students can create a comparison chart featuring content in one column and representative movements that portray the concept in another. As a formative assessment strategy, creating a movement phrase can provide checks for understanding and can reflect spatial relationships, linking mind and body. The teacher can create a rubric that includes some of the following criteria:

- Concepts are translated into movement.
- Key ideas from the text are embodied and students demonstrate through movement their understanding of content.

- Students discuss their artistic choices using the elements of dance (body, energy, space, time).
- Students identify the qualities of movement they have used (percussive, sustained, vibratory, suspension, collapse, swing).
- Students create clear movements or gestures linked with intentional transitions.

Debrief questions. The following questions can be used in debriefing the lesson:

- What artistic choices did you make in creating the movement phrase?
- How did your movement phrase illuminate ideas from the text explored?
- What did you notice in the work of your peers? Use the vocabulary of dance in your descriptions.

Extended learning. Some possible extended student activities for students include the following:

- Create their own movement phrases for content in small groups and share performance interpretations.
- Build choreographic thinking by integrating movement.
- Create movement pathways, such as straight, zig-zag, curve, spiral, circle, that show how the body moves through space.
- Observe a piece of artwork to determine specific lines (straight, curved, and so on). By making the connections to visual arts, students can translate these lines through movement. Students can bring to life a piece of artwork, a photograph, or an excerpt from text.

STRATEGY 5: ROLE-PLAY

Overview of the Strategy

Role-play is a "collection of drama-based instructional strategies which invite students to embody a character in a given set of circumstances" (Dawson., n.d., 0:08). Through this strategy students are invited to step into the shoes of a character in a situation or context. Improvisation allows actors to create a scene in the moment, entering an imaginary world. Characters explored can include real-world roles or fictional characters. Role-play can foster the exploration of perspective, emotions, and conflict while developing communication and language skills.

Role-play is a foundational element in dramatic work. "Role play and drama can offer an authentic context for students to engage in new discourses. These contexts can provide situations where students can be comfortable to speak, respond, initiate ideas, argue, be tentative and reflect" (Harden, cited in Victoria State Government, n.d., "Role play and drama" section.) Using drama during a learning sequence keeps the focus on the process of exploration rather than on creating a polished final performance. The goal is learning. "This strategy is useful for: recalling events, exploring character emotions and actions, developing empathy, asking questions, inferring, analytical thinking, exploring concepts" (Victoria State Government, n.d., "Hot seat strategy" section).

One possibility is to create a space in the classroom designated for cooperative play and dramatic activities. This space provides an environment for social and emotional skill building, collaboration and problem solving, and language and thinking skills. The following excerpt from Scholastic Parents (Scholastic Parents, n.d.), expands on the benefits of cooperative play and dramatic activities for young children as a means for expanding social and emotional learning as well as other skills:

> The process of pretending builds skills in many essential developmental areas. . . When your child engages in pretend (or dramatic) play, he is actively experimenting with the social and emotional roles of life. Through cooperative play, he learns how to take turns, share responsibility, and creatively problem-solve. When your child pretends to be different characters, he has the experience of "walking in someone else's shoes," which helps teach the important moral development skill of empathy.

Similarly, for older students, incorporating a set protocol for role-playing can be utilized in the middle or end of a lesson across the curriculum. While there may not be a designated space for the role-play, a teacher can set a context in a problem/solution format, which is a means of writing and/or discussing a problem and proposing one or more solutions. The problem/solution format allows students to explore a variety of perspectives, personas, and characters by enacting these either in improvisations or in planned role-playing scenes.

Once students know the structure of the strategy, it can be easily implemented as a teaching moment or a means of formative assessment. Most often students need prior, background knowledge and content in order to role-play. As teachers monitor the portrayal of characters, they can determine if the student is accurately portraying the character. While role-play can be a formative task to check for understanding, it helps to define criteria that include dramatic elements such as posture, character development, eye contact, and diction (if the character is portrayed through dialogue or monologue). For students who may not be comfortable acting, there are other roles that can be assigned such as director, props master, or set designer.

Everyone can find a place that feels comfortable to join in the unfolding drama.

Role-playing is especially helpful in understanding different cultures, values, and mores. As students learn to "walk in someone else's shoes," they can learn that there is not always just one perspective. One of the most powerful outcomes of using this strategy is that it allows for reflection and discussion.

As you consider implementing this strategy, the following are three approaches to role-play:

- *Teacher in role*. In this approach, the teacher takes on the role of a character, both modeling role-play for students, as an invitation to participate in a dramatic exploration, and serving as a facilitator, guiding the drama as it unfolds. "It is a good idea to have a signal that you are going in or out of role, e.g. putting on or taking off a hat, a scarf or a pair of glasses" (EAL Nexus, n.d.). Another way to begin or end a role-play is to have the teacher say "Scene" at the beginning and end of the sequence. This can signal a clear beginning and ending. A video example can also prove valuable in showing how role-playing can be used to amplify perspective, mood, conflict, and/or resolution.
- *Student in role*. Students take on the role of characters exploring context and circumstance. This can also include taking on the role of an expert in an exercise that asks the student to become an expert in a specific field or profession. In this "mantle of the expert" students imagine they have a particular area of expertise and share why they are an expert. This would require research and/or curation to build the content knowledge prior to the role-play.
- *Character in the Hot Seat*. A student takes on a character role and is interviewed by other students. This usually occurs when a student is asked to sit in a chair in front of the class and to assume a character, historical figure, or imaginary person. This translation of the strategy allows students to explore a character's background, values, and insights by "closely examining a character's motivation and responses. Before the hot-seating, they need to discuss what it is they want to know and identify questions they want answered" (Centre for Literacy in Primary Education [CLPE], n.d.).

In addition to the above examples, students can create a dramatic scene through improvisation—creating the character portrayal through words and actions in the moment. Here students are "physically embodying characters and exploring their characteristics, emotions and reactions to story events" (CLPE, n.d.).

Through improvisation, students learn problem solving and also employ a range of creative skills as they create scenarios in "real time." An improvisation could be a solo role-play or involve more than one student. When students are given a prompt with a situation, or key elements to explore, they are able to bring to life a scene that is tied to literary works, historical events, and other relevant life situations. Sometimes students can rehearse their improvisations to refine their role-play and then move it into a more planned performance. By setting parameters for what content and language is acceptable, the teacher establishes guidelines for the improvisations which helps with classroom management.

We want to point out that role-play can be used to dramatize not only characters but also inanimate objects (that take on human characteristics) or related concepts. An example of an easy role-play is the activity called Pass the Object. The teacher begins the process by holding up an item from the classroom like a scarf. She says as she moves the scarf, "I wanted you to see my belt. I received it from my grandmother when I was twelve." She then passes the object. A student takes the scarf, manipulates it in a new way, and might say, "This is my sling. I hurt my arm in football practice, and I went to the nurse's office, and she wrapped my arm in this." The student passes the scarf on, and the progression continues until each student has explored a way to role-play with the object. Items that are easy to use are a roll of masking tape, a bracelet, a small box, a belt, or a scarf.

An example of using role-play to "represent a concept or process" is to ask students to use their bodies to represent a bar chart. First, members of the class should arrange themselves by height and then in that order lie down on the floor of the hall. The teacher or a designated student can draw around them in chalk (EAL Nexus, n.d.). When the students stand up, the outline of a bar chart remains.

Grade level(s). All

Space needed. An open space for performance to unfold

Materials needed. Props and costume items will help set the stage for dramatic work, but often students can create imaginary objects through movement and gesture.

Subject addressed in this strategy. This strategy can be incorporated in subjects across the curriculum, as it provides a wide spectrum of application possibilities. Since students study characterization in Language Arts, this strategy can be applied as students are introduced to different curricular areas, for example, as a character in a story, or a witness to an event; it is also very useful for history, geography, and so on (EAL Nexus, n.d). Drama can be used to act out a scientific concept such as states of matter (e.g., solid, liquid, and gas), bring a moment in a story or historical scene to life, or create context for math (e.g., have students imagine they are mathematicians designing a display for a museum). Drama can be used to invite interaction with content in a variety of ways, such as "When a group is performing a scene they have devised, it is useful to create a freeze-frame at a decisive point in the story to involve the rest of the class in asking questions or predicting what will happen next" (EAL Nexus, n.d.).

Learning Outcomes. Students will be able to:

- Use the elements of drama (space, time, imitation, characterization, action, language, energy) in discussing their artistic choices
- Create believable characters through portraying physical traits and verbal expressions through posture, gestures, vocal inflection and emphasis, and movement
- Describe characters in a story or in a historical or current event (traits, backgrounds, and motivations)
- Demonstrate their understanding of events, stories, circumstances (either real or imaginary) through re-creating elements that bring them to life
- Analyze text including an understanding of plot and structure (e.g., chronology, comparison, cause and effect, problem and solution)
- Create a sense of setting and circumstance by creating physical clues (e.g., shivering to create the sense of cold weather)
- Show their understanding of influential factors that motivate choice and human behavior
- Discuss the influence of context and situation on character choices
- Assimilate written facts and textual information by bringing a character to life and by showing different perspectives

Steps for Facilitating This Strategy

Preparation. Identify the text and characters you would like students to explore. Curate examples of role-play using video clips or short monologues and readers theater samples to share with students.

Procedure. Depending on the age level of your students, you can use this as a whole-group activity, an individual exploration, or a partnership activity. Ask each student to step into the role of a character and explore how characters interact with each other in a scene dramatizing a certain situation or event.

- Introduce the elements of drama (character, plot, perspective, gesture, space, time, imitation, action, language, energy).
- Explain the idea of role-play.
- Demonstrate a role-play or show a video example of students role-playing.
- Share a topic or issue that you wish students to explore and ultimately act out.
- Engage students in a discussion about the topic at hand to generate ideas.
- Discuss the process of how the role-play will be created, reviewed, and shared.
- Work with students to identify character and establish a background and motivation. You may explore how a character moves or speaks before launching the role-play. This is a great opportunity to discuss all the ways a person can bring a character to life through the way a person stands, moves, gestures, and talks.
- Introduce a specific setting and set of circumstances for students to engage with. At the heart of strong dramatic work is conflict. Set up a problem the character(s) will solve.
- Invite students to improvise the scene. This can be done in pantomime (physical movement without words), or if students are comfortable adding speech, they can improvise action and dialogue. Adding costumes and props can support the drama. Some role-plays are equally compelling without props or costumes. It often depends on the grade level and the experience of the students.
- Debrief with students on their dramatic choices in both self-reflection and peer review. Invite discussion focused on the content of role-plays to reinforce key ideas and to allow students to make discoveries.

Culturally responsive learning. Children are willing to suspend disbelief as part of the way they approach play. Stepping into the role of a character different from oneself develops empathy. Exploring another perspective through role-play can be used across the curriculum and is especially beneficial for "challenging children to develop a more sensitive understanding of a variety of viewpoints whilst sharpening their language and movement skills. By adopting a role, children can step into the past or future and travel to any location, dealing with issues on moral and intellectual levels" (Farmer, n.d.). Exploring perspectives different from one's own can also help students locate their own identity, values and beliefs.

Dramatic work can foster the development of problem-solving skills and also promotes language development. Owocki (2001) notes that "Dramatic play benefits language in many areas: stimulates language innovation by introducing new words and concepts (especially valuable for second-language learners), motivates language use and practice, develops linguistic awareness, and expands content and concept knowledge."

Teaching example. A teacher takes on the role of a museum director hiring a designer for a new exhibit to feature the use of engineering practices. Then students are engaged in devising an innovative exhibit featuring the importance of math and science in engineering and are tasked with "pitching" their design ideas to the director after immersing themselves in research and the creation of a proposal.

Assessment possibilities. You can incorporate a variety of formative assessments when using this strategy in order to check students' understanding of key concepts, people, and circumstances, or to determine if students are able to differentiate ideas and points of view. You will be able to observe students' abilities to break down and analyze key similarities and differences as well as the new insights students gain from comparing and contrasting concepts. Formative assessments might include comparison charts, rubrics for performances, and/or improvisations that also include criteria related to the subject content you are covering. Graphic organizers can be used to help students break down and compare differences of character. Students can create student profiles that demonstrate their investigative skills that are supported by evidence in the text. Reflection journals allow students to write at different stages in the process. Photographs and videos can be used to capture and curate evidence of student work.

Debrief questions. The following questions can be used in debriefing the lesson:

- How did you incorporate the elements of drama in creating your role-play?
- What choices did you make in creating the character?
- What choices did the character make? What was the result?
- Why does the character make the choices they did?
- How was the problem or conflict explored?
- What words in the text (or other media) that we studied helped you to make decisions about your character?

Extended learning. Some possible extended student activities include the following:

- Create a character's inner thoughts by engaging with "thought tracking" in which characters share what they are thinking when the action is frozen. The teacher taps on a student and then the character speaks a few lines.

- Learn new information before moving into role-play through research, curation, and synthesis of key information. For example, students research a character from literature and discover other influencing factors such as background, time period, education, and events that may have occurred in the person's life. If observing film or video, students observe different characteristics such as a person's posture, gestures, movement qualities, and speech patterns.
- Create a character profile by determining the character's background, age, education, family situation, ethnicity, and life story. Students then can create 6-line scenes where they develop and perform with a partner a short dialogue.

STRATEGY 6: SOUNDSCAPE

Overview of the Strategy

We live in a world of sound: from birdsong to car alarms, from road noise to the rumble of our stomachs, the bark of a dog to a clap of thunder. Stop for a second and listen, really listen: what do you hear? (St. John, 2018)

In this strategy, "students create a sense of setting through the layering of sound effects in producing a soundscape" (Bogard & Donovan, 2013, p. 99). Canadian composer Murray Schafer (1977) defined the idea of *soundscape* as "the acoustic structure of an environment" (as cited in St. John, 2018).

Students are guided to analyze an event or situation through the lens of sound. Students imagine what isolated sounds would be heard in a specified circumstance or setting and then re-create it by using found objects. Some students create sound performances while other students assume the role of the audience and listen to the performance with eyes closed. Student performers are successful if they are able to bring a setting to life through their identified sounds combined together to create audial representations of what one might hear. The classroom audience becomes immersed in the sounds that transport them to places such as a bustling prairie town at the turn of the 20th century, a moment in World War II, or when women marched on behalf of the suffrage movement. The strategy is particularly helpful when students are studying and analyzing literary or historical works. The challenge for the students is to select and create sounds in a sequence in a way that produces an accurate reproduction of the sound environment they are trying to bring to life (Donovan & Pascale, 2012).

This strategy allows learners to contextualize content by adding auditory components. Students apply critical thinking skills to problem-solve and personalize learning through the manipulation of objects to create sounds relative to content within a lesson. House (2014) suggests that "listening is imperative to the educational setting. Children need to be able to use their auditory senses to succeed in a general education classroom" (p. 2). If students have an auditory impairment, you can work more in depth with the idea of vibration and creating scoring with items that can be manipulated. Also, students may alternatively bring the environment to life through another sensory medium, such as a visual representation (St. John, 2018).

Engaging with soundscapes in the classroom can bring learning to life in new ways. Akbari (2016) notes that "by manipulating, compiling, composing and presenting these sounds, we can develop soundscape compositions that allow us to listen to the familiar world in fresh and exciting ways. Engaging in this process is a contemplative exercise that calls on the listener to reflect on how we experience the world around us, and our relationship to it" (p. 1). At the heart of the soundscape is the attention to sensory listening, which often motivates a deeper awareness of the various sounds that surround us. Through various listening exercises students can also imagine the sounds in different stories or historical events:

> In order to tune into soundscapes, [Murray] Schafer proposed two exercises: ear cleaning and the sound walk. Ear cleaning is also known as 'active listening,' where the listener remains silent and focuses in on the sound around them: those which may be taken for granted, for example. If ear cleaning encourages attentiveness to your soundscape, then sound walks take it for a wander, prompting the listener to explore the changing soundscapes of an area through walking and listening. (St. John, 2018)

Grade level(s). All

Space needed. Space for working in small groups

Materials needed. Students will work with found sounds. This can be supplemented with simple musical instruments if you wish.

Subjects addressed in this strategy. Soundscapes can be used across the curriculum. This strategy is particularly effective in illuminating content by adding sound effects. Students actively experience learning such as creating an environment of a story, exploring the setting of a poem, creating the sounds of a significant historical moment, or determining the sounds in the life of a scientist. Students are brought into the environment experientially through the sense of sound and movement. Soundscapes can also be used to bring an image to life, explore a monologue, or create sounds that bring a scientific concept to life, inviting us into the environment being investigated.

Learning outcomes. Students will be able to:

- Explore and identify qualities of sound (pitch, timbre, intensity, and duration) by using found objects to create sound effects
- Read and analyze either a literary work or an artistic work to identify key messages of the author or the artist
- Identify how sounds help create a sense of setting, mood, and feeling
- Create an immersive environment through the layering of sounds
- Compose a soundscape score, graphing the symbols for their composition
- Listen closely to environmental sounds in a sound walk
- Listen closely to the soundscapes created by peers to decipher sounds and environment, mood and setting

Steps for Facilitating This Strategy

Preparation. Prior to the lesson, have students collect sounds for homework. Their job is to find objects that make interesting sounds and bring them to class the next day. Each student should bring in one or two items. Give them examples of items they could find, such as an athletic shoe that squeaks, kitchen utensils that could be struck and rubbed against each other, or tinfoil to be crunched. You should also gather a couple of items to add variety to the collection or to give to students who forget to bring one.

Procedure.

- Discuss the meaning of found sounds by having students share their sounds. Provide time for students to experiment with the "instruments" in small groups and explore different ways they can be used to make sounds. Encourage students to find more than one way to make a sound with each item. For example, they can blow on the top of a bottle, shake it with pennies or pebbles inside, or roll it. Provide time for students to share their discoveries about new ways to make sounds.
- Discuss the elements of music (pitch, duration, dynamics, tone color, form, texture) and encourage students to explore how

each element can enhance their composition and enhance their understanding of the story, environment, or historical moment to be explored.

- Divide students into pairs and assign each pair to create an acoustic environment. Tell students that they will work with their partners to collect items to be used as found sounds. Give students a time frame that allows them to find and test sounds and then come together to compose their soundscape. Give them a shorter amount of time than you think will be necessary—you can listen in on their planning and provide more time as necessary.
- Share examples of musical scoring. Tell students they can create their own approach to documenting the composition and the types of instruments or found sounds they are incorporating.
- Give students time to create and score their soundscapes. Have partners share their soundscape as the rest of the class listens with their eyes closed.
- Facilitate a peer review of each soundscape, and give students engaged in the creation of the soundscape the opportunity to discuss the music elements used, their artistic choices, and their scoring choices. Students can then be given time to rework their compositions including feedback they feel is useful. (Adapted from Bogard & Donovan, 2013, pp. 125–126)

Culturally responsive learning. The rich sensory world created by a soundscape transcends language and offers an often emotional and visceral experience. The strategy also provides a shared sensory process for learners and invites them to experience a particular moment, context, culture, or environment through attention to sound.

Guzy (2017) makes the case that though sound is one of our primary senses, it is easy to lose track of its impact because "one of the core properties of sound is its ephemerality—it does not endure long past its production, and even a recording is but a subjective representation of reality." Arts educator Ehsan Akbari (2016) notes: "One thing I have learned in particular from making videos is the importance of sound in setting mood and conveying meaning" (p.19).

His research has explored a variety of approaches to engage students in listening deeply and discerning the role of sound in lived experience. He advocates for engaging the sense of sound in education and suggests that exploring multiple senses "can lead to an enriching educational experience, and provide fertile ground for creative exploration" (p. 22).

By drawing attention to sounds, students are making new sensory decisions and becoming mindful of the impact of sound on the environment. They are also demonstrating understanding of varied texts and researching and curating sounds to create a soundscape.

Teaching example. In an elementary classroom, students analyzed written content about the California Gold Rush. They then studied the images in a painting depicting this era. Through exploration and collaboration, students created sounds of horses pulling carriages, men talking, pails clanging, and sand and water being sifted, and developed a composition that brought the image to life. Students reported that while listening to each other's soundscape, the sounds made them feel as if they were there, in that time period, in that town, in that very moment. The writing they did as a follow-up was markedly more descriptive and filled with the language about the sights and sounds that brought this time period to life for them. This was juxtaposed with the soundscape of Native American life during the same period. This allowed for a rich conversation about varied perspectives during the same historical frame. For another example of the use of soundscape, see Chapter 5, Map 1.

Assessment possibilities. This strategy can be used to check for understanding of content in a lesson or unit. Students demonstrate their learning by creating the context of an event or fictional circumstance by identifying the sounds and background. Students will need to support their decisions based on their understanding of text and other resources that the teacher may have curated for the students.

This strategy could be part of a performance assessment that culminates at the end of a lesson or unit. It could be paired with other formative assessments such as writing samples, sound charts, video or audio tapes of collected sounds, and/or written or video- or audio-taped reflections where students interpret the meaning of the sounds.

Teachers can incorporate reflections, problem-solving tasks, charts, and graphics, all in tandem with this strategy. Once students know the strategy, they can use it in many other contexts and with other content.

Debrief questions. The following questions can be used in debriefing the lesson:

- How did making new sounds help you understand your section of the story?
- How did the soundscape establish a particular mood or environment?
- In what ways was reading the story together with the sounds like a musical composition in which sounds are played together?
- How do sounds impact your experience of the story? (Adapted from Bogard & Donovan, 2013, pp. 229–230.)

Extended learning. Some possible extended student activities include the following:

- Create a gallery walk or curated exhibit to display soundscapes.
- Rehearse and refine soundscapes and then add narrative text to be presented by students.
- Investigate media to create digital sounds that represent a specific time period and create digital soundscapes with other sounds.
- Play the role of an orchestra conductor and point to different people to create their sounds and then combine sounds by asking others to make their sound at the same time. Try different variations.

STRATEGY 7: STORYBOARD

Overview of the Strategy

A *storyboard* creates a visual story through a sequence of images that are connected to the text. It is a flexible strategy that can serve as a graphic organizer of text and images or as a visual narrative communicating a story. As a formative assessment strategy, it provides students opportunities to capture their knowledge and creativity through visual representation of images. Students learn to sequence information and to create or represent text both individually or in a group. In this strategy, "students create and arrange images in sequence to tell a story or create a narrative. The story can be told through images alone, or the pictures can interact with text." (Bogard & Donovan, 2013, p. 200). Students create visual narratives that can show their thinking on a topic. New insights are gained as students translate concepts into visual form.

Teaching artist and researcher Wendy Strauch-Nelson (2011) notes that students "seemed drawn to the complementary relationship between the linear style of words and the layered nature of images" (p. 9).

In addition to building reading skills, storyboards also provide an opportunity for assessment. "Since reading is an internal process, a difficulty exists for the classroom teacher in diagnosing how students are progressing. When students compose storyboards while reading, the visuals become an artifact of their reading, detailing their interpretations of what is being read. Student understandings (or misunderstandings) of the reading are made explicit because teachers can see a visual record of the students' reading" (Bruce, 2011, p. 79).

Storyboarding is a skill that has been critical for movies, animation, computer games, comics, and more. Now, increasingly educators are seeing its value as a flexible strategy in arts-integrated learning in education. Abram (2008) says that "it's a powerful way to visualize and understand the ultimate experience of your story, whether it ends up in a print, comic, game, or film format. . . . It also uses the core skills we teach, such as creative writing for purpose. It can allow visual learners to create and build skills that align with their own special talents." As Bruce notes (2011), storyboarding can also be used flexibly across the curriculum.

He explains that storyboards are a multimodal approach that can create a visual representation of students' thinking as they interact with text. In the process of composing storyboards, students will often go back and forth between the text they are reading and the visuals they are creating. The storyboard is an artifact that details how students interpret and understand. "Creating storyboards encourages students to engage and interact—or in a reader-response term, *transact*—with the text" (Bruce, 2011, p. 79).

In summing up the storyboarding process, it is important to remember that the storyboard is an organizational tool to bring complex components of a story or narrative together to create a unified whole. Storyboards can be created through the use of a storyboard template that includes separate boxes (similar to a comic strip) to help students develop a chronological sequence. Other helpful tools are index cards and Post-it notes that can be moved around to make sequencing and editing easy for students. For students who may have trouble with fine motor skills, other students can assist in moving the index cards or Post-it notes to represent the desired sequence of events.

Grade level(s). All

Space needed. Space for art making

Materials needed. Drawing and collage materials of all kinds, storyboarding template

Subjects addressed in this strategy. Storyboards can be used as a planning and mapping approach or as a graphic organizer for one's ideas for a project or prewriting tool. They work well for both individual and group work. Storyboarding is a terrific strategy for planning or breaking down scenes. Images and text from a story can be cut out and scrambled for the students to order in sequence for a familiar or unfamiliar story. Storyboarding also provides a great way into exploring media arts. Students can create a script for drama or video. Heffernan et al. (2018) suggest using storyboards as a media arts project to write and film commercials.

Students can depict stages of a scientific process, list a step-by-step set of instructions, or create a series of moments from history that show the impact of cause and effect. Students can create a series of images using the elements of visual art (line, shape, color, form, texture, value, and space) to create a visual narrative. Thus students can examine and create narratives in a variety of ways, addressing the goals of Universal Design for Learning that provide students with wide opportunities to engage with content and express their understanding of content.

Learning outcomes. Students will be able to:

- Create a point of view about the content explored
- Link image and text in the communication of a story
- Create a sequential narrative including text and image to communicate a story
- Create a narrative that integrates characters, plot, conflict, and resolution
- Communicate a clear message for an intended audience
- Visually represent key concepts in the topic or theme
- Use the language of the elements of visual art and the principles of design to discuss compositional and artistic choices
- Demonstrate understanding of visual arts elements
- Demonstrate the ability to apply principles of design

Steps for Facilitating This Strategy

Preparation. Select sample storyboards to share with students. Discuss with students what they notice as they observe the examples. Ask them to notice how images and text work together, what composition ideas the illustrators use to draw audience interest, and how they steer focus from frame to frame. After reviewing the examples, the teacher and students together create a list of ideas that students can use for their own storyboards.

Procedure.

- Explain that a storyboard tells a visual story through sequenced images. Share examples of visual narratives that you have curated and chosen that show how an artist was able to capture a story through images. Discuss how the boxes (or panels) represent key and important events in a sequence.
- Explain to students that they will be creating a storyboard to communicate key ideas in a story. Share that it is important to think about the intended audience who will be reading or observing the storyboard.
- Invite students to begin thinking about the images for their stories.
- Ask students to consider how the story or message should be structured. Invite students to consider how they will break up their own stories into sections. Help students do this by asking questions such as the following: What do you think is the most essential information in the story? What characters are important to include? What settings are important to establish? What sequence makes sense?

- Talk as a class about how illustrations can amplify the meaning of a story or message. Continue to use your visual narrative example to point out how the illustrations connect with the text.
- Guide students in creating the composition of their images by using thumbnail sketches to plan for composition.
- Discuss the elements of design and what makes a powerful image in a storyboard (movement, balance, repetition, gradation, proportion, emphasis, contrast, variety).
- Create captions or embed dialogue to bring an image to life and assist in communicating meaning.
- Have students review their planning storyboards to evaluate how well they conveyed the story and edit or add visual detail as necessary.
- Ask students to create an artist statement and discuss the choices they made in creating the story through words and images.
- Engage students in a gallery walk inviting peer review of work and encourage each student artist to discuss their work artistically and from the perspective of the theme explored.
- Invite students to consider the feedback they have received and to integrate revisions they feel would refine their work. (Adapted from Bogard & Donovan, 2013, p. 203)

Culturally responsive learning. Storyboards can support culturally and linguistically responsive learning as a way to support language acquisition by learning visually and linking images and text to communicate. They can help students express understanding and engage with image and text in a hands-on way, decoding and encoding frame by frame. Reading and analyzing a wide range of graphic novels can help provide support and visual guideposts for understanding narrative and text.

The use of storyboards helps break the process of planning and writing down into more manageable chunks, enabling students to organize their thoughts. "Storyboards are useful tools for visual/spatial learners and even tactile/kinesthetic learners" (Nardolillo et al., 2014).

Brett Brigham (2018) points out, "So often, we think of a visual as something that goes along with a story—an afterthought to push the narrative along. But for those struggling with language, a visual can be, in a way, the rough draft of what they're trying to share." He goes on to suggest that students can create "a visual 'list' of all the important things about which they need to write. For students who struggle and get lost writing, and aren't sure what to do next, this visual will be a great reference."

Teaching example. One example is shared in the lesson "Dr. King's Legacy and Choosing to Participate," which is housed on the Facing History and Ourselves website (https://www.facinghistory.org/resource-library/memphis-1968/dr-kings-legacy-and-choosing-participate).

To understand the civil rights movement and also to understand the words of Dr. Martin Luther King, students read and analyzed Dr. King's Mountaintop speech. Students were asked to create a storyboard that detailed the imagery and historical references in the speech using the storyboard strategy. Students sketched the main idea or image for each paragraph and then wrote a summary or selected a quotation from the text to coincide with the images. Students were asked to share their storyboards in a gallery walk, which allowed them to observe other students' creations. After they observed the interpretations, students discussed the meaning of the speech. One of the discussions following the storyboard exercise was prompted by this question: "What do you think it takes to see a situation from someone else's perspective? What advice might Dr. King give you about deciding how to respond when you observe something that you think is unjust or unfair?" Students reflected on the visions for the kind of world they would like to live in and discussed how history could shape understanding and personal responsibility.

Assessment possibilities. This strategy can be used to assess students' understanding of sequence, story, or key moments in a progression. One formative assessment method might include creating a word wall where students contribute to a list of key words and phrases that represent significant points within a chronology of a story, novel, or series of historical moments or events. Students can also use graphic organizers to create timelines and prioritize key moments that are critical in a sequence of fictional or historical events.

Another idea is to have students create a 3-2-1 summary at the end of a class, which summarizes three things that they learned, two things that they would like to learn more about, and one thing that they liked about the lesson or unit (prompts might vary aligned to content). Exit tickets, which students use to summarize a takeaway from the class, can be a quick way for the teacher to gain an understanding of student progress. Rubrics that feature criteria for visual elements of design, use of images and space, and literary elements can help students understand more fully the components involved in the strategy.

Debrief questions. The following questions can be used in debriefing the lesson:

- How did you use the principles of design as you organized your composition?
- How did you incorporate the elements of visual art as you translated ideas from the topic into visual form?
- How does the storyboard communicate your interpretation of the content?
- How does your sequence of text and image communicate a story or idea for a specific audience?

- If you were to do this again, what would you add or change?
- In the sequence, what part was the most descriptive? What was most difficult to capture?
- How do images and text work together to tell a story?

Extended learning. Some possible extended student activities include the following:

- Move the storyboard from paper to a digital storyboard using media arts. Many digital applications are available for students to create storyboards.
- Create a story based on the storyboard that expands the storyboard and fills in key story elements.
- Work with other students to curate content to create a video based on the storyboard.
- Develop a fully developed graphic novel or comic complete with text and colored images.
- Research how storyboard is used in many careers.

STRATEGY 8: TABLEAU

Overview of the Strategy

Tableau is an art-integrated teaching and formative assessment strategy that helps students bring text to life through creating frozen statues that depict a person, place, or object. The term is short for *tableau vivant* (from French, literally, living picture) and can also represent the creation of a scene usually presented on a stage by silent and motionless costumed participants.

As a classroom strategy, tableau is the theatrical convention in which actors freeze in poses that create a picture of one important moment in the play. Actors form frozen poses to create compelling stage pictures. Often the frozen actors come to life and move to form other compelling stage pictures. Similarly, students create frozen poses to depict a character or inanimate object either alone or with other students. Rosalind Flynn, Professor of Practice and Head of Masters in Theater Education Program at The Catholic University of America and national expert in arts integration (2019), writes about the power of tableau in the classroom:

> Stillness and silence are the hallmarks of Tableau, making it understandable as to why it appeals to teachers for classroom use. But to really get the most out of this drama strategy in conjunction with the reading of a story, novel, or play, student actors have to do a deeper reading, thinking, and rehearsing. They need to work like actors who explore the text and experiment with a variety of alternatives before they choose their final poses. They need to practice focus and

commitment so that they pose with an expression on their faces and energy in their bodies. The best Tableaux show evidence of comprehension of text combined with strong acting skills.

Students are asked to read and analyze text, and define key elements of the literary work with a small group to re-create a point in the text that could be brought to life. Then the student actors must read and reread text, analyze it, and then pull out essential information that informs the creation of the frozen moment. The teacher is very observant of how students are processing information and gathering clues to create a tableau based on text.

Deirdre Moore (2016) writes, "There is just something about tableau that makes it a really accessible, flexible and useful tool for teachers. Although the tableau can also be used as a teaching tool . . . you may be needing or wanting to review information or check for understanding and the tableau is an engaging way to do it."

The strategy of tableau can be used with the whole class or small groups. While having the whole class practice the strategy of tableau, the following settings can be used:

- Reporters and photographers who sight a big celebrity
- Fans—both happy and angry—at a sporting event
- Tourists looking at a famous site
- People watching fireworks

Once students understand the procedure of creating a tableau, try breaking students into smaller groups and follow similar steps. Provide a prompt and allow students to collaborate to create a frozen tableau. The prompts could focus on a scene from a story or an event from a historical period. Once students are familiar with the process, provide prompts that work with the subject matter and learning sequence. After each group shares their tableau, check for student understanding of the content and spend time in reflection and discussion.

Grade level(s). All

Space needed. Create an open space by moving desks or moving to an area where students can work either as a large group or in smaller groupings.

Materials needed. No materials are needed.

Subjects addressed in this strategy. Tableau can be used across the curriculum at different grade levels. In the language arts classroom, teachers use the strategy to bring to life a story, poem, or circumstance. In a social studies classroom, the tableau strategy can be implemented to bring to life a historical moment. In visual arts, students can recreate a frozen pose of a piece of artwork or depict a potential moment following what happened in a particular artwork. Tableau can be used with the study of literature to depict beginning, middle, and end of a literary work. Other applications might include using tableau to create an image of a vocabulary word or creating a frozen picture of a geographic setting, such as what one might see in Hawaii, Alaska, or another part of the world. This frozen image can tell a story, show relationships between characters, or create metaphoric meaning.

Learning outcomes. Students will be able to:

- Use a frozen picture to reinforce an educational concept such as a historical moment or a moment in a story
- Explore deeper meaning through physicalizing and collaboration
- Demonstrate understanding of key theater terms such as tableau, gesture, eye contact, levels, concentration, and body position
- Analyze the meaning of text
- Collaborate to determine how to create a visual representation (of a topic or concept)
- Learn and demonstrate concentration skills
- Synthesize learning by showing understanding of a concept

Steps for Facilitating This Strategy

Preparation. The teacher should determine what part of a text would be appropriate for using a strategy that creates a frozen re-enactment of a point in a story, event, or circumstance. Research the topic, as there are many renditions of the tableau strategy and many applications. Because of the flexibility of the strategy, it will be important to investigate how other practitioners have used the tableau.

Procedure. The following is one way to introduce this drama strategy to students. The sequence below will provide a nonthreatening way for students to begin to learn the strategy and increase the likelihood that they will participate productively in creating a tableau.

- Begin by engaging all students simultaneously in asking them to agree to pretend to be in a situation in which each of them will play a role.
- With students seated at their desks or in chairs, describe an imaginary circumstance and setting that might have many people involved, such as people at a ball game, the state fair, or at a cultural celebration. Ask students to pretend that they are in the situation. A prompt might be: What kinds of activities do you see at a big football game (sports fans cheering, marching band

performing, vendors selling food, and so on)? Imagine you are all sports fans at the stadium watching a game. What would that look like? Let's all assume a pose of fans watching the game.

- Discuss what possible feelings and reaction there might be if all of a sudden there was a thunderstorm at the stadium with lots of wind and rain.
- Engage in a discussion about what kinds of reactions people might have in this situation. Ask students to describe how someone might feel. What adjective would they use to describe the feeling? Ask students to imagine that they were a person at the stadium and think about the kind of reaction they would likely have at the time they experienced rain and wind.
- Then ask the students to imagine that a photographer was about to snap a photograph of them in the situation. Ask them to "act" out what they would be doing at the time of the snapshot.
- Explain how you will cue the students to strike and hold their poses. Ask them not to make any noise when they freeze, but rather imagine what they might be hearing. The intent is that the pose will be in silence.
- Tell the students that you will say, "Action- 1-2-3-Freeze!" This will indicate that the students should freeze their pose. Encourage them to count 1-2-3 and then say, "Relax." Ask students what they saw, and what they noticed. You may want to provide another scenario or ask students to refine their poses by trying the exercise again. Compliment them for their cooperation. You may want to reinforce what makes a great tableau such as using exaggerated expressions and gestures, using high, middle, and low body placement so that there are different levels, and keeping open positions so the imaginary photographer can capture students' placement and expressions. *Open position* is a theater term that means making your body and expressions visible to the audience. Other suggestions for students include keeping silent when the tableau is formed, expressing high energy to create "larger than life" poses and exaggerated expressions and gestures.
- Invite the students to incorporate your dramatic coaching points and re-create the tableau so that it is theatrically more powerful. The second re-enactment of the tableau is often stronger.
- Take time to debrief the process and reflect on the creations of the students.

Culturally responsive learning. Tableau allows students of all ages to examine and gain a greater understanding of human experience through creating physical representations that bring a text or event to life. Students explore different topics, points of view, perspectives through collaborating on a tableau. Teachers can unpack significant moments of a story or event as students learn to read the visual clues that point to meaning. This can spur deeper analysis of the motivations that cause people to make the choices they do. For students who are struggling with language, the tableau allows for visual representation of ideas. Using prints of artwork representative of other cultures is a pathway into understanding both the individuality and universality of human expression impacted by a variety of external conditions. It is important to be:

- Intentionally connecting new learning to students' background knowledge and experiences.
- Helping students bridge from prior knowledge/learning to new learning.
- Challenging students and providing opportunities for them to "stretch," expanding their potential to do more complex thinking and learning. (Sanchez et.al., 2017, p. 14)

Teaching example. Yuyi Morales, in her book *Dreamers* (2018), tells her personal journey of immigrating to the United States with her son. The memoir is a short but compelling story told with poetic language and symbolic, collage illustrations. In one classroom, students were invited to create a series of tableaux in three different explorations: First, students were asked to depict the beginning, middle, and end of the journey. In the next tableau students explored the vocabulary that represented intangible concepts such as hope, fear, and resilience. Finally, the main character in each of the three images was pulled out and a new collective image is created to explore her evolution over the journey. (For more information regarding use of tableau with examples, see Crooks, 2016.)

Assessment possibilities. Tableau is a powerful formative assessment strategy that allows students to translate their understanding of content through physicalization, collaboration, and imagination. Teachers can observe the image and apply a checklist of criteria to assess drama learning as well as learning in other nonarts content areas. Reflection is a key component as students debrief, share knowledge, and begin to become critical observers. For example, teachers can incorporate reflection by referring back to criteria and also content that was covered and portrayed. Many other formative assessment strategies can be used such as short writing prompts and character profile sheets depicting characters in literature or in history. Teachers also find that writing after the strategy helps students draw from the knowledge highlighted through the tableau process.

Students engage with the text more deeply by analyzing and curating key moments or facts that should be incorporated in the tableau. Once you are clear about the evidence you are looking for from students and intentionally design your lesson, you can identify ways to draw out evidence of learning through the processes and products of tableau. Here are three examples of student assignments by subject:

Social Studies

- Examine and discuss the story of the perspectives of a new immigrant experience set against assumptions about immigrants.
- Identify how a journey can change and affect one's sense of self.
- Consider what it means to "belong."
- Identify what creates a sense of "home."

English Language Arts

- Examine how memoirs bring the complexities of personal experience to life.
- Identify how verb examples in the text bring to life the actions of the characters. What are those action verbs? How might you re-create the actions in tableau that represent the verbs in the text?

Theater

- Use the elements of drama and theater vocabulary to discuss artistic choices.
- Create an image with dramatic tension inviting engagement with an audience.
- Create an image showing relationships and action bringing a story to life.

Debrief questions. The following questions can be used in debriefing the lesson:

- Using the elements of drama, describe the artistic choices you made to create your image.
- How were levels, space, frozen action, focus, and so on used to create a compelling image?
- How does your frozen image depict ideas from the topic you were exploring?
- What dramatic choices do you see in the images created by your peers?
- What connections to the topic being explored do you see in the images created by your peers?

Extended learning. Some possible extended student activities include the following:

- Create a tableau chain by developing tableaux in a series. Students create movements to move from one frozen moment to another.

This can be adapted to align with a sequence of events in a story, so that students highlight key moments in the plot.

- Activate the tableau that moves into a live, short scene with dialogue. Students can end the scene in a different tableau to mark the conclusion.
- Write a story about what happened before or after the tableau moment.

CREATIVE FORMATIVE ASSESSMENTS

Figure 7.1 is a helpful tool as you begin to incorporate creative formative assessment practices in the classroom. The checklist provides elements to think about when designing formative assessment measures that can also be paired with artistic work in the disciplines of dance, media arts, music, theater, and visual arts as well as other artistic expressions such as poetry. We included principles of studio habits of mind (Hetland et al., 2007) and Universal Design for Learning (CAST, n.d.) to help you blend key theoretical approaches within a lesson or unit.

The strategies in this chapter are representative of the wealth of creative formative assessment approaches available to you. As you research and curate resources that can be used in your curriculum, you will find new opportunities that include innovative, creative practices. While the steps included in each strategy provide a sequence that can be adapted to the grade level you are teaching, we suggest that you pull out the processes in the strategies to coincide with the curriculum you are teaching and make the modifications that work for you. These flexible strategies can be incorporated into the classroom in a variety of ways, and we encourage you to explore new innovative applications and/or translations for your students. Once students are familiar with the strategies, they will welcome opportunities to revisit them again with other topics within your curriculum.

Figure 7.1. Assessment Checklist

This checklist can be used or adapted to help determine processes for formative assessment.

Subjects Addressed

- ☐ Dance and movement
- ☐ Media arts
- ☐ Music
- ☐ Theater
- ☐ Visual arts
- ☐ Integrated learning with more than one discipline
- ☐ Other subjects covered: e.g., science, arts, English Language Arts, etc.

Arts-Integrated Learning

- ☐ Standards are met in more than one discipline or subject
- ☐ Demonstration of knowledge and skill through a creative process or art form
- ☐ Includes vocabulary and skill building of more than one discipline or subject
- ☐ Students know and are able to use the vocabulary of content areas covered
- ☐ Students demonstrate an understanding of the techniques and processes inherent in the art form and connect them in meaningful applications
- ☐ Subjects that are integrated are equal in rigor
- ☐ Students demonstrate understanding of content through integrating arts processes

Evidence Collection Methods

- ☐ Written reflection
- ☐ Oral reflection
- ☐ Mapping sheets
- ☐ Feedback forms
- ☐ Interviews
- ☐ Learning logs
- ☐ Concept maps
- ☐ Journals
- ☐ Self-evaluations
- ☐ Writing samples
- ☐ Presentations
- ☐ Performances
- ☐ Discussion
- ☐ Videos
- ☐ Audio tape
- ☐ Photographs of student work
- ☐ Portfolios
- ☐ Digital portfolios
- ☐ Group collaborative process
- ☐ Other: _____

Culturally and Linguistically Relevant Teaching

- ☐ Provides opportunities for student expression, agency, and voice
- ☐ Encourages students to be reflective and honor different points of view, traditions, and values
- ☐ Builds a broad array of language, literacy, cross-cultural, and multimedia communication skills
- ☐ Celebrates, respects, and appreciates language and cultural diversity
- ☐ Encourages students to view social problems or issues from multicultural perspectives

Habits of Mind

☐ Develop Craft: Learning to use tools, materials, artistic conventions; and learning to care for tools, materials, and space

☐ Engage and Persist: Learning to embrace problems of relevance within the art world and/or of personal importance, to develop focus conducive to working and persevering at tasks

☐ Envision: Learning to picture mentally what cannot be directly observed and imagine possible next steps in making a piece

☐ Express: Learning to create works that convey an idea, a feeling, or a personal meaning

☐ Observe: Learning to attend to visual contexts more closely than ordinary "looking" requires, and thereby to see things that otherwise might not be seen

☐ Reflect: Learning to think and talk with others about an aspect of one's work or working process, and learning to judge one's own work and working process and the work of others

☐ Stretch & Explore: Learning to reach beyond one's capacities, to explore playfully without a preconceived plan, and to embrace the opportunity to learn from mistakes

☐ Understand Arts Community: Learning to interact as an artist with other artists (in classrooms, in local arts organizations, and across the art field) and within the broader society (Hetland et al., 2007)

Application of Universal Design for Learning Principles

☐ Allows for visual representation
☐ Allows for audio representation
☐ Allows for kinesthetic representation
☐ Provide multiple means of action and expression
☐ Provide multiple means of engagement

_____

(*Note.* Based on the work of CAST, a nonprofit education research and development organization that works to expand learning opportunities for all individuals through Universal Design for Learning.)

Conclusion

> Imagination is as important in the lives of teachers as it is in the lives of their students. (Greene, 1995, p. 36)

Thomas Hoerr (2016) writes that the urgent often drowns out the valuable, beginning his column, "We must focus on what's truly important—not just what's urgent" (p. 90). In our attempt to focus on what's important, urgent issues often demand a quick response. Hoerr encourages us to realize that not every urgent demand is important. As we get up every day, we have an open slate of opportunities to impact the lives of others, inlcuding our family, our students, our colleagues, our friends. As educators, we struggle to find time for the important and often rely on the easy or predictable rather than take the risk to find the valuable.

In this text we invited you to slow down and focus intentionally on teaching methods that can serve to enhance instructional practice and provide new points of access, inspiration, and meaning-making for our students. We have explored arts integration as a way to get to deep learning, covered the importance of arts-based formative assessment, and reviewed curatorial practices that strengthen teaching and assessment. We promoted the need for careful documentation by starting with the tools at hand—the lesson plan and the many curated resources. We showcased how to annotate learning moments and collect student and teacher reflections. We also highlighted how learning stories are a vehicle to share our own expertise as educators as well as the good work of our students.

Teachers ultimately are the most important vehicle for change. By creating space for quality learning and creativity (with careful attention to planning, organization, and documentation), educators provide opportunities for students to engage, metacognitively reflect, and document their work and progress. This deep work, which builds self- and social awareness, critical thinking, and achievement, happens in an ongoing cycle of improvement. By trusting in the critical insights that emerge from this deep work, much can be found in the layers that are lingering below the surface.

THE ARTS AS VERBS IN THE CLASSROOM

> Contrary to conventional wisdom, art has not always been a noun, a valuable
> object relegated to a museum or a ticketed event in a performance hall. At
> the birth of the word "art," it was a verb that meant "to put things together." It
> was not a product, but a process. If we can reclaim that view of art—as a way
> of looking at and doing things, as a series of experiences and experiments—all
> of us gain a fresh grasp on the proven, practical ways to construct the quality
> of our lives. (Booth, 2001, p. 5)

This is active work. As teachers challenge themselves to find the verbs in
their classrooms—providing their students with opportunities to engage, to
explore, to reflect, to problem-solve, to create, to synthesize, to express their
understanding in various ways—they create cultures that value opinions
and perspectives of others. Teachers allow students to create their own stories and learn unique stories (of people past and current) and apply learning
to their own contexts. These experiential components, which are valuable
and essential, anchor learning and bring classrooms to fruitful, positive,
and productive environments. Stories have power. The stories teachers tell
help empower diverse learners and build equitable learning solutions for
students. David Heathfield (n.d.) writes, "I know of no other medium which
can give language learners such insight into another culture as the sharing
of stories. Storytelling acts as a celebration of cultural diversity, provides
students with support in their language learning and builds self-esteem."
Teachers have the power to tell the stories of what transpired in a learning
moment and the stories of the students who need to find their voice.

Research continues to point to the impact that arts learning has on
the lives of students and their overall achievement. We maintain that arts
learning—both in the discrete learning of the art forms and in integrated
lessons—provides the binding agent that actualizes learning—the verbs of
the classroom. Thoughtful practitioners who curate learning through formative assessment that also includes artistic expression as a way of "showing knowing"elevate learning so students can inquire, predict, wonder, and
ponder, and understand.

THE ARTISTRY OF TEACHING

> The artistry of teaching is a commitment to the idea that there is more to
> teaching than the application of principles of teaching that have emerged out
> of research and practice. (Hassard, 2013)

Beyond the latest standards, the newest pedagogies, the latest educational
trends, as teachers, we find that there is always an intersection between

theory and practice and that in our ever-evolving quest for quality (in our lives and the lives of our students) we take many twists and turns in our "hero's journey." In each chapter of our professional growth, we find that at the core, we are wanting to refine our skills, master our craft, and make a difference in the lives of our students. We agree with Sheila Fitzgerald (1986) that

> Artistry may well be the most promising antidote to the frustration, dissatisfaction, and despair which have begun to affect many of the nation's teachers. Additional regulation in the form of mandatory methods can only result in more disillusionment and further blunting of the imagination. It would be far better one would think to encourage higher expectations, greater pride in craft, and teaching behavior which is genuinely self-actuating. (p. 5)

Whether a veteran teacher or a new teacher entering into the profession, as you begin to dig more deeply into the layers of your own lesson and design, and collect the evidence of students' understanding, you are bringing a new level of artistry to your classroom. You are taking risks to find and cultivate the valuable. The learning that you cultivate in the lives of your students and through your self-reflective practice can truly be a remarkable catalyst for change.

KEY NUGGETS

We have discussed many different parts of a complex puzzle of integration, curation, and assessment, and provided ways that teachers are finding new insights into the search for deeper meaning in their instructional practice. Teaching is a practice. Like yoga you never actually arrive at perfection, but instead you cultivate the process of returning to the mat, time and again, honoring and honing your skills with incremental build and focused attention. Having joined us in the journey through this book, we hope that you will take away these nuggets:

- *Intentionality.* It takes intention and mindfulness to disrupt mental models and move beyond the status quo, develop practice, and facilitate engagement opportunities for students. The intentional teacher goes beyond the curriculum established in textbooks or curricula and purposely integrates relevant material and engagement opportunities that reach beyond borders.
- *Curatorial mindset.* By collecting, analyzing, synthesizing, organizing, and making meaning of resources, standards, assessment measures, and evidence, the curatorial teacher leads an ever-evolving cycle of evaluation, analysis, reflection, insights, and improvement. At the core of a curatorial approach is a careful

tending to the needs of diverse students and creating space for
many ways of knowing. The goal is to bring in more voices and
new examples, so students see themselves and trust that their
experiences are valued. We encourage you to continue to evolve
as you bring new processes and techniques to your classroom and
give special attention to clues students provide about how students
learn and what they need to succeed.

- *Creativity.* Integrating the arts into the curriculum fosters
  innovation, divergent thinking, and deep engagement that impacts
  students' discovery, problem-solving, and decisionmaking.

- *Reflection.* Reflection is central to student and teacher self-growth
  and a critical element in arts-integrated learning as students
  translate ideas across symbol systems, unleashing surprising
  connections and personal relevance. In curatorial practice,
  attending to decisions made in selecting, organizing, analyzing,
  and documenting content, as well as reviewing the evidence of
  learning, opens layers of realizations and insights for teachers and
  their students. Increasing opportunities to reflect in process as
  well as at the end of a lesson yields the kinds of aha moments and
  insight we have cited across this text. As one teacher shared, "This
  work puts the thinking back into teaching and learning."

- *Formative Assessment.* Collecting evidence of learning throughout
  the learning process provides ongoing feedback about teaching
  and learning, what's working and what needs to be tweaked.
  Formative assessment can keep you focused on all that evidence
  conveys about what is unfolding, about your process, about
  the learning and needs of your students. This kind of in-process
  assessment is enhanced by a curatorial approach, documentation,
  reflection, and creative work.

- *Documentation.* When teachers document their work, they create
  an archive of learning that can inform their methodologies. They
  learn from their investigations and from the work that their
  students produce. Critical observations during documentation
  can reveal evidence of learning and help you improve your own
  classroom practice.

MEANINGFUL LEARNING EXPERIENCES

We know that teachers want academic excellence in their teaching. The as-
piration of having our students develop their intellectual and creative capacities to impact the world is an altitudinous but important goal. As you look
for ways to create meaningful educational experiences for your students,
we suggest that empowering students to become actively involved in the

classroom can ignite their thirst for learning and provide new ways for them to innovate and investigate. Through arts and creative endeavors, students find their voice. Curating and employing authentic assessments and arts-based strategies will foster mastery of content and higher forms of student thinking and discovery. The actions that teachers take can be the catalyst for change in the lives of students.

We hope that this book has unlocked some insights for possible translation and application for creativity, arts, and innovation in your teaching. As you curate and knit together arts learning strategies, assessments, and inquiry-based learning, you are creating a tapestry of learning for your students . . . and for yourself. This metaphor speaks to the renaissance that can be created at all grade levels when thoughtful, creative methods are woven together for collective impact. Yes, we educators can be vital agents of change as we continue to strive for the valuable treasures in each student. Our students need us, and their future depends upon the creativity of our teaching.

References

Abram, S. (2008, May 1). The pipeline: Storyboarding: Comics, graphic novels, and engaging learners. *Internet @ Schools: An Educator's Guide to Technology and the Web, 15*(3), 25–27. http://www.internetatschools.com/Articles/Column/The-Pipeline/THE-PIPELINE Storyboarding-Comics-Graphic-Novels-and-Engaging-Learners-61027.aspx

Adobe. (2018, January). *Creative problem solving: Essential skills today's students need for jobs in tomorrow's age of automation.* cps.adobeeducate.com/

Adobe. (2019, November 5). *Get hired: The importance of creativity and soft skills.* https://www.adobeforeducation.com/higher-ed

Akbari, E. (2016, June 7). Soundscape compositions for art classrooms. *Art Education, 69*(4), 17–22. https://doi.org/10.1080/00043125.2016.1176480

Alexander, S. (n.d.). *Learning stories: What is a learning story? And is it a good way of assessing a child's learning?* My ECE: Early Childhood Education. https://www.myece.org.nz/educational-curriculum-aspects/227-learning-stories

Alrubail, R. (2015, January 3). Scaffolding student reflections + sample questions. *Edutopia.* https://www.edutopia.org/discussion/scaffolding-student-reflections-sample-questions

Anderson, L. W., Krathwohl, D. R., & Bloom, B. S. (2001). *A taxonomy for learning, teaching, and assessing: A revision of Bloom's taxonomy of educational objectives.* Longman.

Appel, M. P. (2006, November/December). Arts integration across the curriculum. *Leadership, 36*(2), 14–17.

Arts Assessment for Learning. (n.d.). *About formative assessment.* http://artsassessmentforlearning.org/about-assessment/

Battelle for Kids. (2019). *The Partnership for 21st Century Skills: Framework for 21st century learning.* http://static.battelleforkids.org/documents/p21/P21_Framework_Brief.pdf

Beers, S. Z. (2011). *Teaching 21st century skills: An ASCD action tool.* Association for Supervision and Curriculum Development (ASCD).

Beghetto, R. (2018/2019, December/January) Taking beautiful risks in education. The arts and creativity in schools. *Educational Leadership, 76*(4), 18–24.

Bellisario, K., & Donovan, L. (2012). *Voices from the field: Teachers' views on the relevance of arts integration.* Lesley University (Cambridge, MA). https://www.mcla.edu/Assets/MCLA- Files/Academics/Undergraduate/AMGT/lesley_voices-fromthefield.pdf

Berger, R. (2013). Austin's butterfly: Building excellence in students' work. Models of excellence. [Video]. The Center for High Quality Student work, EL

Education: Models of Excellence. https://modelsofexcellence.eleducation.org/resources/austins-butterfly

Bertling, J. G. (2019). Layered collaborative visual reflection: Sharing lived experiences and making meaning. *Art Education*, 72(3), 28–38. https://doi.org/10.1080/00043125.2019.1578022

Bogard, J. M., & Donovan, L. (2013). *Strategies to integrate the arts in language arts*. Shell Education.

Booth, E. (2001). *The everyday work of art*. iUniverse.com.

Briggs, S. (n.d.). The importance of content curation, and tips for teachers and students. *The Learning Scientists*. https://www.learningscientists.org/blog/2016/9/13-1

Brigham, B. (2018, September 6). Putting thoughts on paper: Start with a storyboard. *Tchers' Voice (Teaching Channel)*. https://www.teachingchannel.com/blog/start-with-storyboard

Brookhart, S. (2016, October). Start with higher-order thinking. *Educational Leadership*, 74(2), 10–15.

Brown-Martin, G. (2016, December 19). Assessment is not a spreadsheet, it's a conversation. *Learning {Re}imagined*. https://medium.com/learning-re-imagined/assessment-is- not-a-spreadsheet-its-a-conversation-3d743c754809

Bruce, D. L. (2011, July). Framing the text: Using storyboards to engage students with reading. *The English Journal*, 100(6), 78–85. https://digitalauthorshipuri.files.wordpress.com/2019/01/bruce-storyboarding.pdf

Burnaford, G., Aprill, A., & Weiss, C. (Eds). (2001), *Renaissance in the classroom: Arts integration and meaningful learning*. Lawrence Erlbaum Associates.

Casa-Todd, J. (2018, January 4). *Content curation: A necessary skill for today's learners*.https://jcasatodd.com/content-curation-a-necessary-skill-for-todays-learners/

Cattlin, J. (2016, October 31). *What is curated learning?* Innovative Learning Environments and Teacher Change. http://www.iletc.com.au/what-is-curated-learning/

Center for Applied Special Technology (CAST). (n.d). *About Universal Design for Learning*. http://www.cast.org/our-work/about-udl.html#.Xs2nr8B7mjI

Centre for Literacy in Primary Education (CLPE). (n.d.). Developing ideas through play and role-play. https://clpe.org.uk/powerofpictures/creative-approaches/2

Christensen, L. (2009). *Teaching for joy and justice: Re-imagining the language arts classroom*. Rethinking Schools.

Collins, P. (2008). Using poetry throughout the curriculum. *Kappa Delta Pi Record*, 44(2), 81–84. https://doi.org/10.1080/00228958.2008.10516500

Common Core State Standards Initiative. (2010). College and career readiness anchor standards for reading: 7. http://www.corestandards.org/ELA-Literacy/CCRA/R/7/

Costa, A., & Kallick, B. (2009). *Habits of mind across the curriculum: Practical and creative strategies for teachers*. Association for Supervision and Curriculum Development.

Covey, S. (1989). *The seven habits of highly effective people: Restoring the character ethic*. Simon and Schuster.

Crooks, P., McCormick, S., Urban, A., Sperling, R., & Wells-Famula, R. (2016). Module 9—Problem solving through theatre: Learning 21st century skills via the dramatic arts (grades 6–12). In *Creativity at the Core*. CCSESA Arts Initiative. https://ccsesaarts.org/modules/problem-solving-theatre-learning-21st-century-skills-via-dramatic-arts-grades-6-12/

Curtis, C. P. (n.d.). Teaching strategies: Frozen tableau. In *Teaching multicultural literature: A workshop for the middle grades*. Annenberg Learner. https://www.learner.org/series/teaching-multicultural-literature-a-workshop-for-the-middle-grades/historical-and-cultural-context-christopher-paul-curtis/teaching-strategies/

Davenport, M. (2015, December 17). Enduring understandings: Seeing the forest through the trees. *AtlasNext*. https://www.onatlas.com/blog/enduring-understandings

Dawson, K. (n.d.). *Role play* [Video]. Drama-Based Instruction (DBI Network). https://dbp.theatredance.utexas.edu/content/role-play

Dewey, J. (1934). *Art as experience*. Minton, Balch.

Dodge, J. (2009). *25 quick formative assessments for a differentiated classroom*. Scholastic.

Donahue, D., & Stuart, J. (Eds.). (2010). *Artful teaching: Integrating the arts for understanding across the curriculum*. Teachers College Press.

Donovan, L. (2006). *Ah-Sess* [Unpublished manuscript]. Assessment Conference, New York University.

Donovan, L., & Pascale, L. (2012). *Integrating the arts across the content areas*. Shell Education.

Drost, B. (2016, August 15). Sitting beside the learner: The "me" in assessments. *Aligned*. https://achievethecore.org/aligned/sitting-beside-the-learner-the-me-in-assessments/

EAL Nexus. (n.d.). *Great idea: Drama and role play*. The Bell Foundation. https://ealresources.bell-foundation.org.uk/teachers/great-ideas-drama-and-role-play

Early Learning and Kinder. (2018, April 5). *The 100 Languages of Children*. https://earlylearningandkinder.com.au/the-100-languages-of-children/

Education Technology Insights. (2019, July 16). *How feedback loops boost student learning*.https://www.educationtechnologyinsights.com/news/how-feedback-loops-boost-student-learning-nid-722.html

Facing History and Ourselves. (n.d.). *Dr. King's Legacy and Choosing to Participate*. https://www.facinghistory.org/resource-library/memphis-1968/dr-kings-legacy-and-choosing-participate

Farkas, J. M. (2019, April 13). *Taking blackout poetry to the next level*. National Council of Teachers of English. https://ncte.org/blog/2019/04/blackout-poetry/

Farmer, D. (n.d.). *Role play*. Drama Strategies. https://dramaresource.com/role-play/

Filippini, T., & Castagnetti, M. (2006). The Documentation and Educational Research Center of the Istituzione scuole e nidi d'infanzia, Municipality of Reggio Emilia. *Innovations in early education: The international Reggio exchange, 13*(3).

Finlay, L. (2008, January). *Reflecting on "reflective practice"* (PBPL paper 52). http://ncsce.net/wp-content/uploads/2016/10/Finlay-2008-Reflecting-on-reflective-practice-PBPL-paper-52.pdf

Fisher, D., & Frey, N. (2015, October). Show & Tell: A Video Column / Hope-Building Schools. *Educational Leadership, 73*(2), 80–81. http://www.ascd.org/publications/educational_leadership/oct15/vol73/num02/Hope-Building_Schools.aspx

Fitzgerald, S. (1986). Artistry in teaching. *Language Arts Journal of Michigan, 2*(1). article 2. https://doi.org/10.9707/2168-149X.1745

Flynn, R. (2019, July 28). Introducing the tableau to students. *ThoughtCo*. https://www.thoughtco.com/introducing-tableau-to-students-3938471

Fuglei, M. (n.d.). Start your own learning revolution with transformational teaching. *Resilient Educator.* https://resilienteducator.com/classroom-resources/learning-revolution-transformational-teaching/

Gallo, A. M., Sheehy, D., Patton, K., & Griffin, L. (2006, October). Assessment benefits and barriers: What are you committed to? *Journal of Physical Education, Recreation and Dance, 77*(8), 46–50. https://files.eric.ed.gov/fulltext/EJ794484.pdf

Gandini, L., & Kaminsky, J. A. (2004). Reflections on the relationship between documentation and assessment in the American context: An interview with Brenda Fyfe. *Innovations in Early Education, 11*(1), 5–17. https://pdfs.semanticscholar.org/10f4/4f76367c1aa2e3917e8f16a63d846b05a798.pdf?_ga=2.82163222.1410941597.1594768792-714428769.1594768792

García, J. (2018). Privilege (social inequality). *Salem Press Encyclopedia.* In *Privilege and Intersectionality.* University Libraries at Rider University. https://guides.rider.edu/privilege

Gardner, H., & Hatch, T. (1989). Multiple intelligences go to school: Educational implications of the theory of multiple intelligences. *Educational Researcher, 18*(8), 4–10. http://www.jstor.org/stable/1176460

Gersh-Nesic, B. (2019, March 2). How is collage used in art? *ThoughtCo.* https://www.thoughtco.com/art-history-definition-collage-183196

Gilbert, A. G. (1977). *Teaching the three Rs through movement experiences: A handbook for teachers.* Burgess.

Gillam, B. (1883, February 7). *The protectors of our industries* [Cartoon]. *Puck, 12,* no. 309. Keppler & Schwarzmann. Library of Congress Online Catalog. https://www.loc.gov/item/94507245/

Glass, D., & Donovan, L. (2017). Using curriculum design frameworks for arts integration. In G. Diaz & M. B. Mckenna (Eds.), *Preparing educators for arts integration: Placing creativity at the center of learning* (pp. 41–51). Teachers College Press.

Glass, D., Meyer, A., & Rose, D. H. (2013). Universal design for learning and the arts. *Harvard Educational Review, 83*(1), 98–119 https://www.semanticscholar.org/paper/Universal-Design-for-Learning-and-the-Arts-Glass-Meyer/a182dc37e99e298bcfab81213013fd9465747d8e

Goldberg, M. (2016). *Arts integration: Teaching subject matter through the arts in multicultural settings* (5th ed.). Routledge.

Gonzalez, J. (2017, April 15). To boost higher-order thinking, try curation. *Cult of Pedagogy.* https://www.cultofpedagogy.com/curation/

Gonzalez, J. (2018, February 4). Are you a curator or a dumper? *Cult of Pedagogy.* https://www.cultofpedagogy.com/curator-or-dumper/

González, N., Moll, L. C., & Amanti, C. (Eds.). (2005). *Funds of knowledge: Theorizing practices in households, communities, and classrooms.* Routledge.

Good, R. (2016, July 2). Why curation revolutionizes education and learning. *Content Curation Official Guide.* https://medium.com/content-curation-official-guide/why-curation-revolutionizes-education-learning-5d0130457a81

Goodsir, K. (2017, July 27). An introduction to learning stories [Posted by G. Nixon]. *Educa.* https://www.geteduca.com/blog/learning-stories-introduction/

Gorski, P. (n.d.) *Stages of multicultural curriculum transformation.* Critical

Multicultural Pavilion: Multicultural Curriculum Reform. http://www.edchange. org/multicultural/curriculum/steps.html

Great Schools Partnership. (2014, April 29). Formative assessment. In *Glossary of Education Reform*. https://www.edglossary.org/formative-assessment/

Greene, M. (1995). *Releasing the imagination: Essays on education, the arts, and social change*. Jossey-Bass.

Guzy, M. (2017, May 4). The sound of life: What is a soundscape? *Folklife*. https:// folklife.si.edu/talkstory/the-sound-of-life-what-is-a-soundscape

Hammond, Z. (2015). *Culturally responsive teaching and the brain*. Corwin.

Hammond, Z. (2017, November 6). We all can be authentic merchants of hope. *Culturally Responsive Teaching and the Brain*. https://crtandthebrain.com/ we-all-can-be-authentic-merchants-of-hope/

Hammond, Z. (2018, February 7). Culturally responsive teaching: It begins with re-sponsiveness. *Tchers' Voice (Teaching Channel)*. https://learn.teachingchannel. com/blog/2018/02/07/it-begins-with-responsiveness

Hanley, M. S. (2002). *The scope of multicultural education*. New Horizons for Learning.

Hanley, M. S., & Noblit, G. (2009, June). *Cultural responsiveness, racial identity and academic success: A review of literature* (A paper prepared for the Heinz Endowments). http://www.heinz.org/userfiles/library/culture-report_final.pdf

Hassard, J. (2013, July 13). *The artistry of teaching*. The Art of Teaching Science. http://jackhassard.org/artistry-teaching/

Heathfield, D. (n.d.). Storytelling to celebrate cultural diversity. *Teaching English* (British Council). https://www.teachingenglish.org.uk/article/storytelling-cele-brate-cultural-diversity

Heffernan, M., Hojreh, S., Liscow, W., Longo, S., Marigliano, M. L., Nagel, E., Reece, M. R., Rizzuto, K., Schmid, D., Spicer, W., Sullivan, K., & Ward, D. E. (2018). *New Jersey's art integration think and do workbook. A practical guide to think about and implement arts integration*. http://njpsa.org/documents/ EdLdrsAsSchol2018/artsintegrationWorkbook2018.pdf

Heick, T. (2020, May 1). What is Bloom's Taxonomy? A definition for teachers. *TeachThought*. https://www.teachthought.com/learning/what-is-blooms-taxon-omy-a-definition-for-teachers/

Heritage, M. (2011). *Formative assessment: An enabler of learning*. Michigan Assess-ment Consortium. https://www.michiganassessmentconsortium.org/wp-content/ uploads/FA-Heritage-an-enabler-of-learning.pdf

Heritage, M. (2013). *Formative assessment in practice: A process of inquiry and action*. Harvard Education Press.

Herzog, M. (1990). The art of collage. *SchoolArts*, *89*(5), 23–26.

Hetland, L., Winner, E., Veenema, S., & Sheridan, K. M. (2007). *Studio thinking: The real benefits of visual arts education*. Teachers College Press.

Hetland, L., Winner, E., Veenema, S., & Sheridan, K. M. (2013). *Studio thinking 2: The real benefits of visual arts education* (2nd ed.). Teachers College Press.

Hine, L. (ca. 1912). *Child Labor* [Cartoon]. Library of Congress Online Catalog. Digital ID nclc 04783. https://www.loc.gov/resource/cph.3a53215/

Hoerr, T. R. (2016–2017). Principal connection: What's important. *Educational Leadership*, *74*(4), 90–91.

Hofsess, B. (2015). The map of true places: Moving onward in artistteacher prepa-ration. *Visual Arts Research*, *41*(1), 1–15. doi:10.5406/ visuartsrese.41.1.0001

House, J. (2014). *Soundscape lessons and children's listening* [Unpublished thesis]. Towson University. http://ciufo.org/classes/ae_sp14/student_files/Jordyn_final.pdf

Jackson, Y. (2011). *The pedagogy of confidence: Inspiring high intellectual perfor-mance in urban schools*. Teachers College Press.

Jefferys, A. (2017, March 10). *How to write a dialogue poem*. https://penandthepad.com/write-dialogue-poem-3487.html

Jensen, E. (2000). *Learning with the body in mind: The scientific basis for energiz-ers, movement, play, games, and physical education*. The Brain Store.

Jewitt, C. (2008, February 1). Multimodality and literacy in school class-rooms. *Review of Research in Education*, *32*(1), 241–267. https://doi.org/10.3102/0091732X07310586

Jones, L. (2014, November 21). Harnessing the power of arts integration. *Tchers' Voice (Teaching Channel)*. https://www.teachingchannel.org/blog/2014/11/21/power-of-arts-integration-getty

The Kennedy Center. (n.d.). *What is arts integration?: Explore the Kennedy Center's comprehensive definition*. https://www.kennedy-center.org/education/resources-for-educators/classroom-resources/articles-and-how-tos/articles/collections/arts-integration-resources/what-is-arts-integration//

Koehler, R. (1886). The Strike [Painting]. Library of Congress Online Catalog. https://www.loc.gov/item/90706044/

Kulasegaram, K., & Rangachari, P. K. (2018, November). Beyond "formative": As-sessments to enrich student learning. *Advances in Physiology Education*, *42*(1), 5–41. https://www.physiology.org/doi/pdf/10.1152/advan.00122.2017

Kurani, D. (2016, November 23). *Three ways to design better classrooms and learn-ing spaces*. Getting Smart. https://www.gettingsmart.com/2016/11/three-ways-design-better-classrooms-learning-spaces/

Ladson-Billings, G. (1994). *The dreamkeepers: Successful teachers of African Amer-ican children*. Jossey-Bass.

Larios, J. (2017, November 11). Altered books. *Books Around the Table*. https://booksaroundthetable.wordpress.com/2017/11/11/altered-books/

Lee, D. M. (2012, January 12). Creating an anti-racist classroom: Reflections to level the playing field. *Edutopia*. https://www.edutopia.org/blog/anti-racist-classroom-danielle-moss-lee

Making Learning Visible. (2005). *Learning group and documentation: Definitions and features one-pager*. Making Learning Visible Project at the Harvard Gradu-ate School of Education. http://www.mlvpz.org/files/onepagergldoc609.pdf

Marzano, R. (2007). *The art and science of teaching: A comprehension framework for effective instruction*. ASCD.

Massachusetts Department of Elementary and Secondary Education. (2019). Arts framework. *Massachusetts Curriculum Frameworks—2019*. Massachusetts Dept. of Education. http://www.doe.mass.edu/frameworks/current.html

Massachusetts Department of Elementary and Secondary Education. (2018). *History and social science framework*. Massachusetts Curriculum Frameworks—2018. Malden, MA: Massachusetts Dept. of Education. http://www.doe.mass.edu/frameworks/hss/2018-12.pdf

Massachusetts Department of Elementary and Secondary Education. (2016). Science and Technology/Engineering Framework. Massachusetts Curriculum Frameworks—2016. Malden, MA: Massachusetts Dept. of Education. http://www.doe.mass.edu/frameworks/scitech/2016-04.pdf

Masters, G. (2018, August 27). The role of evidence in teaching and learning. *Teacher*. https://www.teachermagazine.com.au/columnists/geoff-masters/the-role-of-evidence-in-teaching-and-learning

McDermott, M. (2002). Collaging pre-service teacher identity. *Teacher Education Quarterly*, 29(4), 53–68.

McDougall, M., Bevan, B., & Semper, R. (2012). *Art as a way of knowing* [Conference Report]. Exploratorium. https://www.exploratorium.edu/files/pdf/cils/Art_as_a_Way_of_Knowing_report.pdf

McMahon, S. D., Rose, D. S., & Parks, M. P. (2003). Basic reading through dance program: The impact on first-grade students' basic reading skills. Evaluation Review, 27(1), 104–125. https://doi.org/10.1177/0193841X02239021

Meredith, T. (2015, May 15). Starting student feedback loops. *Edutopia*. https://www.edutopia.org/blog/starting-student-feedback-loops-taylor-meredith

Merriam-Webster. (n.d.-a). Curator. In *Merriam-Webster.com dictionary*. https://www.merriam-webster.com/dictionary/curator

Merriam Webster. (n.d.-b). Evidence. In *Merriam-Webster.com dictionary*. https://www.merriam-webster.com/dictionary/evidence

Merriam Webster. (n.d.-c) Tableau. In *Merriam-Webster.com dictionary*. https://www.merriam-webster.com/dictionary/tableau

Miller, J., & Bogatova, T. (2018). Arts in education: The impact of the arts integration program and lessons learned. *Journal for Learning through the Arts*, 14(1). https://doi.org/10.21977/D914128357

Milner, H. R., IV. (2018, February). Assessment for equity. *Educational Leadership*, 75(5), 88–89.

Milwaukee Zine Fest. (n.d.). *What exactly is a zine?* The Bindery. https://www.binderymke.com/what-is-a-zine

Monreal, T. (2017, May 31). Using dialogue poems in history class. *Medium*. https://medium.com/from-a-teacher/using-dialogue-poems-in-history-class-29945aac3861

Moore, D. (2016, May). The magical tool of tableau. *The Institute for Arts Integration and STEAM*. https://educationcloset.com/2016/05/25/magical-tool-tableau/

Morales, Y. (2018). *Dreamers*. Neal Porter Books.

Morin, A. (n.d.). *Universal design for learning (UDL): What you need to know*. Understood. https://www.understood.org/en/learning-thinking-differences/treatments-approaches/educational-strategies/universal-design-for-learning-what-it-is-and-how-it-works

Moss, C. M., & Brookhart, S. M. (2009). *Advancing formative assessment in every classroom: A guide for the instructional leader*. Association for Supervision and Curriculum Development.

Moss, C. M., & Brookhart, S. M. (2012). *Learning targets*. Association for Supervision and Curriculum Development.

Mueller, J. F. (n.d.). Authentic assessment toolbox. http://jfmueller.faculty.noctrl.edu/toolbox/whatisit.htm

Nardolillo, A., Paoloni, M., Passarelli, A., & Patterson, H. (2014, October 4). The use of storyboards in the classroom. *Prezi*. https://prezi.com/ojhzk56ejzf_/the-use-of-storyboards-in-the-classroom/

National Coalition for Core Arts Standards (NCCAS). (2014). *National Core Arts*

Standards: Dance, media, arts, music, theatre and visual arts. https://www. nationalartsstandards.org/

National Dance Education Organization (NDEO). (n.d.). *Philosophy underlying the standards for dance in early childhood.* https://www.ndeo.org/content.aspx-?page_id=22&club_id=893257&module_id=55419

National Education Association. (2012). *Preparing 21st century students for a global society: An educator's guide to the "four Cs."* https://pdf4pro.com/view/an-educator-s-guide-to-the-four-cs-nea-org-39c8.html

National Science Teaching Association. (2014). *Science and engineering practices.* https://ngss.nsta.org/PracticesFull.aspx

Nieto, S. (2006, Spring). *Teaching as political work: Learning from courageous and caring teachers* (The Longfellow Lecture). Child Development Institute, Sarah Lawrence College. https://www.sarahlawrence.edu/media/cdi/pdf/Occasional%20Papers/CDI_Occasional_Paper_2006_Nieto.pdf

Nieto, S. (2010). *The light in their eyes: Creating multicultural learning communities.* Teachers College Press.

Ontario. Ministry of Education. (2009). *The Ontario curriculum, grades 1–8: The arts* [Revised]. http://www.edu.gov.on.ca/eng/curriculum/elementary/arts18b-09curr.pdf

Owocki, G. (2001). *Make way for literacy! Teaching the way young children learn.* Heinemann.

Panik, A. (n.d.). *Make a collage! Collage techniques give students another creative way to express themselves.* Lesson Planet. https://www.lessonplanet.com/article/elementary-art/make-a-collage

Patton, M. Q. (1999). Enhancing the quality and credibility of qualitative analysis. *HSR: Health Services Research, 34*(5 Pt. 2), 1189–1208. https://www.ncbi.nlm.nih.gov/pmc/articles/PMC1089059/

Picken, A. J. (2012). *Using learning stories in secondary social studies: Gathering, analyzing and using evidence to support learners' conceptual understandings* [Master's thesis, Victoria University of Wellington (NZ)]. CORE. https://core.ac.uk/download/pdf/41337742.pdf

Prince, E. (2002). *Art matters: Strategies, activities and ideas to strengthen learning across the curriculum.* Zephyr Press.

Rankine-Landers, M. (2015, March 3). 8 Habits of thinking learned from artists. *Tchers' Voice (Teaching Channel).* https://www.teachingchannel.org/blog/2015/03/03/8-habits-of-thinking

Redman, L. (2016). *Creative movement and dance integration: Their connection to learning third grade math concepts* [Master's thesis, University of Northern Colorado]. Scholarship & Creative Works @ Digital UNC. https://digscholarship.unco.edu/theses/52

Redmond, P. (2014, January 1). Reflection as an indicator of cognitive presence. *E-Learning and Digital Media, 11*(1), 45–58. https://journals.sagepub.com/doi/abs/10.2304/elea.2014.11.1.46

Regents of the University of Minnesota (2006). Dialogue poem. In D. J. Tedick (Ed.), *Proficiency-oriented language instruction and assessment: A curriculum handbook for teachers.* University of Minnesota, Center for Advanced Research on Language Acquisition. http://carla.umn.edu/articulation/polia/pdf_files/dialoguepoems.pdf

Reggio Emilia. (n.d.). *Observation and documentation.* https://reggioemilia2015. weebly.com/observation-and-documentation.html

Rodman, A. (2018, November). Learning together, Learning on their own. *Educational Leadership, 76*(3), 12–18.

Russell, S. (n.d.). *Ancient civilizations dance.* California County Superintendents Educational Services Association (CCSESA) Arts Initiative. https://ccsesaarts. org/lesson/ancient-civilizations-dance/assessment

Sánchez, F., Anderberg, S., Mitchell, J., Rice, M., Taylor, P., Tiwater, L., Waddell, G., Young, S., Davis, S., Winlock, S., Fenner, D., Tyler, H., Zschaber, A., Bryan, A., Enriquez, S., Crooks, P., De La O, A., Wilkins, S. (2017). *Culturally & linguistically responsive arts teaching and learning in action: Strategies that increase student engagement and achievement.* California County Superintendents Educational Services Association (CCSESA) Arts Initiative. https://ccsesaarts.org/ wp-content/uploads/2019/08/Culturally-Responsive-Guide.pdf

Scholastic Parents. (n.d.). *The importance of pretend play: Imagination-driven play builds your young child's developmental skills.* https://www.scholastic.com/ parents/kids-activities-and-printables/activities-for-kids/arts-and-craft-ideas/ importance-pretend-play.html

Schön, D. A. (1983). *The reflective practitioner.* Basic Books.

Serra, R. (2015, March 11). What is reflective teaching and why is it important? *RichmondShare Blog.* https://www.richmondshare.com.br/what-is-reflective-teaching-and-why-is-it-important/

Sharma, M. (2019, November 7). Why creativity is the superpower for tomorrow's workforce. *Adobe Blog.* https://blog.adobe.com/en/2019/11/07/why-creativity-is-the-superpower-for-tomorrows-workforce.html#gs.fpgogt

Sickler-Voigt, D. C. (Ed.). (2018, July 31). Introduction. *Assessment white papers for art education.* National Art Education Association. https://www.arteducators.org/learn-tools/assessment-white-papers-for-art-education

Siemens, G. (January 27, 2008). *Learning and knowing in networks: Changing roles for educators and designers.* Presented to ITFORUM. https://www. academia.edu/2857165/Learning_and_knowing_in_networks_Changing_ roles_for_educators_and_designers

Silverstein, L. B., & Layne, S. (2010). Defining arts integration. The John F. Kennedy Center for the Performing Arts. http://www.artsintegrationpd.org/wp-content/ uploads/2017/07/What-is-Arts-Integration.pdf

Simmons, N., & Daley, S. (2013). The art of thinking: Using collage to stimulate scholarly work. *The Canadian Journal for the Scholarship of Teaching and Learning, 4*(1), 1–13. http://dx.doi.org/10.5206/cjsotl-rcacea.2013.1.2

Skoning, S. (2008). Movement in dance in the inclusive classroom. TEACHING Exceptional Children Plus 4(6). https://eric.ed.gov/?id=EJ967723

Snyder, L., Klos, P., & Grey-Hawkins, L. (2014). Transforming teaching through arts integration. *Journal for Learning through the Arts, 10*(1),1–24. https://doi. org/10.21977/D910119308

Sousa, D. (n.d.). *How the arts develop the young brain.* AASA, The School Superintendents Association. https://www.aasa.org/SchoolAdministratorArticle. aspx?id=7378

Souto-Manning, M. (2013). *Multicultural teaching in the early childhood classroom.* Teachers College Press.

Spencer, J. (2017, November 18). Getting started with content curation in the classroom. *John Spencer [Blog]*. http://www.spencerauthor.com/content-curation/

St. John, R. (2018, August). The soundscape. *Sound Matters*. https://beoplay.squarespace.com/journal/the-soundscape

Starting Point: Teaching Entry Level Geoscience (Carleton College). (n.d.). *A short glossary of assessment terms*. https://serc.carleton.edu/introgeo/assessment/glossary.html

Sterrenberg, S. (n.d.). *It's about balance*. California County Superintendents Educational Services Association (CCSESA) Statewide Arts Initiative. https://ccsesaarts.org/lesson/its-about-balance/assessment/

Strahan, D., & Rogers, C. (2012). *Formative assessment practices in successful middle level classrooms: Researach summary*. Association for Middle Level Education. https://www.amle.org/BrowsebyTopic/WhatsNew/WNDet/TabId/270/ArtMID/888/ArticleID/108/Formative-Assessment-Practices.aspx

Strauch-Nelson, W. (2011). Book learning: The cognitive potential of bookmaking. *Teaching Artist Journal. 9*(1), 5–15.

Tavangar, H. (2017, November 8). Creating an inclusive classroom. *Edutopia*. https://www.edutopia.org/article/creating-inclusive-classroom

TEDx. (2013, June 19). *The myth of average: Todd Rose at TEDx Sonoma County* [Video]. YouTube. https://www.youtube.com/watch?v=4eBmyttcfU4

Tolisano, S. R., & Hale, J. A. (2018). *A guide to documenting learning: Making thinking visible, meaningful, shareable, and amplified*. Corwin.

True Heroes Films (2015, September 22). *The making of an editorial cartoon*. https://www.youtube.com/watch?v=X1rNCO6Zu5I

Turner, T., & Wilson, D. G. (2010). Reflections on documentation: A discussion with thought leaders from Reggio Emilia. *Theory Into Practice, 49*(1), 5–13. https://doi.org/10.1080/00405840903435493

U.S. Department of Education, Office of Planning, Evaluation and Policy Development, Policy and Program Studies Service. (2016). *The state of racial diversity in the educator workforce*. https://www2.ed.gov/rschstat/eval/highered/racial-diversity/state-racial-diversity-workforce.pdf

Valenzuela, C. A. (2017). Sonic borderland literacies: A re/mix of culturally relevant education. *Journal of Pedagogy, Pluralism, and Practice, 9*(1)32–56. https://digitalcommons.lesley.edu/jppp/vol9/iss1/

Victoria State Government. (n.d.). *Role play and drama*. https://www.education.vic.gov.au/school/teachers/teachingresources/discipline/english/literacy/speakinglistening/Pages/exampleroleplay.aspx

Wager, A. C., Poey, V. M., & Berriz, B. R. (2017, Fall). Art as voice: Creating access for emergent bilingual learners. *Journal of Pedagogy, Pluralism, and Practice, 9*(1), 5–32. https://digitalcommons.lesley.edu/jppp/vol9/iss1/1

Walsh, J., & Sattes, B. (2005). *Quality questioning: Research-based practice to engage every learner*. Corwin Press.

Watanabe-Crockett, L. (2019, July, 5). 10 innovative formative assessment examples for teachers to know. *Wabisabi Learning*. https://www.wabisabilearning.com/blog/formative-assessment-examples

West Ed. (n.d.). Five evidence gathering routines: Activity 3.7. *Formative Assessment Insights: A Digital Professional Learning Experience for Teachers*. https://www.

oregon.gov/ode/educator-resources/assessment/Documents/five_evidence_gathering_routines.pdf

Wiggins, G., & McTighe, J. (1998). *Understanding by design*. Association for Supervision and Curriculum Development.

Wiggins, G., & McTighe, J. (2008). *Understanding by design* (2nd ed.). Association for Supervision and Curriculum Development.

Wiggins, G., & McTighe, J. (2013). *Essential questions: Opening doors to student understanding*. Association for Supervision and Curriculum Development.

Workman, E. (2017, September 6). *Beyond the core: Advancing student success through the arts* (Education Trends) [Policy report]. Education Commission of the States. https://www.ecs.org/wp-content/uploads/Beyond_the_Core_Advancing_student_success_through_the_arts.pdf

Young, A. (1910). *Eleven Hours a Day* [Cartoon]. In J. Simkin (2020, January), Art Young. *Spartacus Educational*. https://spartacus-educational.com/ARTyoung.htm

Zambon, K. (2013, November 12). *How engaging with art affects the human brain*. AAAS, American Association for the Advancement of Science. https://www.aaas.org/news/how-engaging-art-affects-human-brain

Zeichner, K. M., & Liston, D. P. (1996). *Reflective teaching: An introduction*. Lawrence Erlbaum Associates.

Index

About the Authors

Lisa Donovan is a professor in the Fine and Performing Arts Department at the Massachusetts College of Liberal Arts (MCLA) in North Adams, Massachusetts. Previously she was an associate professor of education and the director of the Creative Arts in Learning Division at Lesley University in Cambridge, Massachusetts. Lisa has broad experience working as an arts educator and administrator in a variety of organizations including Jacob's Pillow Dance Festival; Berkshire Opera Company; Barrington Stage Company; University of Massachusetts' Department of Theater; and Boston University's Theater, Visual Arts, and Tanglewood Institutes. She is spearheading several projects that foreground the use of the arts as a strategy for regional change—as Director of the Creative Compact for Collective Impact project to create a blueprint for arts education for Berkshire County, Codirector of the Berkshire Regional Arts Integration Network funded by the National Department of Education and Innovation, and Director of the MCLA Institute for Arts and Humanities funded by the Andrew W. Mellon Foundation. She has published widely on arts integration and rural arts education.

Lisa served as executive director of the Massachusetts Alliance for Arts Education and is the coeditor and author of a five-book series on arts integration published by Shell Education, *Strategies to Integrate the Arts Series*. She recently conducted research on leveraging change for arts education in rural areas. Lisa was voted Best Professor in 2017 as part of the Berkshire Eagle's Best of the Berkshires competition and was a finalist in the 2018 Berkshire Trendsetters Award for Creative Economy Standout.

She has a BA in psychology from the State University of New York–Oneonta, an MA in communications from Boston University, and a PhD from Lesley University. Contact Lisa at Lisa.Donovan@mcla.edu.

Sarah Anderberg currently serves as Director for the California County Superintendents Educational Services Association (CCSESA) Statewide Arts Initiative. CCSESA represents California's 58 County Superintendents of Schools and their respective county offices of education that connect to over 1,000 school districts in the state. Through this infrastructure, Sarah directs grant programs that expand arts learning in pre-K-12 classrooms throughout California with a focus on regional, county, and local arts leadership, capacity building, curriculum, professional development, and technical assistance. She is also the director of the *Creativity at the Core* initiative and oversees the development of arts education professional learning resources developed by county offices of education in partnership with arts organization partners throughout California. She is currently working on a rural arts initiative to increase student access to the arts in rural communities across California. Sarah's leadership experience includes secondary and postsecondary teaching and administration. Highlights include working at the University of California–Davis as Director of Arts Education and Professional Development for the Robert and Margrit Mondavi Center for the Performing Arts and serving as the Director of the Sierra Arts Project at the School of Education, where she taught arts education courses, directed arts education programs, and led institutes for educators.

Sarah serves on the Policy Advisory Council for the California Alliance for Arts Education and on the Leadership Council for Create CA, a broadbased statewide coalition involving CCSESA, the California Department of Education, the California Alliance for Arts Education, the California State PTA, and the California Arts Council, and other arts and education leaders. She is the past chair of Create CA.

Sarah Anderberg has a BA from the University of South Dakota and an MA from the University of Minnesota. She has completed postgraduate work at the University of California– Davis; California State University–Hayward; California State University–Stanislaus; and California State University–Sacramento. Contact Sarah at sanderberg@ccsesa.org or sarahmarieanderberg@gmail.com.